David Brog has written a timely and important book. His keen insight into the relationship between evangelicals and Israel is a must-read. I believe at this critical time in the history of Israel, David has provided a valuable resource that will be a benefit to all of us that are concerned with the land of Israel and its survival.

—Jay Alan Sekulow, Chief Counsel
American Center for Law & Justice

This important, persuasive book argues that "Christians who embrace the Jews as the elect of God are ascendant both theologically and politically. In twenty-first-century America, the righteous Gentiles have taken over the church." Brog explains how and why "evangelical Christians have become a powerful pro-Israel force in America." He also challenges the American Jewish community to recognize the change and take it to heart. An eloquent and well-crafted presentation of an urgent proposition.

—Jacob Neusner
Research Professor of Theology
Senior Fellow, Institute of Advanced Theology
Bard College

STANDING *With* ISRAEL

DAVID BROG

Most Strang Communications/Charisma House/Siloam/FrontLine products are available at special quantity discounts for bulk purchase for sales promotions, premiums, fund-raising, and educational needs. For details, write Strang Communications/Charisma House/Siloam/FrontLine, 600 Rinehart Road, Lake Mary, Florida 32746, or telephone (407) 333-0600.

Standing With Israel by David Brog
Published by FrontLine
A Strang Company
600 Rinehart Road
Lake Mary, Florida 32746
www.frontlineissues.com

Cover design by Judith McKittrick
Author photograph by Paul Wharton, Wharton Photography

International Standard Book Number 978-1-59979-050-3

08 09 10 11 12 — 9 8 7 6 5 4 3 2
Printed in the United States of America

To my parents,
Judah and Barbara Brog,
who taught me
to stand with Israel

Acknowledgments

WRITING IS A solitary pursuit, and it is during such moments devoid of the constant interruptions and distractions of a busy office when one needs and appreciates the people in his life more than ever. As always, my family has been my greatest support. My parents Judah and Barbara, my brothers Steven and Michael, my sisters-in law Amy and Judy, and my nephews Daniel, Justin, Jeremy, and Sammy have provided me with an abundance of love, laughter, and encouragement. I thank and love all of you. I also want to thank all of my Washington friends for the crucial support and distraction they provided during the writing process. Special thanks go to Rachel Schwartz and Charles Robbins for helping me to presume that I could write a book, and to Erin Streeter, Gretchen Birkle, and Chris Israel for the carrot of a book party in the country.

I'd like to thank my agent, Andrew Stuart, for his wise counsel, strong encouragement, and excellent work in pitching an unorthodox proposal from a first-time author. Thanks also to Rick Mallen, Dan Shapiro, Scott Siff, and Neil McBride for reviewing early drafts and providing helpful insights. I also want to express my appreciation to Peter Collier at Encounter Books for his early support for this project.

I owe a great deal to some of the Christian Zionists I met along the way who both helped me understand their theology and inspired me to tell their story. In particular, I'd like to thank Tom Bowman for providing an early and profound example of Christian love, Larry and Romey Hubner for their hospitality and warmth, Susan Michael for her encouragement and suggestions, Gary Bauer for making time to talk to an unknown writer, and Pastor John Hagee for his support and stirring inspiration.

Finally, I'd like to thank the good people at Strang Communications. It has been a pleasure to work with Bert Ghezzi, Barbara Dycus, and Lillian McAnally. And I'd like to express special appreciation to Stephen Strang, both for his interest in this book and for serving as an inspirational example of the righteous Gentile I seek to describe herein.

Contents

Foreword by John Hagee . . . . . . *xi*

Preface . . . . . . *xiii*

Introduction: The Righteous Then and Now 1

PART ONE
Theology and Other Motives

1 The Rise of Replacement Theology 17

2 The Return of the Jews 41

3 Motives 65

PART TWO
Before the Revolution: Early Christian Zionism

4 The Deep Roots of Christian Zionism: Hechler and Blackstone 91

5 Three Christian Zionists Who Helped to Create Israel: Balfour, Wilson, and Truman 107

PART THREE
After the Revolution: Christian Zionism Ascendant

6 Christian Zionism in Washington 133

7 Christian Zionism's Good Works 159

PART FOUR
The Jewish Response

8 The Response From the Jewish Mainstream 179

9 Evangelical Anti-Semitism? 203

10 Toward a New Approach 227

Conclusion: Strange Bedfellows or Blood Brothers? 251

Notes 257

Index 275

Foreword

IT IS MY great pleasure to highly recommend David Brog's powerful and penetrating book *Standing With Israel.* This is the book I thought would never be written in my lifetime.

Standing With Israel is a comprehensive exposé of the roots of Christian anti-Semitism, the birth and development of Christian Zionism, and the death of replacement theology written by a Jewish author.

David Brog explains why the Jewish community has largely withheld its embrace from Christian Zionists in times past. He encourages his fellow Jews to break free from their fixation on past traumas and embrace their Christian allies who fight anti-Semitism as passionately as do the sons and daughters of Abraham, Isaac, and Jacob.

This book is a must-read for all Christians and Jews searching for a better understanding of each other and a more excellent way to defend and stand with Israel in common cause.

—John Hagee, Senior Pastor
Cornerstone Church, San Antonio, Texas

Preface

THIS IS A book about politics and religion, Christians and Jews, anti-Semites and righteous Gentiles. It would be difficult to find more emotional and controversial topics about which to write. Anyone who wants to objectively analyze my ideas on these difficult subjects will need to factor in my background and the biases I may bring to my analysis. I thus owe it to you, the reader, to state at the outset just who I am and why I have written this book.

Starting with religion, I am a Jew. I am not a Messianic Jew or a Jew for Jesus—I don't believe that the Messiah has ever appeared on Earth. Nor am I an alienated or self-hating Jew. I embrace my Jewish faith and seek knowledge of my Creator through the paths and texts provided to me by my Jewish ancestors. While I do not observe all of the *Halacha* (Jewish law), I do recognize the *Halacha* as a central component of my religion. If there be fault in my failure to observe it, the fault lies with me, not with the law.

Moving on to politics, I am a Republican. Yet it is important to note that I spent my entire career in politics working for the most "liberal" of Republican senators, Arlen Specter. I worked for Senator Specter for more than seven years, first as his chief counsel and later as his chief of staff. Senator Specter is a vocal champion of causes that are anathema to the Christian Right, namely legalized abortion and embryonic stem cell research. While I do not share my former boss's certainty on these issues, I represented him zealously the entire time I was in his employ. Thus I write this book not as a stalwart of the Christian Right, but as one who has seen difficult combat with the Christian Right.

My curiosity about the topic of Christian Zionism stems from my years working on Capitol Hill. During this period, I was privileged to meet a number of Christian Zionists who impressed me by their devotion to Israel and their apparent love for the Jewish people. If there is one great theme to Jewish history, it is our lonely walk through the centuries. The Jews have known no great allies, no stalwart friends—we have lived and died facing a hostile world alone. Thus I found it intriguing to think that, finally, we had some very big friends standing on our side.

Yet the media told me not to get my hopes up. Television, newspapers, and magazines all informed me that Christian Zionists were not real friends of the Jews but enemies in disguise who supported Israel out of a sick desire to see the Jews killed or converted at the end of days. I started researching this book in a simple quest to discover the truth, to see if these purported friends were what they claimed to be.

What I learned in the course of my research far surpassed what I had expected to find. I became convinced that the evangelical Christians who support Israel today are nothing less than the theological heirs of the righteous Gentiles who sought to save Jews from the Holocaust. This book represents the fruits of my search for the truth. This book is also my attempt to thank those whom the truth has vindicated and exalted. It is my great hope that this book can contribute in some small way to a reconciliation between Christian and Jew, which is long overdue.

This book has been a labor of love. And like all expressions of love, it has left my heart bigger than it was before I began. I hope that it will have the same effect on you, dear reader.

Introduction

THE RIGHTEOUS THEN AND NOW

WHEN THE GERMANS occupied France in World War II, historian Jules Isaac was fired from his post as France's Inspector General of Education. Isaac had been a fixture of French intellectual society for decades. His seven-volume *Cours d'histoire* served as the standard history text in most French high schools and universities. Isaac was also a decorated World War I veteran and patriotic Frenchman. While Jules Isaac never denied his Jewish identity, he did not define himself by it.

As the Nazis implemented their "final solution" in France, Isaac turned his historian's mind to the question of anti-Semitism. *How,* he thought, *could the Holocaust be happening in societies that have been Christian for nearly two thousand years?* At first, Isaac managed to maintain his characteristic academic detachment from his subject. But his subject refused to maintain its detachment from Isaac. While he was away from home one day in 1943, the Gestapo arrested Isaac's wife, daughter, son, and son-in-law. Of the four, only his son would return home from the death camps. Before being deported from France, Madame Isaac managed to send a note to her husband exhorting him to, "Save yourself for your work; the world is waiting for it."[1]

On the run and in hiding, Jules Isaac devoted himself to fulfilling his wife's last wish. Isaac's writing became to him a "cry of an outraged conscience, of a lacerated heart."[2] By the war's end, he had completed a six-hundred-page manuscript titled *Jesus and Israel.* In wrestling with the question of how the Holocaust could happen in a Christian Europe, Isaac had reached an unexpected conclusion. While German soldiers serving a neo-pagan Nazi ideology were the ones who carried away his family, Jules Isaac pointed the finger of ultimate blame not at the Nazis, but at the Christian church. He wrote that while the German responsibility for the Holocaust was "overwhelming," it was only a "derivative responsibility."[3] The real culprit, Isaac asserted, was the centuries-old tradition of Christian anti-Semitism. In his words:

> Christian anti-Semitism is the powerful, millennial tree, with many and strong roots, onto which all the other varieties of anti-Semitism—even the most antagonistic by nature, even anti-Christian—have come to be grafted in the Christian world.[4]

Isaac traced the source of this Christian anti-Semitism to the church's traditional teaching on the Jews and Judaism, what Isaac named the "teaching of contempt." In *Jesus and Israel,* Isaac thoroughly documents and then rebuts this corpus of anti-Jewish beliefs. At the heart of this teaching of contempt was the claim that the Jews "as a whole" had rejected and then crucified Jesus, and that Jesus in turn had rejected and condemned the entire Jewish people. Central also was the church's uniform denial of Jesus' Jewish identity and Christianity's Jewish roots.

Isaac concludes *Jesus and Israel* with the following, haunting statement of his thesis:

> The glow of the Auschwitz crematorium is the beacon that lights, that guides all my thoughts. Oh my Jewish brothers, and you as well, my Christian brothers, do you not think that it mingles with another glow, that of the Cross?[5]

ALTHOUGH HE CONDEMNED the Christian teaching of contempt for the Jews, Jules Isaac never condemned Christianity. Despite all he suffered, Isaac persisted in the optimistic belief that if it would only end this teaching of contempt, the church would produce Christians who would save Jews, not kill them. On this point he did not rely upon mere conjecture. For much of the time he was writing *Jesus and Israel,* Jules Isaac was hiding from the Nazis in a Catholic home. His rescuer, a woman named Germaine Bocquet, received her Catholic education from a teacher who had purposely removed anti-Semitism from his lesson plan.[6] When asked why she risked her life and that of her husband to save the life of a Jew, Germaine Bocquet replied:

> The religious education I had received had instilled in me respect for the Jewish people, and gratitude that they have given us the prophets, the Virgin Mary, Christ, and the apostles. Jews were for me people of the Covenant, of God's promises. Jesus, the Messiah, was a faithful son of the Law, which he had come to bring to perfection, not to abolish. I had never heard the Jews spoken of as Christ-killers; I had been taught that our sins crucified Jesus.[7]

Tragically, Mrs. Bocquet's religious education was not the standard catechism in the churches of Europe. While she believed that the Jews were still beloved of God and the beneficiaries of God's holy covenant, the Christian majority embraced the teaching of contempt and a "replacement theology," which held that the church had superceded the Jews as God's chosen people. While Mrs. Bocquet saw the Jews as the family and followers of Christ, most Christians viewed the Jews as the enemies and murderers of Christ. While Mrs. Bocquet risked her life to save a Jew, an entire continent of Christians was killing Jews or standing by and letting it happen. By removing the Jews from God's love, the dominant Christian theology of the day left them vulnerable to man's hate.

Thirty-five years after the Holocaust, the Israeli air force destroyed an Iraqi nuclear reactor at Osirak, outside of Baghdad. The Israelis had determined that Iraq was using the reactor to develop a nuclear bomb, a weapon this implacable enemy might one day use against them. Israeli Prime Minister Menachem Begin justified the action to the world by declaring that he would not permit "another Holocaust in the history of the Jewish people."[8] Israel was universally condemned for the Osirak raid, including by its ally the United States.

In San Antonio, Texas, a pastor named John Hagee was dismayed by the loud outcry against Israel's action. He decided to counter the chorus of criticism with a public show of support. With the help of a fellow pastor and two rabbis, Pastor Hagee organized a "Night to Honor Israel." The day after he held a press conference to announce the upcoming event, someone phoned Pastor Hagee's church and said, "Tell that preacher he'll be dead by Friday."

As the evening of the event drew near, someone shot out the windows of Pastor Hagee's car while it was parked in front of his house.[9]

The Night to Honor Israel went ahead as scheduled. After the speeches, Hagee presented a $10,000 check to the president of the local chapter of Hadassah. Then, at 9:27 p.m., Hagee was handed a note. Someone had phoned the *San Antonio Express News* threatening to blow up the auditorium at 9:30 p.m. The room was quickly evacuated.[10]

Despite this troubled start, Hagee's Night to Honor Israel became an annual event. Over the years, the size of the crowd grew, and a massive television audience was added. And the checks got bigger. At the 2004 Night to Honor Israel, Pastor Hagee presented checks totaling $2.25 million to two Jewish organizations that fund the immigration of Jews to Israel and one that supports Israeli orphans.

When asked why he so staunchly supports Israel, Pastor John Hagee speaks of a "biblical mandate to bless the Jews" and of a Christian "debt of gratitude" to the Jewish people. Pastor Hagee notes that:

> The Jewish people gave to us the patriarchs, Abraham, Isaac, and Jacob. The prophets, Elijah, Daniel, Zechariah, etc.—not a Baptist in the bunch. Every word in your Bible was written by Jewish hands. The first family of Christianity, Mary, Joseph, and Jesus, were Jewish. Jesus Christ, a Jewish rabbi from Nazareth, made this statement: "Salvation is of the Jews." The point is this: If you take away the Jewish contribution to Christianity, there would be no Christianity.[11]

If these words are reminiscent of those spoken by Germaine Bocquet, Jules Isaac's rescuer, this is no coincidence. Pastor Hagee and Mrs. Bocquet share the same theology. Like so many of the righteous Gentiles who saved Jews during the Holocaust, Hagee roundly rejects the teaching of contempt and replacement theology; he believes that the Jews are still God's chosen people. When Pastor Hagee looks at Jews, he does not see a rejected people or a deicide people; he sees the family and friends of Christ.

DESPITE THE SIMILARITIES, however, there is one difference between Pastor John Hagee and Germaine Bocquet, and it is a difference of enormous significance.

In her day, Mrs. Bocquet's theology represented the thinking of a small group on the fringes of Christendom—it was the minority report. A generation later, Pastor Hagee's theology represents the dominant strain of Christian thinking in America. Replacement theology is on the decline; its adherents have lost their power and momentum. Christians who embrace the Jews as the elect of God are ascendant both theologically and politically. In twenty-first-century America, the righteous Gentiles have taken over the church.

Today's righteous Gentiles confront a world in which the threats facing the Jewish people have changed but not disappeared. Despite a recent and troubling rise in European anti-Semitism, most Jews in the Christian world no longer live in physical peril and need not seek refuge in Christian homes. Instead, the great existential threat facing the Jews today is the one confronting their Jewish State. Since the day it declared its independence in 1948, Israel has lived under the threat of physical destruction from its Arab neighbors. As Israel's prowess in conventional arms grew, its enemies pursued weapons of mass destruction with sufficient success to ensure that Israel continues to confront annihilation. Since 2000, Israel has been besieged by a new danger in the form of a sustained campaign of suicide bombings by Palestinian terrorists. Israelis, strong and independent in their own land, now face a day-to-day physical danger that once haunted their forebears in Europe.

The modern-day righteous Gentiles exemplified by John Hagee recognize the current threats facing the Jews and have responded to them with an outpouring of support for the Jewish State. Evangelical Christians have become a powerful pro-Israel force in America. In fact, when Republicans hold the balance of power in Washington, evangelical Christians become *the most* powerful pro-Israel force in America. Evangelical leaders speak to the White House and Congress as the representatives of the largest single voting block within the Republican Party. Outside of politics, evangelical Christians raise millions of dollars every year for Israel and for poor Jews around the world. So many Christians visit Israel each year that the Jewish State often receives more Christian tourists than Jewish ones.

Of course, neither lobbying for Israel nor sending checks to the United Jewish Communities qualifies as an act of heroism. While Pastor Hagee and others have taken risks to support Israel, the threats they faced were from a few extremists, not a brutally efficient regime. Referring to Christian Zionists as modern-day righteous Gentiles does not mean that their actions are as noble as those who risked their lives to save Jews during the Holocaust. The times do not currently demand sacrifices so sublime from any of Israel's friends, Christian or Jewish. The reference is intended simply to recognize the fact that today's Christian Zionists share the same theology as their heroic forebears, and that they have thus far chosen to act on this theology to the extent demanded by the times. If the Christian Zionists and other friends of Israel do their job properly now, no one may ever need to discover to what heights of heroism they might rise under more exigent circumstances.

WITH LIMITED EXCEPTIONS, the American Jewish community has responded to this epochal change in Christian theology toward the Jews with a collective yawn. For the most part, they simply haven't noticed. Because they have failed to recognize this change, America's Jews persist in assuming that Christian attitudes toward the Jews today are substantially similar to those of prior centuries. It is no wonder, therefore, that so many Jews are suspicious when Christians profess to love them so deeply. When American Jews see a cross, they often see it, as did Jules Isaac, bathed in the glow of the Auschwitz crematorium.

In their failure to recognize radically changed circumstances, American Jews resemble those legendary Japanese soldiers stationed on remote Pacific islands during World War II. Japan surrendered in 1945, and her people went to work building a democracy and a modern economy. Japan rapidly became a major ally and trading partner of the United States. Yet, oblivious to these changes, many of these soldiers continued to prowl the jungles in search of the American enemy.

Many in the American Jewish community are also living in the past, stuck not in Pacific jungles but in European ghettos. In an alternative reality built on traumatic communal memories, millions of Jews continue to crouch, fingers on their triggers, surrounded by bloodthirsty Christians who view them as a replaced, deicide people. Yet the world has changed dramatically in recent decades, and the enemy they fear has long since become a friend. These Jews are fighting ghosts.

In focusing on Isaac's cross, the Jewish community misses Isaac's point. Jules Isaac not only looked back into a dark past, but he also looked forward. He looked forward and saw a door open to him. That door led to the home of a Catholic woman willing to save his life. Jules Isaac walked through the door, and he survived.

Today, the Jewish community owes it to six million victims to look back into history and remember the evil that was done. But like Jules Isaac, the Jewish community must also look forward. American Jewry must look forward and find that there is a door open to them. The door leads to the churches and homes of millions of Christians who want to stand with the Jews and with their small, embattled State of Israel. It is a door through which they should walk.

To many American Jews, the proposed alliance with evangelicals in support of Israel is a Faustian bargain. They are reluctant to grasp the devil's hand. Their hesitation, they argue, is driven not by past trauma but by present policy.* American Jews, still overwhelmingly liberal, often view evangelical Christians as bitter political opponents. On a series of domestic social issues from abortion to assisted suicide, evangelical Christians champion positions that are anathema to most Jews. Even when it comes to Israel, evangelical Christians often support Israeli policies and politicians that liberal Jews cannot abide.

Here again, the example of Jules Isaac proves instructive. For Isaac, seeking refuge in the home of a Catholic did not require a vow of silence or acquiescence in Catholic teachings to which he objected. He faced no Hobbesian choice between survival and conscience. On the contrary, in the shelter provided by his Catholic rescuer, Jules Isaac wrote a work that placed ultimate responsibility for the Holocaust upon the Catholic Church.

Not only did Isaac criticize the church, but he also changed it. After the war, Isaac dedicated the remaining years of his life to encouraging a Christianity that would reflect his rescuer more than it reflected his tormentors. He worked closely with sympathetic Catholics to draft reforms that would eliminate the teaching of contempt from the Catholic catechism. In his effort to secure adoption of these reforms, Isaac met with a number of Catholic

* The extent to which Jewish communal memories magnify and exacerbate present-day policy differences will be explored in later chapters.

leaders, including Pope Pius XII and Pope John XXIII. Isaac's 1960 meeting with Pope John XXIII proved to be historic. Here Isaac persuaded the pope to take steps that culminated in the Vatican's official condemnation of anti-Semitism and the charge of deicide against the Jews.[12] There is thus a direct line from Isaac's writing about the teaching of contempt to the decision by the Catholic Church to end the teaching of contempt.

For American Jews today, joining hands with evangelical Christians will not require ignoring significant policy disagreements. Christian friendship is not being offered at the price of Jewish silence or acquiescence. Each community can continue to pursue its own vision of what is best for America and Israel from within the same tent. While America's Jews may not be able to change Christian politics the way that Jules Isaac changed church doctrine, they may find that collaboration works to blunt differences and foster respect. As Jules Isaac did, American Jews should reach out to their Christian brothers. This time, there is already an outstretched hand waiting to receive theirs.

WHEN THE NAZIS extended their control to a new country, one of their first acts was to require the Jews of that country to wear a yellow Star of David on their clothing. The yellow star was part of the process of dehumanization and subjugation. By separating the Jews from their fellow citizens in this fashion, it would be easier to later extract them from the general population and then murder them.

A wonderful story is told about King Christian X, the king of Denmark during World War II. Legend has it that when Hitler ordered Denmark's Jews to wear the yellow star on their clothes, King Christian protested by placing a yellow star on his own jacket. The Jews were fellow Danes, his subjects, and he would not permit such discrimination against them. According to the story, thousands of Danes followed their king's lead, thus thwarting Nazi efforts to single out the Jews.

While the tale is apocryphal, the heroism of the Danes is not. When the Nazis were arranging the deportation of Denmark's seventy-five hundred Jews, their plans were leaked to a few Danish leaders who promptly informed the Jewish community. Almost all Danish Jews went into hiding, and, eventually, more than seven thousand of them were ferried to safety in neutral Sweden by a flotilla of Danish fishing vessels. Ordinary Danes provided the hiding places, the boats, and the crew for the transport. When Nazi soldiers visited every Jewish address in Denmark, they found very few Jews at home. King Christian and his subjects wore the yellow star on their hearts if not on their clothing.

Such heroism flowed naturally from a people whose church had never embraced the replacement theology so popular in sibling churches across the border. In the midst of the Danish rescue of the Jews, for instance, the bishop of the Lutheran Church of Denmark proclaimed:

> Wherever persecutions are undertaken for racial or religious reasons against the Jews, it is the duty of the Christian Church to raise a protest against it... because we shall never be able to forget that the Lord of the Church, Jesus Christ, was born in Bethlehem, of the virgin Mary into Israel, the people of His possession, according to the promise of God.[13]

Imagine if there would have been more King Christians during World War II. Imagine if there would have been more Germaine Bocquets. Imagine if the majority of Christians in Nazi Europe would have remained true to the Christian message of love instead of the false theology of hate. It may well have been impossible to perpetrate the Holocaust in a Europe so populated.

Today, there is no need for such an exercise of the imagination. Something truly extraordinary is taking place here and now. American Christianity is being taken over by righteous Gentiles. Unlike during the Holocaust, the Jews aren't being abandoned to their fate. Across America, church by church, one by one, Christians are putting on the yellow star. They are standing with the Jews. This time, they are determined not to leave the Jews or their nation, Israel, to fight alone.

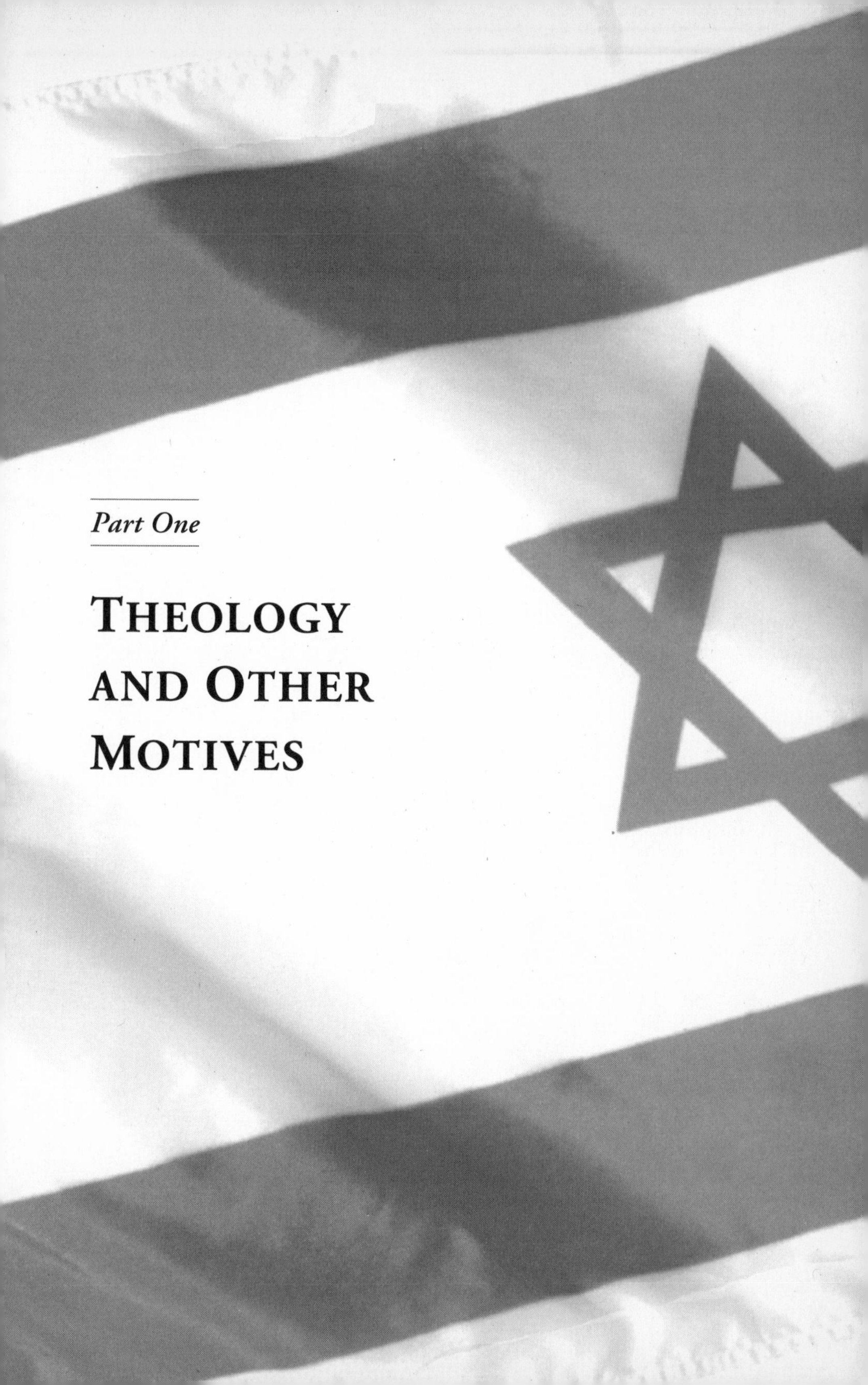

Part One

Theology and Other Motives

During the twentieth century, there was a revolution in Christian theology in America. This revolution produced the greatest shift in Christian attitudes toward the Jewish people since Constantine converted the Roman Empire. This new theology has driven millions of Christians to embrace the Jews and their Jewish State of Israel. Consequently, evangelical Christians may well be the most powerful pro-Israel force in America today.

This tectonic theological shift was the result of something that might strike the uninitiated as insignificant: a new interpretation of one word in the Bible. That word is *Israel*. The Bible relates that God made a series of promises to Abraham and his progeny, referred to collectively as "Israel." Yet like so many religious words and concepts, the question of who exactly is "Israel" has been the subject of protracted controversy. Christian attitudes toward the Jews throughout the centuries have turned largely on this basic question of interpretation.

The identity of Israel is so important because so very much is at stake. While God makes many promises in the Bible, it is with Israel that God makes His most significant and intimate covenant. God promises to make Israel a "great nation," as numerous as the stars in the sky, and to grant Israel a Promised Land as its inheritance. God also provides this great nation with a great mission, promising that through Israel all the nations of the earth will be blessed. In the shorthand that has been used throughout the centuries, God makes Israel His chosen people.

Judaism teaches that the Jews are the chosen people to whom God promised so much. When parsing the words "Abraham and his descendants," the Jews have employed a literal interpretation. The Jewish people claim the mantle of Israel through their *physical* descent from Abraham.*

For most of its history, from the middle of the second century through the middle of the twentieth, the Christian church embraced a different interpretation. Christians maintained that when the Jews rejected Christ as the Messiah, the church replaced the Jews as the beneficiaries of the Abrahamic covenant. Thus the church—the true *spiritual* descendants of Abraham—became the new Israel. The technical term for this view is *supersessionism*, that

---

* It is true that other nations, including the Arabs, also trace their lineage back to Abraham. But for the Jews, Genesis 17:19 clarifies the matter when God tells: "Sarah your wife shall bear you a son, and you shall call his name Isaac; I will establish My covenant with him for an everlasting covenant, and with his descendants after him." Only the Jews claim descent through Isaac.

is, the belief that the church superseded Israel as God's chosen people. This view is more commonly and more simply known as *replacement theology*.

It is possible to imagine a replacement theology that stripped Jews of their divine inheritance but otherwise accorded them full respect as human beings and children of God. Yet while certain Christians at certain junctures embraced such a tolerant outlook, it typically remained a minority view. In most places where it held sway, replacement theology led inexorably to anti-Semitic opinion, legislation, and action. Rejected by God, the Jews found little mercy from man.

In the early nineteenth century, dissident Protestants began to embrace an alternative, literal interpretation of the Abrahamic covenant. Under this theology, the Jews were never replaced—they are still the Israel who will inherit all that God promised in the Bible. Accordingly, the birth of the State of Israel is viewed as the fulfillment of the Abrahamic covenant and of numerous biblical prophecies. In twentieth-century America, a domestic religious upheaval combined with unprecedented tragedy abroad to transform this minority interpretation into the dominant Christian view. More than any other single factor, this theological shift—the decline of replacement theology in postwar America—explains the rise of Christian Zionism.

A POPULAR PILGRIMAGE for Jewish tourists has come to be known as the "March of the Living." The trip starts in Poland, at the site of Auschwitz. After contemplating the greatest tragedy in Jewish history at the epicenter of the Holocaust, the participants fly to Israel. There they celebrate the greatest miracle of Jewish history: the resurrected Jewish State. Having started in the deep valley, the heights no doubt appear even more glorious.

This book follows a similar itinerary. Chapter one reviews the birth of replacement theology and its very bitter legacy for the Jewish people. Chapter two then relates the rejection of replacement theology and the rise of Christian Zionism. The remainder of this book is devoted to a review of the actions and implications that have flowed from this theological shift. When viewed in light of the centuries of Christian anti-Semitism that preceded it, it becomes clear that this new Christian theology toward the Jews is a shift and an opportunity that must not be ignored.

The cornerstone of Christian Anti-Semitism is the superseding or displacement myth, which already rings with the genocidal note. This is the myth that the mission of the Jewish people was finished with the coming of Jesus Christ, that "the old Israel" was written off with the appearance of "the new Israel." To teach that a people's mission in God's providence is finished, that they have been relegated to the limbo of history, has murderous implication, which murderers will in time spell out.[1]

—Franklin Littell, 1975

Chapter One

THE RISE OF REPLACEMENT THEOLOGY

WHEN NAPOLEON'S ARMIES conquered Rome in 1809, they entered a city where Jews were forced to wear a yellow star on their clothes, forbidden to eat, drink, or converse with Christians, and were literally locked behind their ghetto walls each night. True to the ideals of the French Revolution, Napoleon opened the gates of the ghetto and granted the Jews full rights of citizenship. It appeared that, for Rome's Jews, the Middle Ages had finally ended.

Such optimism was short lived. After a series of military defeats, Napoleon's regime collapsed in 1814. In the power vacuum that followed, the Vatican regained control of Rome and its neighboring territories and reestablished a Papal State. Upon his return to power, Pope Pius VII reinstated all of the prior restrictions upon the Jews. The Jews were forced back into the ghetto. The Inquisition was revived. Jewish students were expelled from the universities.[2]

The Vatican's anti-Jewish regime was no sudden paroxysm of hate—it was the culmination of centuries of anti-Jewish edicts and pronouncements. Such church policies toward the Jews flowed directly from church theology regarding the Jews. The Roman church had for centuries embraced replacement theology. In teaching that it had replaced the Jews as God's chosen people, the church asserted a divine rejection of the Jews that opened the door to human imitation. The ghetto followed logically.

THE BIRTH OF REPLACEMENT THEOLOGY

JESUS WAS JEWISH. His disciples were Jewish. In the prevailing Christian view, the Bible was written by forty authors. Of these, thirty-nine were Jewish. The fortieth, Luke, was likely a convert to Judaism. None of these earliest Christians believed that they were starting a new religion. They merely sought to spread the news that Jewish prophecy had been fulfilled by the arrival of the Jewish Messiah.

Even when some of the early church fathers began to turn outward and preach the gospel to the Gentiles, they continued to cling to the Jewish roots of their faith. Many early churches required their Gentile members to be circumcised and to observe the full breadth of Jewish law. Jerusalem remained the physical and spiritual center of the nascent church. So long as they viewed themselves as Jewish, Christians continued to embrace the traditional view that the Jews were the beneficiaries of God's covenant with Abraham.

Christians did not continue to view themselves as Jewish for very long. The Christian leaders who believed that the church must follow Jewish law quickly lost the argument to those who believed that such rituals were no longer necessary. Once these barriers were eliminated, the early trickle of Gentile converts quickly grew into a steady stream. As the first century gave way to the second, Christianity became a Gentile religion in which Jews played an ever-declining role.

As this demographic shift took place, a theological one followed. The flow of Gentile converts into the church created a pressure to broaden the covenant beyond one specific bloodline. Some of the church fathers began to assert that the criterion for inclusion in the covenant was not blood but belief: so long as the converts accepted Christ, they became part of the chosen people. Yet this assertion implied a corollary. If faith in Christ was the basis for inclusion within the covenant, then Jewish blood alone was no longer sufficient in the absence of such faith. Indeed, by the mid-second century, this implication was made explicit. The language that had once been used to argue for Gentile *inclusion* within the Abrahamic covenant was increasingly used to argue for Jewish *exclusion* from the covenant.[3] Thus replacement theology was born.

The apostle Paul's struggle

The life and teachings of the apostle Paul capture in real time the demographic and theological transformation of the early church into a Gentile institution. Paul (née Saul) was born into a Jewish family in Tarsus, a Roman province on the southeastern coast of modern-day Turkey, around A.D. 1. A devout Jew, Paul traveled to Jerusalem to study with Rabbi Gamaliel, one of the giants of the rabbinic period, and he became active in the effort to combat the spread of Christian teachings among the Jews. When Christians started making inroads among the Jews of Damascus, Paul set off for that city to fight back.

Then something happened on the road to Damascus. Paul saw a vision of Christ and immediately converted. From that day forward, he redirected his zeal from fighting the church to building it. At a time when most Christians still sought converts from among the Jews, Paul turned outward and devoted himself to preaching the gospel of Jesus Christ to the Gentiles. He traveled the Mediterranean world preaching, converting, and building Gentile Christian communities. In addition to personal visits, he pursued his missionary work through letters. From A.D. 51 through A.D. 65 Paul wrote a series of letters to Gentile Christian communities that were later enshrined in the New Testament.

Paul preached an inclusive message to the Gentiles. He argued forcefully against the need for Gentile converts to follow Jewish law. To justify this position, Paul dismissed the importance of the "outward" signs of being Jewish, such as following Jewish ritual or being circumcised "of the flesh." He instead stressed the importance of being a Jew "inwardly" and of being circumcised "of the heart" through faith in Jesus Christ. After Christ, argued Paul, the old Jewish rituals were merely impediments to the growth of the church.

Paul carried this distinction between the physical and the spiritual over into his interpretation of the Abrahamic covenant. He stressed that the Gentiles could, through their faith in Christ, become full participants in God's covenant with Israel. In his Epistle to the Romans, Paul illustrated this point by analogizing God's covenant with Israel to an olive tree. According to Paul, the Jews were the original branches, many of which were "broken off" due to "unbelief." The church, he wrote, is a wild olive shoot that was "grafted" into the Jewish olive tree and thereby became "a partaker of the root and fatness of the olive tree."[4]

Paul thus opened the Abrahamic covenant to all who believe in Christ without regard to Jewish descent or practice. In so doing, he also laid the rhetorical foundation for Jewish exclusion from the covenant. It was Paul who enshrined the idea that the failure of the Jews to accept Christ was a basis for exclusion from the covenant when he referred to the Jews as the original branches of the olive tree that were "broken off" due to "unbelief." Likewise it was Paul who embraced the concept that blood alone was not a sufficient basis for inclusion in the covenant when he wrote that:

> They are not all Israel who are of Israel, nor are they all children because they are the seed of Abraham.... those who are children of the flesh, these are not the children of God; but the children of the promise are counted as the seed.[5]

Perhaps anticipating the arguments for Jewish exclusion that could flow from his own words, Paul sought to preserve a special status for his people "of the flesh." After comparing the church to the wild shoot grafted into the olive tree, he famously cautioned the Gentiles:

> Do not boast against the branches. But if you do boast, remember that you do not support the root, but the root supports you.[6]

Paul also invokes his own identity on behalf of the Jews:

> I say then, has God cast away His people? Certainly not! For I also am an Israelite, of the seed of Abraham, of the tribe of Benjamin. God has not cast away His people whom He foreknew.[7]

He later returns to this theme a third time:

> I say then, have they [the Jews] stumbled that they should fall? Certainly not!... Concerning the gospel they [the Jews] are enemies for your sake, but concerning the election they are beloved for the sake of the fathers. For the gifts and the calling of God are irrevocable.[8]

In perhaps the ultimate statement of love for his own Jewish people, Paul states that he wishes he could be "accursed from Christ" so that his brethren "according to the flesh" might be saved.[9]

THERE IS A tension underlying Paul's defense of the Jews. Such tension is perhaps unavoidable given the task Paul took upon himself of opening the

Abrahamic covenant to all who shared faith in Christ while preserving a special status for the Jewish people.[10] Once faith is made the fundamental criterion for entry into the covenant, the status of Jews lacking such faith is tenuous at best. Christian theology carried within it the seeds of supersessionism from its earliest days.

Paul believed that Christ's Second Coming was imminent. He never envisioned centuries or millennia separating the first and second comings. He likely felt no need, therefore, to find a definitive resolution to the tension between the continued election of the Jews and their rejection of Christ since Christ Himself would soon be on hand to settle the issue.[11] When Christ tarried, these tensions were resolved by men with far less tolerance for ambiguity than Paul.

Justin Martyr and full-blown replacement

In the mid-second century, approximately one hundred years after Paul wrote his Epistle to the Romans, the church abandoned Paul's struggle to preserve a special status for the Jews in favor of a clear and clean replacement theology. By this time, the split between Judaism and Christianity had hardened, and the flow of Jewish converts into Christianity had largely stopped. While there would continue to be Judaizers in the church seeking to bring it back to its Jewish roots, they had lost their hold over the new religion and would never regain it.

The foremost spokesman of this early replacement theology was one of the leading theologians of the period, Justin Martyr. Justin, a Gentile convert to Christianity, lived in various Christian communities around the Mediterranean. As his name indicates, he ultimately met with an untimely end at the hands of the Romans. One of Justin Martyr's most important works was his *Dialogue with Trypho.* Here Justin debates theology with Trypho, a fictional Jewish scholar. In Dialogue 11, Justin claims the mantle of Israel for the church:

> We [Christians] have been led to God through this crucified Christ, and we are the true spiritual Israel, and the descendants of Judah, Jacob, Isaac, and Abraham who, though uncircumcised, was approved and blessed by God because of his faith and was called the father of many nations.[12]

In Dialogue 44, Justin makes clear that Christian inclusion is accompanied by Jewish exclusion:

> You [Jews] are sadly mistaken if you think that, just because you are descendants of Abraham according to the flesh, you will share in the legacy of benefits which God promised would be distributed by Christ.[13]

Finally, in Dialogue 119, Justin expands upon the implications of Jewish replacement:

> We Christians are not only a people, but a holy people... nor just any nation... but the chosen people of God.... For this is really the nation promised to Abraham by God when He told him He would make him a father of many nations.... And we [Christians] shall inherit the Holy Land together with Abraham, receiving our inheritance for all eternity, because by our similar faith we have become children of Abraham.... Thus, God promised Abraham a religious and righteous nation of like faith, and a delight to the Father; but it is not you [the Jews] "in whom there is no faith."[14]

To Justin, the dispossession is complete. The Jews—physical Israel—will inherit none of the benefits of the Abrahamic covenants, *not even the physical benefits.* Everything once promised to the Jews, including the land of Israel itself, will now flow to the church.

St. Augustine's shelter

In 387, a man named Augustine was baptized outside of Rome. "After Constantine, the conversion of Augustine may be the most momentous in the history of the Church."[15] When the Roman emperor Constantine converted to Christianity, he made his new faith the official religion of his vast empire. When Augustine converted, he began a career of prolific writing that would make him the most influential Christian thinker of his day. Augustine's views became the official doctrine of the newly ascendant church.

When it came to the Jews, Augustine embraced replacement theology, declaring the Jews to be "the House of Israel which [God] has cast off."[16] Augustine thus elevated replacement theology to official church doctrine, where it would remain enshrined for over a millennium and a half. It would take a tragedy on the scale of the Holocaust to cause the Catholic Church to reexamine this issue.

Yet much like Paul before him, Augustine sought to carve out a special status for the Jews. By Augustine's day, the issue was no longer the abstract one of saving for the Jews a place within God's covenant, but the far more immediate one of saving their lives.[17] With Christianity now the official religion of the Roman Empire, religious minorities throughout the realm faced increasing peril. Christian leaders of the day were already preaching violence against the Jews, and such violence inevitably followed. In 414, a full-scale pogrom occurred in Alexandria, the largest Jewish community in the world at that time. The Jews were expelled from the city and their synagogues destroyed. During this era, pagans and other religious minorities were persecuted into extinction.

It is thus of great significance that Augustine asserted a justification for the continued existence of Jewish communities in Christian lands. Augustine argued that Christians faced a credibility problem. He wrote that the Old Testament is filled with so many clear predictions of the coming of Christ that skeptics would likely dismiss the work as a Christian forgery. However, he asserted, such an argument against the authenticity of the Bible is conclusively rebutted by the fact that this book is preserved by the Jews, the very people who rejected, crucified, and "daily blaspheme" Christ.[18] In this context, the Jewish rejection of Christ becomes a Christian asset. The Jews were witnesses to the truth of Christianity.

For Augustine, the destruction of Jerusalem and the dispersion of the Jews throughout the Roman Empire both confirmed and enabled their new mission. In his words:

> For if they lived with that testimony of the Scriptures only in their own land, and not everywhere, the obvious result would be that the Church, which is everywhere, would not have them available among all nations as witness to the prophecies which were given beforehand concerning Christ.[19]

Having found for the Jews a continuing divine mission, Augustine exhorted his followers to spare their lives. In reference to the Jews, Augustine quotes the Psalms, "Do not slay them, lest at some time they forget your Law; scatter them by your might."[20] While the exhortation "do not slay them" is hardly a warm ecumenical embrace, these words likely enabled Jewish survival in Christian Europe up to the Enlightenment.

AUGUSTINE PLACED DIVINE significance upon the "dispersion" of the Jews. Under a pure interpretation of Augustine's replacement theology, therefore, the Jews could have been dispersed, but not despised. Yet simpler minds inevitably added to Augustine's formula a component of degradation. The Jews would serve as a witness to the truth of Christ not only by their dispersion, but also by their suffering in dispersion.

Much like the apostle Paul before him, therefore, Augustine's effort to preserve a limited status for the Jews contained within it an ambiguity that would elude the masses and the mob. The overriding message of replacement overpowered any subtle caveats placed before it. As Catholic writer James Carroll has noted, "Augustine's relatively benign attitude toward Jews is rooted in assumptions of supersessionism that would prove to be deadly." Carroll added that:

> For a thousand years, the compulsively repeated pattern would show in bishops and popes protecting Jews—but from expressly Christian mobs that wanted to kill Jews because of what bishops and popes had taught about Jews. Such a teaching that wants it both ways was bound to fail, as would become evident at every point in history when Jews presumed, whether economically or culturally or both, to even think of thriving.[21]

Replacement theology thus evolved, inexorably, into a rationale for persecuting the Jews. Exclusion from God's covenant led to exclusion from Christian society, and then led, too often, to exclusion from the human family. This shift from *replaced* to *despised* was made most explicitly by a contemporary of Augustine named Saint John Chrysostom.[22]

John Chrysostom and anti-Semitic violence

In the year 387, Saint John Chrysostom, the bishop of Antioch, delivered a series of anti-Jewish sermons to his flock. Chrysostom enthusiastically embraced replacement theology and added to it a new and ominous charge. For Justin Martyr and Augustine, the Jews had been replaced because they lacked faith in Christ. While both men invoked the charge of deicide against the Jews, neither emphasized it. For Chrysostom, however, deicide was the ultimate Jewish crime, and he made it a central plank of replacement theology. Addressing the Jews, Chrysostom asserted:

> It is because you killed Christ. It is because you stretched out your hand against the Lord. It is because you shed the precious blood that there is now no restoration, no mercy anymore and no defense.... Through your madness against Christ you have committed the ultimate transgression. This is why you are being punished now worse than in the past.... If this were not the case God would not have turned his back on you so completely.[23]

Having traced the cause of replacement to the bloody crucifixion, Chrysostom calls for bloody retribution. In Chrysostom, the link between *replacement* and *elimination* is made explicit. In one example of his oratory, Chrysostom analogizes the Jews to gluttonous "pigs" who understand only how to "gorge themselves and get drunk." The analogy thus established, Chrysostom escalates his rhetoric. The foreshadowing is chilling:

> When animals have been fattened by having all they want to eat, they get stubborn and hard to manage.... When animals are unfit for work, they are marked for slaughter, and this is the very thing which the Jews have experienced. By making themselves unfit for work, they have become ready for slaughter. This is why Christ said, "As for my enemies, who did not want me to reign over them, bring them here and slay them before me."[24]

In a pattern that would tragically repeat itself throughout the centuries that followed, anti-Jewish rhetoric inevitably inspired anti-Jewish action. Chrysostom preached at the close of the fourth century. In the early fifth century there were a series of violent pogroms against the Jews in Chrysostom's city, Antioch. The great synagogues of the city were destroyed. During this same era, the first recorded charge of ritual murder against the Jews was made in Antioch. These eruptions of anti-Jewish violence continued into the sixth century until the Jews were finally expelled from Antioch altogether.[25] So it began.

FOR THE NEXT millennium and a half, up until the twentieth century, Christian treatment of the Jews would alternate between the two poles established by Chrysostom and Augustine in the fourth century. At times, the church embraced Augustine's approach, content to separate the Jews but not murder them. At other times, Augustine's exhortation not to slay the Jews was lost in the anti-Semitic frenzy whipped up by the charge of deicide, blood libels, and other invective. Sometimes permitted to survive, never permitted to thrive, the Jews would spend centuries in Christian Europe clinging to a second-class status in the best of times.

The codification of replacement theology

In 313, the emperor Constantine converted to Christianity and made his new religion the official religion of the Roman Empire. Overnight, Christianity went from a persecuted religious minority to the state religion of the greatest empire on earth. Christians now had a vast state apparatus and powerful army at their command. This marriage of Christian theology with state power would prove disastrous for the Jews. Replacement theology and the degradation that flowed from it were gradually transformed from abstract theological concepts into the law of the land. In the words of Jules Isaac, "The fate of Israel did not take on a truly inhuman character until the fourth century A.D. with the coming of the Christian Empire."[26]

Constantine himself initiated the transformation of anti-Semitic doctrine into anti-Semitic law. In 315, the new emperor issued an edict making it a crime for Jews to proselytize. At the Council of Nicaea held in 325, Constantine ordained that the date of the Christian Easter should no longer be linked to that of the Jewish Passover, declaring, "It is unbecoming that on the holiest of festivals we should follow the customs of the Jews; henceforth let us have nothing in common with this odious people."[27]

Building on what Constantine had started, Christian synods and councils continued to translate replacement theology and related doctrine into the law of the realm. From the Council of Nicaea in 325 up until the Council of Basel in 1434, the church gradually built a legal regime that removed the Jews from Christian society and locked them behind ghetto walls.* The following are merely the highlights:

- Synod of Clermont (535): Jews are prohibited from holding public office.
- Synod of Orleans (538): Jews are barred from owning Christian slaves or employing Christian servants.
- Synod of Gerona (1078): Jews are obligated to pay taxes for support of the church to the same extent as Christians.
- Third Lateran Council (1179): Jews are prohibited from suing or being witnesses against Christians in the courts.
- Fourth Lateran Council (1215): Jews are required to wear distinctive dress (eventually implemented by means of a yellow badge).
- Council of Oxford (1222): Construction of new synagogues is prohibited.
- Synod of Breslau (1267): Jews are forced to reside in ghettos.
- Synod of Ofen (1279): Christians are prohibited from selling or renting real estate to Jews.
- Council of Basel (1434): Jews are barred from obtaining academic degrees.[28]

As early as the fourth century John Chrysostom demonstrated that anti-Jewish pronouncements lead inexorably to anti-Jewish violence. Throughout the centuries of these anti-Jewish edicts and legislation, the truth of this tragic law of human nature was proven time and time again. The long history of anti-Semitic violence in Christendom is well known and has been well documented. During these dark centuries, Christian authorities visited upon the

* A few anti-Semitic measures actually predated Constantine. In 306, most notably, Christian leaders meeting at the Synod of Elvira prohibited intermarriage, sexual intercourse, and the sharing of meals between Christians and Jews.

Jews the organized violence of the Crusades and the Inquisitions, most notoriously that of Spain. Christian leaders also inspired more sporadic violence in the form of countless local pogroms and Easter massacres. In different places and at different times, Jews repeatedly faced the choice of conversion to Christianity or death. Quite often, the option of conversion was not provided.

The Reformation: An opportunity missed

When Martin Luther nailed his *95 Theses* to the door of his church in the early 1500s, he shattered the Catholic Church's monopoly on Christian theology in the West. Out of Luther's critique grew the Protestant Reformation and the rise of new Christian sects freed from the theological control of Rome.

This break from Roman orthodoxy opened the door to a new theology toward the Jews. Yet this was a door through which Martin Luther did not walk. Despite significant theological differences in other areas, Luther and his followers did not challenge Rome's position on the Jews. It took centuries before certain minority Protestant sects would take advantage of their theological freedom to arrive at a different view of the Jews.

Instead of rejecting replacement theology, Martin Luther embraced it and contributed to the rhetorical erosion of Augustine's protective teachings. Some of the most anti-Semitic writings in the history of the Christian church came from Luther's pen. In a work bearing the less-than-subtle title *The Jews and Their Lies*, Luther sets forth a program for dealing with the Jews that foreshadows future tragedy:

> First, their synagogues or churches should be set on fire, and whatever does not burn up should be covered or spread over with dirt so that no one may ever be able to see a cinder or stone of it. And this ought to be done for the honor of God and of Christianity in order that God may see that we are Christians.... Secondly, their homes should be broken down and destroyed. Thirdly, they should be deprived of their prayer books and Talmuds in which such idolatry, lies, cursing and blasphemy are taught.
>
> Fourthly, their Rabbis must be forbidden under threat of death to teach any more.... Fifthly, passport and traveling privileges should be absolutely forbidden the Jews. Let them stay at home. Sixthly, they

> ought to be stopped from usury. For this reason, as said before, everything they possess they stole and robbed from us through their usury, for they have no other means of support. Seventhly, let the young and strong Jews and Jewesses be given the flail, the ax, the hoe, the spade, the distaff, and spindle, and let them earn their bread by the sweat of their noses as is enjoined upon Adam's children.
>
> If, however, we are afraid that they might harm us personally, or our wives, children, servants, cattle, etc., then let us apply the same cleverness as the other nations such as France, Spain, Bohemia, etc., and settle with them for that which they have extorted from us, and after having it divided up fairly let us drive them out of the country for all time.[29]

Thus the Reformation provided the Jews no shelter from replacement theology and its consequences. Up until the Enlightenment, with limited exceptions, the pattern of anti-Semitic edicts and anti-Semitic acts continued in Protestant lands much as it did in those still under Rome's sway.

THE HOLOCAUST

NAZISM WAS NOT a Christian ideology. Quite to the contrary, Nazism was the antithesis of true Christianity. Christians worship Jesus Christ, the Lamb of God who turned the other cheek and willingly went to the cross. The Nazis worshiped blood. They built an altar to their own Aryan blood and upon this altar made millions of human sacrifices. The Nazis rightly recognized true Christianity as an enemy, and thousands of Christian martyrs suffered and died alongside Jews at Nazi hands.

It was modern, neo-pagan Nazism that perpetrated the Holocaust. Yet there is evidence of a Christian core beneath the pagan patina. Christian responsibility for the genocide of Europe's Jews exists at two levels, one historical and one contemporaneous. At the historical level, centuries of Christian anti-Semitism prepared Europe to so readily and enthusiastically embrace Nazi anti-Semitism. For most Europeans, Nazism was merely a new variation on an old and very familiar theme. At the contemporaneous level, the Holocaust was committed by Christians in the heart of Christendom. According to a survey conducted in 1939, 95 percent of Germans belonged to a Christian church.[30] None of the many Catholics in the Nazi leadership, including Hitler himself, were excommunicated by the Catholic Church during or after the war.[31] Nazi soldiers were buried in Christian graves.

An honest analysis of the consequences of replacement theology cannot avoid confronting the Holocaust.

The Catholic Church and the Holocaust

Nazism, along with its race-based anti-Semitism, was a relatively new ideology in Europe. Yet this ideology instantly and deeply resonated with the European masses. In searching for an explanation for this rapid adoption, it is difficult to avoid the conclusion that Nazism flourished in soil fertilized by centuries of Christian replacement theology.

This connection between Christian religious anti-Semitism and Nazi racial anti-Semitism is at its most explicit in the realm of anti-Jewish legislation. Upon coming to power in 1933, the Nazis immediately went to work reversing the Enlightenment and extracting the Jews from Aryan society. One of the first Nazi initiatives was to pass a series of racial laws that reduced the Jews to a separate, degraded existence. As the Nazis conquered neighboring countries, they imposed, or had their puppet regimes adopt, similar racial codes.

In most places in which these anti-Jewish laws were promulgated, they were not revolutionary concepts but merely a return to the legal regime that had only recently been replaced. As historian Raul Hilberg has demonstrated, the anti-Jewish laws passed by the Third Reich and its allies all had clear precedents in church law. Indeed, almost every anti-Semitic provision passed by the various church councils and synods throughout the centuries found new life in Nazi legislation.[32] While the Nazi-era laws had a new, racial justification, they fit neatly into a preexisting space in the European imagination.

BEYOND SETTING IDEOLOGICAL and legal precedents, the Catholic Church also played a more direct, real-time role in the Holocaust. The first official action of the Catholic Church toward the new Nazi regime was to recognize it. On July 8, 1933, the Vatican signed the Concordat with Hitler. This agreement was Hitler's first bilateral treaty with a foreign power, and it was for him a significant diplomatic victory. Under this agreement, the Vatican recognized

Hitler's regime and agreed to remove the Catholic Church and the political parties affiliated with it from the political opposition. German bishops were obligated to swear an oath of allegiance to the Nazi state. Throughout the war, even as news of atrocities and genocide made their way into common knowledge, the Vatican never repudiated the Concordat.

The Catholic Church in Germany complied obediently with the role assigned it under the Concordat. Although the church condemned other aspects of Nazi policy, such as the euthanasia of the mentally ill, it never officially protested any of the Nazi policies toward the Jews. On the contrary, Catholic churches actually helped the Nazis to identify Jews by providing them access to church genealogical records. Throughout the war years, even after the fate of deported Jews was common knowledge, these churches continued to share these vital records.[33]

When the final solution came to Italy and Rome itself, the church continued its silence. In the fall of 1938, Mussolini's Fascist government adopted a set of anti-Jewish racial laws modeled on the Nuremberg laws. In defending this legislation, the Fascists invoked the clear similarity of this new code with the Catholic Church's traditional anti-Jewish codes. Roberto Farinacci, a member of the Fascist Grand Council, noted that until the French Revolution, all states had excluded "Jews from public offices, from the schools, from university degrees, from exercising professional business positions. All this in harmony with the dispositions sanctioned by the Church through its councils and papal bulls."[34]

Neither the pope nor any other church authority publicly opposed the Fascist legislation in its declaration or implementation. The Italian government's representative to the Holy See reported back to his government that the new laws "have not, on the whole, found an unfavorable reception at the Vatican."[35] When the pope did finally speak out against the legislation, he limited his critique to the application of these laws to Jews who had converted to Catholicism. Catholic converts, argued the pope, were no longer Jews and therefore should not be subject to these restrictions.[36] The pope thus objected to the one and only provision of the new laws that went beyond the church's traditional anti-Semitism.

Church acquiescence continued even when the Nazis came to take away Rome's Jews. On October 16, 1943, German SS units rounded up all of Rome's Jews in the central square of the Jewish ghetto. On October 18, these prisoners were driven to the train station and loaded onto cattle cars bound for Auschwitz. The journey to Auschwitz that followed was practically a public spectacle.

As the train departed Rome, it was attacked by Allied aircraft seeking to stop it. The attack failed. As the train passed through Padua, in northern Italy, the local bishop saw the condition of the Jews in the cattle cars and begged the pope to take urgent action. When the train reached Vienna, the Vatican was informed that the prisoners were begging for water.[37]

Five days after the train had set off from Rome, all but 196 of the 1,000 passengers were gassed to death at Auschwitz. Of the 196 admitted to the camp to work, only 15 survived the war. All of the survivors were men, except for one woman. She suffered a fate worse than death as the subject of Dr. Josef Mengele's sadistic medical experiments.[38]

The pope made no public statement about the roundup and deportation until after most of the Jewish deportees were already dead. When he did speak, his references were veiled and mentioned neither the Jews nor their deaths. He instead lamented "the suffering of all innocents in the war" and the "increased suffering of so many unfortunate people."[39]

THE VATICAN'S DEFENDERS take exception to the argument that the Catholic Church did not do enough to save Jews during the Holocaust. They note, accurately, that the rolls of the righteous Gentiles are filled with Catholics who risked their lives to save Jews. Among the rescuers were Catholic priests, monks, and nuns who often hid Jews on church property. The pope himself gave refuge to no less than three thousand Italian Jews in his summer residence at Castel Gandolfo.[40] Some of the Vatican's defenders have further argued that the pope needed to maintain his relative silence so as not to jeopardize these ongoing rescue efforts.

Without wading too deeply into this hot controversy, it is sufficient for present purposes to note that even the church's defenders recognize some level of Catholic responsibility. The Catholic Church itself, through its words and deeds, has acknowledged a link between church anti-Semitism and the

Holocaust. The Vatican framed the issue well in its 1998 document, *We Remember: A Reflection on the Shoah*:*

> But it must be asked whether the Nazi persecution of the Jews was not made easier by the anti-Jewish prejudices embedded in some Christian minds and hearts. Did anti-Jewish sentiment among Christians make them less sensitive, or even indifferent, to the persecution launched against the Jews by National Socialism when it reached power?

While the Vatican does not directly answer this question in this document, it provides a series of *dots* that can be connected into a tacit acknowledgment of responsibility. The Vatican recognizes that "certain interpretations of the New Testament regarding the Jewish people as a whole," that is, replacement theology, led to discrimination, expulsion, forced conversion, violence, and massacres against the Jews. The Vatican further notes that Christians did not engage in resistance to Nazism that "might have been expected from Christ's followers." The document then concludes, "For Christians, this heavy burden of conscience of their brothers and sisters during the Second World War must be a call to penitence."

Other church bodies have been less reticent in noting the link between Christian anti-Semitism and Nazi success. In a landmark 1997 statement, the Catholic bishops of France acknowledged that:

> In the process which led to the Shoah, we are obliged to admit the role, indirect if not direct, played by commonly held anti-Jewish prejudices, which Christians were guilty of maintaining. . . . In the judgment of historians, it is a well-proven fact that for centuries . . . an anti-Jewish tradition stamped its mark in differing ways on Christian doctrine and teaching, in theology, apologetics, preaching and in the liturgy. It was on such ground that the venomous past of hatred for the Jews was able to flourish. Hence, the heavy inheritance we still bear in our century, with all its consequences, which are so difficult to wipe out. Hence our still open wounds.

* The Vatican here used the Hebrew word for the Holocaust.

More importantly than its words, the Vatican has recognized the link between replacement theology and the Holocaust in its deeds. Within a generation of the Holocaust, the Vatican officially renounced replacement theology. Even if the reason was not explicitly acknowledged, the timing of such a dramatic theological change speaks volumes.

The church's new approach to the Jewish people was one of the many reforms to emerge from the Second Vatican Council. In 1965, the Council issued a declaration entitled *Nostra Aetate* addressing the church's relationship with non-Christian religions. In this document the Vatican boldly and clearly rejected both replacement theology and the related charge of deicide by pronouncing that:

> What happened in His [Christ's] passion cannot be charged against all the Jews, without distinction, then alive, nor against the Jews of today. Although the Church is the new people of God, the Jews should not be presented as rejected or accursed by God, as if this followed from Holy Scriptures.

This document elsewhere notes that "God holds the Jews most dear for the sake of their Fathers; He does not repent of the gifts He makes or of the calls He issues..." *Nostra Aetate* also reminds believers of the Jewish roots of Christ, the Virgin Mary, the apostles, the early disciples of the church, and the Old Testament. This document invokes Paul's words in Romans by noting that the church "draws sustenance from the root of that well-cultivated olive tree onto which have been grafted the wild shoots, the Gentiles."

The Protestant role

Like the Catholic Church, Protestant churches also bear a historical and contemporaneous responsibility for the Holocaust. Much like the Catholic Church, the major Protestant denominations had embraced and preached replacement theology for centuries. Martin Luther rivaled and quite possibly surpassed John Chrysostom in the vitriol of his anti-Jewish rhetoric. Because the Lutheran church was the major Protestant denomination in Germany, the views of Martin Luther had a particular resonance with Germans. Hitler cited Martin Luther in *Mein Kampf.* Julius Streicher, the publisher of Hitler's newspaper, *Der Stuermer*, quoted Luther in his own defense at the Nuremberg trials.

It was not only the Nazis themselves who invoked Martin Luther to justify their anti-Semitic program. Protestant leaders often echoed the call. After the Kristallnacht anti-Jewish pogroms of November 1938, for example, Bishop Martin Sasse of Thuringia published a compendium of Martin Luther's anti-Semitic writings. In his foreword to the book, Bishop Sasse expressed joy that the Germans were carrying out the program of Luther, whom he referred to as "the greatest anti-Semite of his time, the warner of his people against the Jews." Bishop Sasse noted the happy coincidence that, "On November 10, 1938, on Luther's birthday, the synagogues are burning in Germany."[41]

As Hitler gained popularity in Germany, a group of his followers formed a group named the *Deutsche Christen* [German Christians] as the voice of Nazi ideology within Germany's Protestant churches. The German Christians supported removing all things Jewish from Christianity. They proposed that the church end its efforts to proselytize Jews and that all non-Aryans be barred from becoming ministers and teachers. They further advocated the removal of the "Jewish" Old Testament from the Bible.

When Hitler rose to power in 1933, he moved quickly to consolidate his hold over the major institutions in German society, including the churches. Toward this end, Hitler decided to unite Germany's regional Protestant churches into one unified Reich Church. The regional churches agreed to the unification and participated in the July 1933 elections to select delegates to a new national synod. In the run up to the elections, the Nazi party openly supported the German Christian candidates. On election eve, Hitler himself made a nationally broadcasted radio speech in support of the German Christians. On election day, the German Christians won two-thirds of the vote* and gained control of the national synod as well as regional synods throughout Germany.[42]

The first meeting of the national synod in September 1933 became known as the "brown synod" since so many of the delegates in attendance wore their

---

* The Nazis had by this point begun to persecute Protestant leaders who opposed the German Christians, no doubt contributing to the German Christian margin of victory.

brown Nazi uniforms. This synod elected the German Christian candidate Ludwig Muller to the new office of Reich Bishop. The synod also adopted the controversial "Aryan paragraph," which required that all Protestant pastors and their wives be free of Jewish blood.[43]

In November 1933, the German Christians held a triumphant rally in Berlin. In a stadium decorated with swastikas and packed with twenty thousand German Christians, the movement's leaders proclaimed the unity of Christianity and National Socialism. Speakers called for the full implementation of the Aryan clause and the removal of the Old Testament from the Bible. As one speaker reasoned:

> If we National Socialists are ashamed to buy a tie from a Jew then we must also rightfully feel ashamed to accept from Jews something that is supposed to speak to our soul, to our innermost religious being.[44]

Even when the German Christians later lost their monopoly over German Protestantism, they continued to be an active and influential force in German society. In 1939, the German Christians held a conference in which they formed an official body known as the "Institute for the Research and Removal of Jewish Influence on the Religious Life of the German People."[45] In 1941, Protestant church leaders from seven German regions issued an official proclamation that declared that Jews were not capable of being saved and that they were "born enemies of the world and Germany." The proclamation urged that the "severest measures against the Jews be adopted and that they be banished from German lands."[46] Of all the Protestant bishops of Germany, only one, in a confidential letter to Hitler, protested the slaughter of the Jews.[47]

NOT ALL OF Germany's Protestants permitted their religion to be hijacked by the Nazis. In 1934, the opponents of the German Christians came together to form the Confessing Church. What united these Protestants was their opposition to government interference in church affairs. Yet while the members of the Confessing Church opposed Nazi interference, not all opposed the Nazis. Many members of the Confessing Church were anti-Semites who had voted for the Nazis or were themselves members of the Nazi party. Many continued to try to work within the system and never challenged the legitimacy of the Nazi government.[48]

There were some notable members of the Confessing Church, however, whose opposition to government interference in church affairs led them into open opposition to the Nazi regime. Martin Niemoller, one of the founders of the Confessing Church, began to preach against the Nazi regime from his pulpit. Hitler arrested him in 1937, and he spent the next eight years in concentration camps. Another leader of the Confessing Church, Dietrich Bonhoeffer, participated in the German resistance and helped smuggle a group of Jews out of Germany. Bonhoeffer was caught and hanged by the Nazis in 1945.

MUCH LIKE THE Catholic Church, the Protestant world has through its actions recognized the connection between replacement theology and the horror of the Holocaust. In the aftermath of the Holocaust, most major Protestant denominations have adopted resolutions clearly renouncing this teaching.

Given its proximity to the epicenter, it is not surprising that the Evangelical Lutheran Church in Germany took the lead in charting a new theological course. In 1950, the church leadership declared that "God's promise is valid for his Chosen People, even after the crucifixion of Jesus Christ."[49] The American Lutheran Church followed suit later, along with most of the major Protestant denominations in America.

While most of these church resolutions were silent as to the reasons for the change, others made the motive explicit. The Presbyterian Church, for example, noted the following when it rejected replacement theology in 1987:

> It is agonizing to discover that the church's teaching of contempt [for the Jews] was a major ingredient that made possible the monstrous policy of annihilation of Jews by Nazi Germany.[50]

FOR MORE THAN fifteen hundred years, the Christian churches of Europe taught that when the Jews rejected Christ, the church replaced them as the true Israel and the beneficiaries of God's promises to Abraham. Once the church achieved temporal power in the fourth century, replacement theologians replicated God's rejection in their realms. As if needing to constantly confirm the truth of replacement, successive Christian generations degraded, persecuted, and murdered the Jews. An exiled, reviled people became living proof that God had embraced a new partner in covenant.

Even when the Enlightenment ended the church's political and spiritual monopoly over Europe, replacement theology's influence continued unabated. Hitler inherited an ideological infrastructure and minds open to his message when he put forth an anti-Semitic program that was new only in its underlying rationale. Hitler's debt to replacement theology was deep.

What if the church had preached a different message? What if Christianity's consistent message had been that God loved and would never forsake the Jewish people? What if week after week for century after century Europe's priests and pastors had preached to their flocks that he who blesses the Jews will be blessed, and he who curses the Jews will be cursed? What if they had rejected the deicide charge and had instead taught that Christians owe a deep debt of gratitude to the Jews for providing their Messiah, their apostles, and their Holy Bible? Could such Christians have systematically excluded Jews from society and locked them in ghettos? Could such Christians have murdered Jews in the belief that they were furthering God's will? Could a Europe so schooled have perpetrated a Holocaust?

Any answer to these questions would be pure conjecture. Yet it is possible to make the guess more educated, to grasp what could have been, by examining the behavior of those Christians who have rejected replacement theology. Today, Christians who reject replacement theology are in the ascendance and dominate American evangelical Christianity. It is to these Christians, and a sunnier chapter, that we now turn.

The error of Replacement Theology is like a cancer in the Church that has not only caused it to violate God's Word concerning the Jewish people and Israel, but it made us into instruments of hate, not love in God's Name. Yet, it is not too late to change our ways and rightly relate to the Jewish people and Israel today.[1]

—The Rev. Clarence E. Wagner
Bridges for Peace, 2003

Chapter Two

THE RETURN OF THE JEWS

DURING WORLD WAR II, a Jewish refugee hiding in a French village ventured out to a nearby farm to buy some eggs. Upon entering the farmhouse, she was accosted by the farmer's wife. "You," the wife asked, "you are Jewish?"

In Vichy France, during the height of the Holocaust, this question struck terror in the heart of a Jew. The Jewish woman stepped back, trembling. She became even more frightened as the matron began to shout to her family upstairs, "Husband, children, come down, come down!"

When the family arrived, however, they did not grab the refugee and hold her for the police. They did not kick her out of the house. Instead, the farmer's wife announced, "Look, look, my family! We have in our house now a representative of the Chosen People!" They welcomed this Jewish refugee as an honored guest.

This Jewish refugee had stumbled upon a village of Plymouth Brethren, known in French as "Darbyites" after the movement's founder, John Nelson Darby.[2] Here, in the heart of Vichy France, was a settlement of religious Protestants who rejected replacement theology and believed instead that the Jews were the chosen people of God. In the midst of a genocide, the theology of the Plymouth Brethren led this Christian family to quite literally embrace the Jewish people.

JOHN NELSON DARBY AND THE PLYMOUTH BRETHREN

THE PLYMOUTH BRETHREN movement was founded in the winter of 1827–1828 when a group of devout Protestants began meeting for prayer and Bible study in Dublin. These young churchmen shared religious zeal and a growing disillusionment with the Anglican Church to which they belonged. They believed that their church was "in ruins," corrupted by hierarchy, power, and money, and disconnected from true spirituality. Their response was separation. The Brethren held their own, independent worship services in which the Bible was the sole authority and all members were equal.

The Brethren were one among many dissenting offshoots of the Anglican Church and were in this regard hardly novel. The pilgrims had come to America over a century and a half earlier with a similar list of grievances against the Anglican Church. What made the Plymouth Brethren unique was not their views on the church but their views on the Jews. The Brethren rejected replacement theology and instead embraced a theology that held that the Jews were still the "Israel" to which so much is promised in the Bible. More importantly, the Brethren succeeded in transmitting their minority view of the Jews to Christian groups far larger and more influential than their own. The Christian Zionist movement was built on a foundation of Plymouth Brethren theology.

One of the founders of the Plymouth Brethren was a young pastor named John Nelson Darby. After being seriously injured in a horse-riding accident, Darby spent a prolonged recuperation immersed in a close study of the Bible. Out of these months of study came the seeds of a revolutionary theology. When Darby and his colleagues formed the Plymouth Brethren, the movement embraced Darby's theology as its own.[3]

Darby read the Bible literally. To Darby, a reference to the "descendants of Abraham" or "Israel" meant the literal, biological descendants of Abraham—the Jews. Accordingly, Darby believed that all of the promises that God made to Israel in the Old Testament would be fulfilled in the Jews. It was Jews who would one day be a great people and the Jews who would one day inherit the land promised to Abraham.

Darby saw confirmation of his literal reading of the Bible in the flow of Jewish history. The Old Testament prophets warned repeatedly that

Israel would turn from God and be punished for this sin with exile. The prophets also foretold, however, that God would remember His covenant with Abraham and would one day return the people of Israel to their Promised Land. In Darby's day, the curse of exile had already been fulfilled in the Jews. As the prophets had predicted, the Jews were indeed living as a persecuted minority throughout the world. If the Jews were the people to suffer Israel's punishment of exile, Darby reasoned, then they must also be the ones to inherit Israel's blessing of return.

In so reading his Bible, Darby bumped up against the paradox encountered by the apostle Paul in the church's earliest days. If God chose only one people to fulfill His divine mission, if there was only one "Israel," then divine election was a zero-sum game. If the Jews were still the chosen people, then where did this leave the church? How could the church of Christ be eclipsed in God's eyes by a people who failed to recognize Christ? Despite Paul's efforts to preserve a special status for the Jews, the church decided early on that the only solution was for the church to replace the Jews as God's chosen people.

Darby proposed a novel way out of the paradox. Instead of attempting the seemingly impossible task of finding space for both the church and the Jews within a singular divine plan for humanity, Darby argued that God had two completely different plans for humanity. One plan was for His "earthly" people, the physical descendants of Abraham, the Jews. A second and distinct plan applied to the spiritual descendants of Abraham, God's "heavenly" people, the church. God would use both peoples to achieve His will on earth under two separate plans playing out in two separate ages.

Like all other aspects of his theology, Darby's two-plan thesis flowed from his method of interpreting the Bible. Darby's literal reading led him to conclude that the church is never mentioned or prophesied in the Old Testament—only an allegorical reading could place the church in that ancient book. Confronted with this textual absence, Darby made a theological leap. Since the church is absent from the Old Testament, he reasoned, then the church could not have been part of God's original plan for humanity as set forth in that text. Instead, the church's creation, mission, and ultimate reward must all take place outside the scenario set forth in the Bible.

Why did God need to change plans? According to Darby, the original script laid out in the Old Testament called for the Jews to recognize Christ as the Messiah. When the Jews failed to do so, God needed to find a different vehicle through which to instruct humanity. Thus God temporarily suspended the prophetic timetable set out in the Old Testament and went to work building the church. Darby wrote that our current age, one in which God is working through the church, actually takes place in an unanticipated *great parenthesis* between God's past and future dealings with Israel. At the end of this age, the true believers in Christ will literally be removed from earth to meet Christ in heaven in an event called *the Rapture.* When the church is thus removed from the picture, God will restart the original prophetic time clock, and the Jews will resume their place at the center of God's original prophetic plan.

For Darby, therefore, the Jewish rejection of Christ did not result in their permanent replacement. Having played their role in the opening acts, the Jews were temporarily placed offstage. The Jews are still the stars of the piece, and they will yet return to center stage for the grand finale. And when they return, all of the covenants that God made with Abraham and his seed will be fulfilled through them. Darby's theology was the rare Christian view that placed the Jews back at the center of God's world.

In rejecting replacement theology, Darby laid the groundwork for a far more philo-Semitic Christianity. *Dispensationalism* restored to the Jews the divine mission and divine love that replacement theology had stripped away. In so doing, dispensationalism provided a very different instruction to individual Christians about how they should relate to the Jews living among them. If God never rejected the Jews but still held them dear, then it followed logically and emotionally that man should do the same.

Dispensationalism also prepared the way for Christian Zionism. Replacement theology had abrogated the Jewish inheritance of the land of Israel by replacing the Jews with the church as the ultimate heirs and by spiritualizing the inheritance from an actual strip of land to a more abstract realm. Dispensationalism recognized the Jews as the legal heirs and the land of Israel as their rightful legacy. Christians who believe that it is God's will for the Jews to return to and rebuild Israel will enthusiastically support the enterprise.

DARBY'S THEOLOGY HAS been burdened with the unwieldy title of "premillennial dispensationalism." It is more commonly referred to by the latter of these two words alone.* This title helps illuminate the ways in which Darby's views differ from those that had traditionally dominated Christianity.

Dispensationalism references Darby's broader theories about God's interaction with humanity. According to Darby and other dispensationalists, God has interacted with His creation under a series of different paradigms, or *dispensations*. Each dispensation is characterized by a distinct test for humanity that humanity inevitably fails. The first dispensation, for instance, started with the creation of man. It ended when Adam ate of the fruit of the tree of the knowledge of good and evil and was cast out of Eden. The second dispensation started with Adam's fall and ended when God punished a sinful humanity with the great flood.

Viewed from this perspective, the Jewish failure to recognize Christ as the Messiah was not an unprecedented crime against God. The Jews were merely continuing a well-worn pattern of human failure. The punishment for this failure was not rejection by God, but the end of one dispensation and the beginning of another. The dispensation that followed the Jewish rejection of Christ, the one we are currently living in, is one in which God deals with mankind through the church. When Christ returns, the church will disappear, and the final dispensation of human history will begin.

The modifier *premillennial* describes Darby's views on the timing of events relating to this last dispensation. A central concept in Christianity is the Millennium, a one-thousand-year period when Christ will reign in triumph. Christians differ on a host of issues relating to the Millennium such as whether it will be a literal thousand-year reign of Christ on Earth or a more figurative, symbolic reign of Christ in the hearts of man. Christians also differ on the timing of the Millennium, that is, whether it will occur before or after Christ's Second Coming. Darby was among those who believed that the Second Coming would *precede* the start of the Millennium, and his theology is therefore properly categorized as *pre*millennial.

Darby was not the first theologian to embrace either dispensationalism or premillennialism. He may not even have been the first to combine the two views into one theology. But Darby was the first to combine these views in a theology that insisted upon a strict separation between Israel and the church.

---

* Throughout this work, I will refer to Darby's premillennial dispensationalism as *dispensationalism*.

In the words of theologian Charles Ryrie, the distinction between Israel and the church is the "essence"[4] of Darby's dispensationalism and "probably the most basic theological test of whether or not a man is a dispensationalist."[5]

Darby's separation between Israel and the church is the diametrical opposite of their conflation through the belief that the church replaced the Jews to become Israel. Thus the rejection of replacement theology is not incidental to Darby's dispensationalism—it is the bedrock belief upon which the entire structure rests.

Darby's view of the Jewish people was revolutionary. Yet in the mid-1800s, Darby's theology was known to only a few thousand Protestant intellectuals in Ireland and England. Had dispensationalism remained the theology of the Plymouth Brethren alone, it would have little religious or political significance today. But Darby was an effective and tireless evangelist. In a series of visits to America, he taught dispensationalism to a rising generation of conservative churchmen. In time, Darby's dispensationalism became the dominant theology of America's fundamentalists and would ride to power on their shoulders. To understand the rise of Christian Zionism in America, therefore, it is necessary to trace the rise of the fundamentalist movement.

THE RISE OF FUNDAMENTALISM

FROM ITS INDEPENDENCE until the end of World War I, the United States was characterized by a surprising degree of theological uniformity.[6] During most of this period, America was a predominantly Protestant country. And throughout this period, American Protestantism was dominated in form and substance by evangelicals.[7]

When it came to the role of the Jews in God's plan for humanity, the evangelical Christians who dominated religion in nineteenth-century America shared a common view: they embraced replacement theology.* They believed that God would work through His new people, the church, to usher in the promised Golden Age of the Millennium. As opposed to Darby and other premillennialists, American evangelicals of this era believed that the Second

* It must be noted that American replacement theology of this period was a largely positive one in that it emphasized the election of the church rather than the rejection of the Jews.

Coming of Christ would occur only *after* the Millennium had taken place. These evangelicals are typically referred to, therefore, as *postmillennialists*.

Postmillennialism was first clearly articulated in America by the preeminent prerevolutionary theologian Jonathan Edwards. Edwards is best known today for his fire-and-brimstone sermon "Sinners in the Hands of an Angry God." Despite his severe view of the fate of sinners, however, Edwards' view of the power of Christian believers could not have been rosier. Edwards did not believe that a supernatural intervention by Christ was needed to usher in the Millennium. Instead, Edwards held that Christians could themselves bring the Millennium through "the preaching of the gospel and the use of ordinary means of grace."[8] In practical terms, this boiled down to converting people to evangelical Christianity and eliminating sin, or at least the most public forms thereof, from American society. Adding a note of immediacy to this concept, Edwards preached that the religious revivals of his time marked the "dawning" of the Millennium and that it was likely that America would take the lead in bringing this glorious age to all mankind.[9]

Edwards' postmillennialism was a perfect fit for the optimistic spirit that reigned in America for most of the eighteenth and nineteenth centuries. On the conversion front, it appeared during this period that the church was on a steady march to ultimate victory. A robust Christianity was winning souls in ever-increasing numbers. This was the era of the First and Second Great Awakenings, when evangelical religious fervor descended upon America in enormous waves producing hundreds of thousands of converts. Beyond America, Christian missionaries were taking the good news of Christ to every corner of the globe, winning entire new peoples over to the Christian faith.

On the domestic morality front, evangelical Christians appeared to be succeeding in their efforts to eliminate the last bastions of vice and sin in America. Evangelical Christians were the prime movers behind the temperance movement. Through their efforts, they secured passage of myriad local prohibition laws and, eventually, ratification of the Eighteenth Amendment to the Constitution banning the manufacture and sale of alcoholic beverages in the United States.* Evangelicals also led the Sabbatarian movement, responsible for blue laws across the country forcing most businesses to close on Sundays.

---

* Prohibition was repealed with ratification of the Twenty-first Amendment in 1933.

To many evangelicals, the institution of slavery was America's darkest sin and the greatest barrier to bringing the Millennium. Northern evangelicals thus became the driving force behind the abolitionist movement. Beyond supplying many of its leaders and foot soldiers, evangelical Christianity supplied the movement with its most potent rhetorical weapon, the novel *Uncle Tom's Cabin*. Harriet Beecher Stowe, the devout daughter of one of the most prominent evangelical ministers of the century, wrote this novel that inflamed popular sentiment against slavery.

Given this view of slavery, northern evangelicals viewed the Civil War—a war to end slavery in America—in deeply religious terms. The northern anthem during the Civil War, "The Battle Hymn of the Republic," was actually a postmillennial Christian hymn. The author of the song, Julia Ward Howe, was a deeply religious Christian and a devoted abolitionist. The famous first line of her song, "Mine eyes have seen the glory of the coming of the Lord," immediately associates the Civil War with the Second Coming of Christ. The final stanza of the song emphasizes the higher purpose of the Civil War in stirring terms:

> In the beauty of the lilies Christ was born across the sea,
> With a glory in His bosom that transfigures you and me;
> As He died to make men holy, let us live to make men free,
> While God is marching on.[10]

To evangelical Christians in the mid-nineteenth century, the spread of Christianity, reform, and righteousness appeared inexorable.

IN THE AFTERMATH of the Civil War, the broad theological consensus that had characterized the United States since its birth as a nation began a slow but steady disintegration. A series of factors—theological, social, and intellectual—combined to create a crisis in evangelical Christianity in America. After World War I, these long-brewing tensions burst into the open in a series of intradenominational and public policy battles. This conflict marked the end of the postmillennial monopoly over American Christianity. Into the opening thus created entered the fundamentalists, embracing a new theology developed by a British churchman named Darby and a new view of the role of the Jews in God's plan for humanity.

Crisis in the church

Until the middle of the nineteenth century, science was generally viewed as an ally of religious faith: it demonstrated an order and pattern to Creation that only a higher being could have achieved. Then, in 1859, Charles Darwin published *On the Origin of Species* and introduced to the world his theory of evolution. Darwin's theory that human beings were the product of millions of years of natural selection directly contradicted the biblical account that God created man in one day. Darwin's theory forced Christians to choose between science and their traditional religious views.

While Darwin invoked natural science to challenge the Bible's accuracy, other scholars of the era were employing the tools of literary criticism to question its divine authorship. In the years following the Civil War, German *higher criticism* began to gain a following in America. This discipline employed a detailed analysis of the diction and style of the biblical text to uncover evidence of its date and place of composition. Some higher critics supplemented these efforts by reference to history and the growing field of biblical archeology. While differing on details, higher critics largely agreed that the Bible was composed by many authors over the course of centuries, each author adding their own particular vision of God to the tapestry.

American evangelical Christianity had been built on the core belief that the Bible was the perfect and inerrant Word of God. The dual attack from evolution and higher criticism shook the evangelical world at its roots. Many Christians responded to these modern challenges by adjusting their faith to accommodate them. This movement, labeled alternatively *modernism* and *liberalism*, grew rapidly. By the early 1900s, the modernists were well entrenched in the major American denominations and were a powerful presence in the leading theological seminaries.

The modernists developed approaches to their faith that no longer demanded an inerrant Bible. Primary among these was an emphasis on morality. The central mission of Christianity, they argued, was to spread the moral teachings of Jesus Christ. Even if the Bible is wrong on many details, it nonetheless succeeds in conveying Christ's core message. Other modernists preached that the Bible was merely the record of the religious experience of the ancient

Hebrews. Christians were thus obligated to improve upon this doctrine in light of the continuing revelation of God through science and scholarship.

Modernists also sought to downplay the supernatural aspects of evangelical faith, which conflicted with emerging scientific rules. In place of the deity of Christ, some modernists argued that Christ was a human who merely reflected the glory of God. In place of the literal resurrection of Christ, some suggested that there would be a spiritual resurrection of Christ through the continued teaching of His doctrine.[11]

The fundamentalist response

While the modernists sought to accommodate the latest learning from the academy, other Christians chose to confront it. Conservative Christians sought to purge the modernists from their ranks and return the church to the golden evangelical consensus that had held sway before the challenges of modernity descended. In their opinion, modernist teachings were a heresy that denied Christianity's core message and abandoned its transformational power. These conservatives would, by the early years of the twentieth century, be more commonly known as *fundamentalists.*

During the decades between the Civil War and World War I, every major Protestant denomination in America was to some extent torn by the struggle between the fundamentalists and the modernists. Characteristic of these battles was the trial of Charles Briggs, a professor at the Union Theological Seminary in New York. In an 1891 address, Briggs questioned the doctrine of biblical inerrancy. Briggs suggested that the Bible contained numerous incidental errors, but that these errors did not dilute its core teaching. The conservative faction within the Presbyterian Church was outraged and called for Briggs' expulsion. Briggs was eventually put on trial by the church and suspended from the ministry.[12]

The fundamentalist/modernist conflict was more famously fought on a second, broader front beyond church walls. Fundamentalists sought to purge modernism not only from their denominations but also from the larger American culture. Under fundamentalist prodding, many states passed laws banning the teaching of evolution in the public schools. When the State of Tennessee passed such a law, a teacher named John Scopes challenged it by openly teaching Darwin's theory to his students. Scopes' trial in the summer of 1925 turned into a dramatic showdown between the two worldviews competing for the soul of the nation.

The prosecution brought in William Jennings Bryan to lead the charge against Scopes. Bryan, one of the leading conservative evangelicals of his day, was a former secretary of state and three-time Democratic presidential candidate. Scopes was defended by Clarence Darrow, considered the leading defense attorney of the day. This monumental ideological clash would be fought by legal titans.

Technically, the fundamentalists won. Scopes was found guilty of teaching evolution and fined $100 (although the decision was subsequently reversed on a technicality). But in the court of public opinion, the Scopes trial did great damage to the fundamentalist cause. Darrow, in his prime, out-lawyered an aging William Jennings Bryan and in the process subjected his fundamentalist creed to ridicule. The press sided so openly with Scopes and Darrow that the *Baltimore Sun* offered to pay Scopes' fine for him. In the popular imagination, fundamentalisms became associated with backwoods hicks and anti-intellectuals afraid to subject their views to the light of modern learning.

AFTER THE DEBACLE of the Scopes trial, the fundamentalists abandoned their efforts to drive the modernists from their schools and churches. While some reconciled themselves to living alongside the modernists, most of the more zealous fundamentalists could not abide such accommodation. Having failed to purge the modernists from their denominations, they now abandoned their denominations and formed their own churches. The fundamentalists became separatists.

While underground, fundamentalism quietly developed and grew. Fundamentalists built churches, schools, colleges, seminaries, mission boards, and publishing houses. As they built up their institutions they continued to evangelize and expand their following. With little fanfare, fundamentalism thus gained an influence over American Christianity that it had failed to secure through open confrontation. When the fundamentalists reemerged as a political power in the 1980s, they spoke with unprecedented power.

DISPENSATIONALISM TAKES OVER FUNDAMENTALISM

WHILE THE FUNDAMENTALISTS and modernists were openly battling for the soul of American Protestantism, another quieter struggle was being waged for control of the fundamentalist movement itself. During the late nineteenth and early twentieth centuries, the followers of John Nelson Darby gradually took over American fundamentalism. Instead of engaging in public debates and trials, dispensationalists gained power through the plodding work of preaching, teaching, and institution building. As dispensationalists assumed leadership roles within the fundamentalist movement, they made their distinctive theology regarding the Jews a core component of the fundamentalist dogma.

John Darby was, in a very real sense, the first fundamentalist. The Plymouth Brethren first banded together to protest some of the same modernist accommodations that sparked the fundamentalist movement when they spread to America a half century later. Darby's belief that the Bible was the inspired, infallible Word of God was central to his theology. And Darby steadfastly embraced a supernatural Christ who was divine, whose death paved the way for human salvation, and who would literally return to earth. As theologian John Walvoord has noted, "Much of the truth promulgated by fundamental Christians today had its rebirth in the movement known as the Plymouth Brethren."[13]

Just as the tension between the modernists and the conservatives in America was starting to escalate, Darby made a series of seven extended visits to the United States and Canada. Between 1862 and 1877, Darby spent a total of seven years in America preaching, teaching, and building relationships with the leading evangelicals of the day.[14] Darby had hoped to win new members to his Plymouth Brethren movement during these visits and was in this regard unsuccessful. American conservatives were not yet ready to leave their denominations.

Yet Darby's conservative theology resonated deeply with evangelicals who were beginning to feel threatened by the rise of modernism. These evangelicals enthusiastically embraced Darby's teachings, including his dispensationalism and his views on Israel. Churchmen thus inspired and influenced by Darby became the leading activists and institution builders in the conservative camp.

The revival movement

American religious life in the decades between the Civil War and World War I was dominated by the great evangelists who held massive revival campaigns in cities across America. Of these, none was more popular or influential than D. L. Moody, who preached in the last quarter of the nineteenth century. Moody had gotten to know Darby during the latter's visits to America. Although the two parted on bad terms after a heated theological disagreement, Moody was nevertheless an early and zealous convert to dispensationalism.[15] As he preached to massive crowds across America, Moody spread dispensationalism to an audience far larger than Darby ever contemplated.

Nearly every major American evangelist and revivalist after Moody embraced his dispensationalism.[16] For example, Billy Sunday, the Billy Graham of his day, was a committed dispensationalist. Sunday was a colorful character, a professional baseball player turned preacher who attracted enormous crowds to his revivals. Over a twenty-one-year career starting in 1896, Sunday conducted more than three hundred revivals with an accumulated estimated attendance of 100 million people.[17] This audience took in a healthy dose of Sunday's dispensationalism along with the baseball analogies and acrobatics that made Sunday's preaching so popular.

The Bible conference movement

In 1875, conservative churchmen organized a two-week retreat for like-minded Christians at Niagara Falls. This first convocation of the nascent fundamentalist movement became an annual event known as the *Niagara Bible Conference*. Dispensationalists figured prominently in the early Niagara Conferences and, within a few years, were firmly in control.[18] When those attending the 1878 Niagara Conference decided to draft a statement of the conservative movement's core tenets, the dispensationalists ensured that it included the following summary of their creed:

> The Lord Jesus will come in person to introduce the millennial age, when Israel shall be restored to their own land, and the earth shall be full of the knowledge of the Lord.[19]

The Niagara conference was so popular that it quickly spawned a national Bible conference movement. Soon conservative Bible conferences were being held across America, from the Boardwalk Bible Conference in Atlantic City to the famous retreats at Winona Lake, Indiana. As had been the case in Niagara, dispensationalists dominated these conferences and ensured that dispensationalism was taught along with the other core beliefs of the emerging fundamentalist movement.[20]

The Bible schools movement

Christian higher education in America had traditionally been dominated by the prestigious northeastern theological seminaries and divinity schools. Toward the end of the nineteenth century, as these theological seminaries came increasingly under modernist control, conservatives decided to create their own institutions of Christian learning to instruct aspiring teachers and lay leaders. D. L. Moody himself led the way by opening the Moody Bible Institute in Chicago in 1886. By 1900, more than fifty such Bible schools had been opened across the country.[21] Some of the largest Bible schools, such as the Bible Institute of Los Angeles and the Philadelphia College of the Bible, were founded shortly after the turn of the century.[22]

As was the case with the Bible conferences, dispensationalists dominated the Bible school movement. Almost all of these schools were founded and administered by dispensationalists, and they taught the next generation of fundamentalist leaders a dispensational interpretation of the Bible.[23] Preachers, teachers, and lay leaders thus schooled in dispensationalism went forth into the Christian world to spread this theology to their fellow congregants and students.

The *Scofield Reference Bible*

After taking over the Bible conferences and the Bible schools, the dispensationalists took over the Bible itself. A pastor named C. I. Scofield wanted to share the lessons coming out of these conservative conferences and schools with the great masses of Christians who were unable to attend either. Scofield decided to publish a Bible with detailed annotations that would provide the reader with the conservative perspective. In 1909, the first *Scofield Study Bible* was published and met with enormous success. The *Scofield Reference Bible* quickly became *the* Bible of the fundamentalist movement and "perhaps the most important single document in all fundamentalist literature."[24]

Scofield was a zealous dispensationalist. He was deeply influenced by Moody and others who had studied directly under Darby. While working on his Bible in England, Scofield regularly prayed with the Plymouth Brethren.[25] Accordingly, the *Scofield Reference Bible* prominently sets forth the dispensationalist interpretation of Scripture. Due to its enormous popularity, Scofield's Bible "contributed more than any other single work to the spread of dispensationalism in the United States."[26] In the words of Ernest Sandeen, a leading scholar of American fundamentalism:

> The *Scofield Reference Bible* combined an attractive format of typography, paragraphing, notes, and cross references with the theology of Darbyite dispensationalism. The book has thus been subtly but powerfully influential in spreading those views among hundreds of thousands who have regularly read that Bible and who often have been unaware of the distinction between the ancient text and the Scofield interpretation.[27]

Confirmation in current events

The postmillennialists had preached that humanity could perfect the world and bring the Millennium through their own efforts. The dispensationalists preached a far more pessimistic message. Dispensationalists believed that the world was in an inevitable decline and that man was powerless to stop it. The final days of the world would be characterized by increasing wars, bloodshed on a massive scale, and the collapse of civil society. Even the church would decline and suffer growing apostasy in the End Times. Such mounting chaos would nevertheless contain a silver lining: it would indicate that the time of Christ's Second Coming was drawing near. In the last days, Christ would return to perfect the world in a way that humans never could.

The course of world events from the Civil War through World War I contradicted the optimistic postmillennialist script and instead provided dramatic confirmation of the dark dispensationalist predictions. Through the slow, incremental work of building institutions and publishing books, dispensationalists were incorporating their views into the standard theology of the fundamentalist movement. The newspaper headlines then intervened to greatly accelerate the spread of dispensationalism both within church walls and beyond.

To THE POSTMILLENNIALISTS, the Civil War was a holy war to rid America of the stain of slavery and create a truly righteous, Christian country. Yet the

Northern victory in the Civil War ushered in not a Golden Age, but the *Gilded Age.*[28] These post–Civil War decades were characterized by blatant political corruption and the gross material excess of the rich on display next to the grinding poverty of the masses.

Despite this disappointment, postmillennialism continued as the dominant strain of Christian theology in America into the early years of the twentieth century. As the country debated whether or not to enter World War I, postmillennialism was still a strong enough force to muster great Christian enthusiasm in support of the war. Postmillennialists had always believed that Americans could help bring the Millennium by spreading their democratic form of government throughout the world. World War I, the war to make the world safe for democracy, offered the means by which to accomplish this holy mission.

If the aftermath of the Civil War planted a seed of doubt about postmillennialism in the Christian imagination, the events following World War I saw the seed grow to full maturity. This great postmillennial battle did not bring an era of peace and light. Instead, a war far bloodier and more barbaric than any that had preceded it produced murky results, bitter resentments, and a new European arms race. The belief in an inexorable march toward progress under Christian stewardship could no longer be reconciled with the muddled and bloody reality.

In addition to these geopolitical disappointments, the postmillennial war for souls abroad also appeared to be faltering. Even though the effort was at an all-time high in terms of the absolute number of missionaries in the field, Christian revivals and missions were not winning the world for Christ. New demographic studies showed that the world's non-Protestant population was growing far faster than the Protestant population. Roman Catholics, Muslims, and "heathens" were not disappearing but thriving.[29]

While chaos reigned in international affairs, Protestant society appeared to be unraveling at home. During this era, America ceased to be a society dominated by small rural communities centered physically and spiritually around the church. Instead, immigration and *in-migration* shifted America's demographic balance to crowded cities plagued by poverty, disease, and vice on an unprecedented scale. From the fundamentalist perspective, the major Protestant denominations themselves fell victim to this cultural decay in the form of modernist heresies.

IN THE MIDST of such general confirmations of dispensational truth, signs began to emerge that the core dispensationalist prediction was also being fulfilled. Since Darby first promulgated his theology, the dispensationalists had taught that the Jews would one day rebuild their nation in their ancient land in accordance with biblical prophecy. Yet, throughout most of the 1800s, the prospects of such a rebirth must have seemed poor indeed. Palestine was a backwater of the Ottoman Empire completely ignored by the great masses of world Jewry.

At the close of the nineteenth century, this situation suddenly and rapidly began to change. In 1896, Theodor Herzl published *Der Judenstaat* and launched the Zionist movement. In 1917, Lord Arthur Balfour, the British foreign secretary, announced Britain's official support for "the establishment in Palestine of a national home for the Jewish people." A little over a month later, British forces entered Jerusalem and accepted the surrender of the Ottomans. The nation that had declared support for a Jewish home in Palestine was now in a position to deliver on that promise. Before this prophecy would be completely fulfilled, another generation would pass and the tragedy of the Holocaust would intervene. Then in 1948, the State of Israel declared its independence and miraculously defeated five Arab armies seeking to crush it.

Each step on the road to the birth of Israel electrified the rapidly expanding dispensationalist camp. These events, more than any others, confirmed for millions that the dispensationalists had tapped into biblical truth through their literal method of interpreting the Bible. Here were the Jews—the literal, biological descendants of Abraham—returning to their ancient homeland in glory. Much as the prophecies of the exile were fulfilled in the Jews, it was becoming increasingly apparent that the prophecies of the great return were also being fulfilled in the Jews. Darby must certainly have been smiling from his grave.

The imagery of Jewish rebirth was as significant a boost to dispensationalism as the underlying events. For centuries, weak, downtrodden Jews living in the ghettos of Europe's cities served as a living confirmation of the truth of replacement theology. The Jews simply looked like a people rejected by God. But with the rise of Israel, a new and very different Jewish image emerged. Tanned and confident Jews were simultaneously making the desert bloom while defending their land from large Arab armies. Modern-day

Davids and Joshuas had emerged from the squalor of the ghetto. Such an image bespoke not replacement but continued election.

DISPENSATIONALISM TAKES OVER AMERICA

QUESTIONS OF CHRISTIAN doctrine rarely capture the popular imagination. The passionate theological debates that periodically rock seminary walls seldom resonate beyond. To this rule, dispensationalism has proven to be a very large exception. Some of the best-selling books of the 1970s, 1990s, and the early twenty-first century have been works about dispensationalism. Through these works, this theology has garnered millions of adherents well beyond the traditional orbit of evangelical Christianity. After taking over American fundamentalism, dispensationalism has proceeded to take over America itself.

The Late Great Planet Earth

In 1970, Hal Lindsey published a book titled *The Late Great Planet Earth*. This book employs a dispensationalist interpretation of biblical prophecy to explain the current events of the day from the cold war to the rise of New Age religions. Israel, of course, figures prominently. In an excerpt quoted opposite the title page, Lindsey states that in Earth's final days, the course of world events will revolve around "the most important sign of all—that is the Jew returning to the land of Israel after thousands of years of being dispersed. The Jew is the most important sign to this generation."[30]

Lindsey invokes Israel's birth in 1948 and Israel's conquest of the Old City of Jerusalem in 1967 as confirmation of both the accuracy of dispensationalist predictions and the impending arrival of the end of days. In the course of his discussion of Israel, Lindsey offers a pointed refutation of replacement theology:

> For many years prior to 1948 some Christian scholars denied the possibility of accepting the prophecies concerning the restoration of Israel as a nation in Palestine. As a matter of fact, many Bible teachers taught that all prophecy relating to Israel's future was fulfilled in Israel's past. Others taught that the promises made to Israel must be applied to the Church (since Israel rejected her Messiah). Some theologians of the liberal school still insist that prophecy has no literal meaning for today

> and that it cannot be taken seriously. It is difficult to understand this view if one carefully weighs the case of Israel's rebirth as a nation.[31]

Lindsey's book was wildly, inexplicably successful. According to the *New York Times*, *The Late Great Planet Earth* was the best-selling nonfiction book of the 1970s.[32] The book has sold more than fifteen million copies to date[33] and has been translated into more than fifty languages.[34] Lindsey even made a film version of the book, narrated by Orson Welles, which appeared in commercial theaters throughout the United States. As was the case with the Scofield Bible, the millions who read *The Late Great Planet Earth* likely accepted its dispensational theology as gospel truth.

Lindsey's particular theological emphasis was no accident. Lindsey is a graduate of Dallas Theological Seminary. The founder of the seminary, Lewis Chafer, was one of the most important dispensationalist thinkers after Darby and Scofield. The Dallas Seminary he founded remains one of the world's leading centers for the study of dispensationalism. In spreading the dispensationalist gospel, Lindsey was carrying on a proud school tradition.

The Left Behind series

In the 1990s, the unprecedented commercial success of *The Late Great Planet Earth* was surpassed by that of a series of books providing a fictional account of the events leading up to the Second Coming according to the dispensationalist script. These books, known as the Left Behind series, have so far sold more than fifty-five million copies.[35] The last six books of the series all debuted at number one on all of the major best-seller lists, including those of the *New York Times*, *USA Today*, *Publisher's Weekly*, and the *Wall Street Journal*. According to *Publisher's Weekly*, the ninth book in the series, *Desecration*, was the best-selling novel of 2001.[36] The Left Behind books have also been adapted into a series of children's books as well as two movies.

The publishing phenomenon that would become the Left Behind series resulted from a momentary dispensationalist musing. Tim LaHaye, the originator of the series, is a fervent dispensationalist who believes that, according to Darby's concept of the Rapture, all believing Christians will be removed from the world prior to the Second Coming of Christ. Dispensationalists view this removal as literal and complete—believers will actually disappear into thin air. Passing the time on an airline flight, LaHaye asked himself, *What if the Rapture occurred while riding on an airplane?*[37] It suddenly occurred to LaHaye that the Rapture and the dramatic events that follow would make for riveting fiction.

LaHaye teamed up with Jerry Jenkins, an experienced ghostwriter, and in 1995 their first book, *Left Behind*, was published. In the opening scene of *Left Behind*, an airline pilot is interrupted by a frantic stewardess who reports that a third of the passengers on their flight have disappeared. Clothes, shoes, and gold fillings are all that remain where these passengers once sat.

In this book and the eleven that follow it, the heroes of the series become born-again Christians and band together to do battle with the Antichrist. Throughout the series, the story line closely follows the dispensational script for the final years leading up to the Second Coming of Christ. And throughout the series, Israel is the center of much of the action, including miraculous Israeli military victories, the Antichrist's last stand, and Christ's return to earth. Heroic Israelis are among the series' main protagonists.

Like Hal Lindsey, Tim LaHaye did not come across his subject matter by accident. LaHaye is an old soldier of the Christian Right. He helped to found the Moral Majority with Jerry Falwell in 1979, and he later formed the American Coalition for Traditional Values, which worked to get out the vote for conservative politicians.[38] After leaving politics, LaHaye became a pastor and Christian educator in California. As was the case with Scofield and Lindsey before him, it is likely that millions of LaHaye's readers accept his dispensationalist version of the end days as the official "Christian" view.

THE INTROSPECTIVE CHURCH

THE DISPENSATIONALISTS ARE no longer the only large block of Christians who reject replacement theology. They now find themselves in very good company. In the aftermath of the Holocaust, almost every major Christian denomination in America engaged in a process of introspection in which they confronted the role of replacement theology in fostering anti-Semitism. In the years that followed, most of these denominations formally renounced this now suspect teaching.[39]

The Evangelical Lutheran Church in Germany set the example when it rejected replacement theology in 1950. The Catholic Church followed in 1965. In 1972, the United Methodist Church stated the Jews were still a "covenanted people."[40] In 1987, the Presbyterian Church concluded that, "this teaching of supersessionism is harmful and in need of reconsideration. . . . God's covenants are not broken. . . . The Church has not 'replaced' the Jewish people."[41] Also in 1987, the United Church of Christ adopted a resolution affirming:

> That Judaism has not been superseded by Christianity; that Christianity is not to be understood as the successor religion to Judaism; God's covenant with the Jewish people has not been abrogated; God has not rejected the Jewish people; God is faithful in keeping his covenant.[42]

In 1993, the Disciples of Christ declared that, "The covenant established by God's grace with the Jewish people has not been abrogated but remains valid."[43]

Yet while these churches have renounced replacement theology, they have stopped short of the enthusiastic embrace of Jewish election that characterizes the dispensationalists. In recognizing the continuing validity of God's covenant with the Jewish people, the mainline churches immediately bumped up against the paradox of Jewish election in a Christian theology that recognizes only one path to salvation. Much like the apostle Paul centuries earlier, these denominations wrestled with, but could not fully resolve, this puzzle. The Presbyterians, for example, noted that:

> The continued existence of the Jewish people and of the Church as communities elected by God is, as the Apostle Paul expressed it, a "mystery." We do not claim to fathom this mystery, but we cannot ignore it.[44]

The Disciples of Christ acknowledged this tension with the following words:

> Although we do not want to say Judaism is for Jews and the Church is for Gentiles, we must acknowledge the continued existence of the Jewish people who do not confess the lordship of Jesus Christ and who see their Jewishness as incompatible with this confession is, as Paul the apostle declares, a mystery.[45]

The United Church of Christ stated simply that, "Our affirmation both of the continuing covenant of God with the Jewish people and of fulfillment of God's promises in Christ appears to be a paradox."[46]

AMBIGUITY IN RELIGION is no vice. Those who possess absolute truth are too often those who seek to impose their version of the truth on others. Those who struggle, who see the complexity of faith, are typically far more tolerant of diversity and dissent. For religious minorities such as the Jews, there is an undeniable appeal to finding themselves in the midst of a mature and conflicted majority religion. For the Jews, Paul's paradoxical view of their status is a most welcome improvement from the bloody certainty of replacement theology.

Yet, as welcome as it is, Paul's "mystery" of Jewish election may be too fragile a peg upon which to hang the solution to so weighty a problem. The human need for certainty strains so precarious an arrangement. In Romans 11, Paul constructed a theological way station for the Jews to protect them from full-blown replacement theology. Yet this shelter was quickly trampled by masses of Christians rushing in to assume their role as the new chosen people. Paul's answer may once again prove to be of limited prophylactic value against a resurgence of replacement theology when memories of the Holocaust are less fresh.

From the Jewish perspective, there is also a more immediate problem with this middle ground. While Paul's solution may foster greater tolerance for the Jews, it does not appear to inspire identification with them. Such an ambiguous view of the theological status of the Jews engenders no zeal for the project of Jewish survival today. Thus when it comes to the major existential challenge now facing the Jewish people—defending the State of Israel—this theology inspires neutrality at best.

The United Church of Christ, for example, was supreme in the eloquence with which it condemned replacement theology. Yet the church could not muster similar clarity or enthusiasm on the issue of support for Israel. The Jews may maintain some vague covenant with God, but when it comes to defining any benefits flowing from this covenant, the church turns stingy:

> We do not see consensus in the United Church of Christ or among our panel on the covenantal significance of the state of Israel. We appreciate the compelling moral argument for the creation of modern Israel as a vehicle for self-determination and as a haven for a victimized people; we also recognize that this event has entailed the dispossession of Palestinians from their homes and the denial of human rights.[47]

The merits of Israel's actions are certainly subject to debate. Many friends of Israel and, for that matter, a large percentage of Israelis themselves passionately object to Israeli policies and actions. Yet most mainline churches have not assumed the position of friends of Israel who wish to provide constructive criticism. Instead, in word and in deed, these churches simply have not taken sides. They have in effect taken themselves out of the game and stand on the sidelines with neither team's pennant in their hands.

On those occasions when the mainline churches have involved themselves in the Arab-Israeli conflict, they have typically done so to criticize Israel and to penalize her partners. In recent years, some of the leading mainline denominations have gone so far as to impose on Israel a form of punishment previously reserved for apartheid South Africa—divestment. In July 2004, the General Assembly of the Presbyterian Church voted to "initiate a process of phased selective divestment in multinational corporations operating in Israel" with a special emphasis on penalizing those companies that supply the Israeli military.[48] In February 2005, the World Council of Churches praised the Presbyterian decision and urged its members to consider similar economic measures to oppose the Israeli occupation of the West Bank and Gaza.[49] Also in 2005, both the United Church of Christ and the Episcopal Church passed resolutions calling for the use of economic leverage to promote peace in the Middle East, including divesting from or otherwise pressuring companies whose products are held to contribute to violence in the region, including companies involved in building Israel's security fence along the West Bank.[50]

THE CHRISTIAN ZIONISTS of today are almost entirely dispensationalists. Dispensationalism erased all ambiguity on the issue of Jewish election. Darby's theology created a solid basis for the continued election of the Jews and restored to the Jews a central role in God's continuing plan for humanity. This certainty has its virtue. Dispensational clarity prevents backsliding toward replacement theology. Of greater immediate import, dispensational certainty generates deep identification with the Jews as they confront challenges to their survival in the world today. Dispensationalism has inspired millions of Christians to stand with the Jews and with the Jewish State of Israel.

The notion that evangelicals are extending themselves this way [on behalf of Israel] because it's part of some sinister theology is the biggest lie that Jews believe today. Why can't we simply accept the fact that these people recognize that God had done a wondrous thing with the birth of Israel and the ingathering of the exiles and allow them to enjoy the fulfillment of prophecy?[1]

—Rabbi Yechiel Eckstein, 2001

Chapter Three

MOTIVES

JOHN HAGEE, THE pastor of the Cornerstone Church in San Antonio, Texas, is one of the most eloquent and forceful Christian Zionists preaching in America today. Hagee's father was a gospel minister who taught his children at a young age that the Jewish people were the "apple of God's eye." Hagee recalls that even during the darkest days of the Holocaust, his father kept reminding his congregants that the time would soon come when Israel would be reborn "in a day" in accordance with their dispensationalist reading of the Bible.

On May 15, 1948, Pastor Hagee remembers sitting "mesmerized" around his kitchen table in Channelview, Texas, as he and his family listened to the radio reports about Israel's Declaration of Independence.[2] Israel was reborn "in a day" just as the prophets, and his father, said it would be. Hagee has been a committed Christian Zionist ever since.

Hagee's story is a common one for Christian Zionists of a certain age range. It is rare that world events conform neatly to one's reading of the Bible. Typically faith, if it is to survive, must rest on a foundation distinct from proofs and facts. Yet in 1948, many dispensationalists and their families received a confirmation of their views as dramatic as the parting of the Red Sea. They sat around crackling radios and listened to the birth of a Jewish State just as they or their parents had predicted. Such a wondrous experience confirmed for them both the truth of their theology and the centrality of Israel to that theology. Even the generations of Christian Zionists who did not live through it are electrified by this clear fulfillment of biblical prophecy.

IN THE POPULAR imagination Israel is still a Jewish issue. Most people are surprised to learn that millions of devout Christians passionately support the Jewish State. This apparent paradox leads to a natural question: Why? What motivates a Christian to care so much about the Jewish State? As the Christian Zionists have become the subject of increasing media attention in the aftermath of September 11, many commentators have stepped forward to explain this mystery to the public. Largely ignorant of Christian theology and history, these commentators have typically provided answers that are superficial at best and slanderous at worst.

As Pastor Hagee's story illuminates, the central motive for Christian Zionism is Christian theology. Christian Zionism is the product of the theological revolution that took place in twentieth-century America. The replacement theology that had dominated Christianity for so many centuries began a steep decline at the start of the century, and the Holocaust dealt it a knockout blow. Dispensationalism—with its view that the Jewish people are the *Israel* to whom the Bible promises so much—has rapidly expanded to fill the theological vacuum. This new theology practically instructs Christians to be Zionists. Without this theological shift there would certainly be some Christians who support Israel, but there would be no Christian Zionist movement.

Yet while theology may be its wellspring, Christian Zionism is not a purely religious phenomenon. Most Christian Zionists, especially those who operate in the secular world of Washington, are typically driven by a broader range of considerations. As modern people educated and fully engaged in the secular world, they naturally embrace concepts and values from the larger American culture. In particular, Christian Zionists often mention two secular motives for supporting Israel: (1) the moral motive of repaying a debt of gratitude to the Jews, and (2) the strategic motive of supporting a key ally.

Neither the moral nor the strategic argument requires religious belief. Indeed, these same arguments are often employed by Israel's Jewish and secular supporters. Yet in embracing these arguments, Christian Zionists typically reflect a worldview shaped in the first instance by their Christian faith. For most Christian Zionists, religious considerations tend to mix with and reinforce the secular ones.

Many Christian Zionists describe their support for Israel as an effort to repay the great debt that Christians owe to Judaism for providing the essentials of their faith: Jesus, the apostles, and the Bible. This moral imperative thrives in a post-Enlightenment society that objectively teaches history and recognizes the important contributions of the Jews to Western civilization. Yet Christian theology certainly helps foster this view. An appreciation of the Jewish roots of Christianity flows naturally from a theology that holds a positive view of Jews and their role in God's plans. When Christianity was focused on replacing the Jews, Christians never bothered to thank them.

During the cold war and again during the current war on terrorism, Christian Zionists have frequently invoked America's national security to explain their support for Israel. In both conflicts, Christian Zionists have viewed Israel as a committed and valuable ally. This strategic motive is a secular consideration that is shared by many of Israel's secular supporters. Yet here as well, religion looms in the background. As activist Gary Bauer has noted, "Conservatives generally and Christian conservatives specifically see our foreign policy in moral terms."[3] Evangelical Christians are more inclined to embrace biblical distinctions between good and evil and to divide the world accordingly. Thus they embrace a worldview in which the Soviet Union was an "evil empire" and the 9/11 terrorists are "evildoers." To those who see the world so sharply divided, Israel has stood out more clearly as a friend.

When asked to explain his support for Israel, former House Majority Leader Tom DeLay gave a typical Washington policy answer. His support for Israel, said DeLay, is "about expanding democracy and fighting the war on terror." But DeLay quickly added an addendum from a very different part of his psyche, noting that, "Jesus Christ was a Jew. The Jewish people were God's chosen people. He has a covenant with them. We ought to appreciate that."[4]

In its diversity, DeLay's explanation expresses a typical Christian Zionist view. In this brief, off-the-cuff remark DeLay starts with a strategic motive of fighting the war on terrorism, moves on to the moral motive of repaying a debt to the people who provided Christians with their Messiah, and ends with a theological motive derived from the dispensationalist view that God has never abandoned His covenant with the Jews. For most Christian Zionists, no one motive stands alone. Each individual combines these motives—the theological, the moral, and the strategic—in a personal mix with their own particular emphasis.

THEOLOGY

THE BIBLE IS filled with promises and prophecies confirming that the people of Israel will inherit the land of Israel. In the Book of Genesis, God promises Abraham on four separate occasions that He will give the land of Israel to him and his descendants. God then repeats this promise to Isaac and then to Jacob.

The Old Testament prophets reiterated this promise and fleshed out the details. The prophets warned that the Jewish people would one day disobey God and that God would punish them for their transgressions by exiling them from their land to the "four corners of the earth." In the words of Jeremiah, "Therefore I will cast you out of this land into a land that you do not know, neither you nor your fathers; and there you shall serve other gods day and night, where I will not show you favor."[5]

These same prophets who predicted the great exile also predicted a glorious return. Moses, Isaiah, Jeremiah, and Ezekiel all prophesied, some of them repeatedly, that the day would come when God would gather His people from "the four corners of the earth" and lead them lovingly back to their Promised Land. In the words of Ezekiel:

> As a shepherd seeks out his flock on the day he is among his scattered sheep, so will I seek out My sheep and deliver them from all the places where they were scattered on a cloudy and dark day. And I will bring them out from the peoples and gather them from the countries, and will bring them to their own land.[6]

Dispensationalists believe that when the Bible says "Israel," it is referring to the Jews. Dispensationalists find confirmation for this interpretation in the fact that the prophecies about the exile were fulfilled in the Jewish people. It was the Jews whom the Romans expelled from the land of Israel in A.D. 70. And it was the Jews who could thereafter be found living in a Diaspora that extended to every region of the globe. To these people of faith, it was obvious that the second half of the plan, the glorious return, would also be fulfilled in the Jewish people.

As Jerry Falwell has noted:

> Any man or woman who takes time to read the Bible will find that it is more up to date than our newspapers. It is filled with prophecies regarding the Jewish people. The Bible clearly prophesized that after more than twenty-five hundred years of dispersion, the Jewish people would return to the land of Israel and establish the Jewish nation once again.[7]

To the extent that religious Christians discern God's will for the world, they will naturally seek to be on God's side. Thus the belief that the creation and existence of Israel is the fulfillment of biblical promise and prophecy leads automatically to Christian Zionism. As John Hagee has asked, "Is it not logical to state that since God created Israel, and defends Israel, that those who fight with Israel fight with God?"[8] In Pat Robertson's words:

> Evangelical Christians support Israel because we believe that the words of Moses and the ancient prophets of Israel were inspired by God. We believe that the emergence of a Jewish state in the land promised by God to Abraham, Isaac and Jacob was ordained by God.[9]

Genesis 12:3

While the biblical promises regarding the inheritance of the land of Israel provide general instruction as to God's will, another passage of the Bible provides a more specific call to Christian action. In Genesis 12:3, God promises Abraham that, "I will bless those who bless you, and I will curse him who curses you." The "you" employed here is a plural, referring to Abraham and his descendants, that is, Israel. To a dispensationalist, therefore, Genesis 12:3 practically commands philo-Semitism and Zionism.

Genesis 12:3 is Christian Zionism in a nutshell. In explaining their support for Israel, Christian Zionists almost always invoke this one sentence from the Bible. Pat Robertson relates that his mother "drilled into" him at a young age that Genesis 12:3 taught: "You do good things to the Jewish people, and God will bless you."[10] Gary Bauer, who typically prefers the language of public policy to that of the Bible, is nonetheless quick to cite Genesis 12:3 as a source of his Christian Zionism.[11] According to Dr. Richard Land, a leading spokesman for the Southern Baptist Convention, "If we want God to continue to bless America, then we need to bless the Jews."[12] Jerry Falwell rarely talks about Israel or the Jews without invoking Genesis 12:3. In Falwell's words:

> I personally believe that God deals with all nations in relation to how these nations deal with Israel. I think history supports this. I premise that on what God said to Abraham: "I will bless them that bless thee, and curse them that curse thee." I therefore think America should without hesitation give total financial and military support for the State of Israel. My political support for Israel is unconditional.[13]

Falwell is so confident in this view that he has used Genesis 12:3 as the basis for some prophecy of his own. In 1981, while the Soviet Union still thrived, Falwell cited Genesis 12:3 to argue that "the Soviet Union makes a terrible mistake in their harassment and persecution of Jews...a fatal mistake."[14] Less than a decade later, Falwell had yet another example of how God keeps His promises to His people.

Texas pastor John Hagee constantly cites Genesis 12:3 in support of his Zionism. In his books and in his sermons Hagee likes to demonstrate how world events have repeatedly proven the bedrock truth of these ancient words. Going back to biblical times, Hagee cites the long list of nations that blessed the Jews and were in turn blessed. Pharaoh blessed Joseph and made him one of the most powerful men in Egypt. Egypt, in turn, became the most powerful nation on earth, controlling the supply of food during a worldwide famine. Post-Enlightenment England blessed the Jews by permitting them unprecedented freedoms and in turn received God's blessings. As long as this good treatment continued, the sun did not set on the British Empire. America has blessed the Jews and is now the most prosperous and powerful nation on earth.

Hagee then takes a walk through the dustbin of history to detail what has become of those nations that have cursed the Jews. Egypt prospered as long as Pharaoh blessed the Jews through Joseph. But when there came a pharaoh who "knew not Joseph" and enslaved the Jews, Egypt's fortunes declined dramatically. God smote the firstborn in each Egyptian household and drowned Pharaoh's army in the Red Sea. Spain thrived and enjoyed a Golden Age during which it was the economic and intellectual capital of the world. Then came the Spanish Inquisition and the expulsion of the Jews. The

Golden Age ended, and Spain began a long decline. Hitler cursed the Jews. Instead of founding a thousand-year Reich, he killed himself in his bunker and, according to Hagee, "stepped into eternity to meet a Rabbi named Jesus of Nazareth as his final judge."[15]

Hagee continues with this theme:

> Where are the Babylonians? Where are the Romans? Where are the Greeks? Where are the Persians? Where is the Ottoman Empire? Where is that lunatic Adolf Hitler and his Nazi hordes? They are all historical footnotes in the bone yard of human history.
>
> Where is Israel? Where are the Jewish people? They are alive and well in the only democratic society in the Middle East. The Jewish people have survived pogroms and persecution. They have outlasted Pharaoh's slavery and Hitler's final solution. They are the living testimonial that there is a God in heaven who keeps His word.[16]

THE DEBT OF GRATITUDE

FOR MOST OF its history, the Christian church has blamed the Jews for crucifying Christ. Century after century, outrage at this alleged deicide sparked the persecution and murder of Jews throughout Europe. Today, anger at the Jews over the Crucifixion is rapidly giving way to gratitude to the Jews for providing Christians with Christ and the other fundamentals of their faith. For many Christian Zionists, their work on behalf of Israel is an effort to repay the Jews for these very precious gifts.

This change in emphasis from Christ's death to Christ's Jewish birth has largely coincided with the decline of replacement theology. When Christian theology was focused on the rejection of the Jews, Christians themselves were transfixed on the act that they believed had caused that rejection: the crucifixion of Christ. When Christian theology shifted its focus to the continuing election of the Jews, Christians likewise shifted their focus to the Jewish roots of their faith. Thus while not a purely theological motive, gratitude toward the Jews flows directly from theology.

LORD ARTHUR BALFOUR was one of the first and most influential Christian Zionists. In 1917, Balfour was instrumental in engineering the official British statement bearing his name that expressed sympathy with Zionist aspirations. With the Balfour Declaration, Britain not only recognized the Jewish right to a home in their ancient patrimony, but also committed itself to working to create such a home. The Balfour Declaration was one of the pivotal events on the road to the birth of Israel.

While Balfour played a central role in committing his government to the creation of a Jewish homeland, he was reticent about the reasons. In fact, during the course of his lifetime Balfour made only one public statement explaining his rationale. In a speech on the floor of Parliament, Balfour declared:

> This is the ideal which chiefly moves me...that Christendom is not oblivious to their [the Jews'] faith, is not unmindful of the service they have rendered to the great religions of the world, and that we desire to the best of our ability to give them the opportunity of developing in peace and quietness under British rule, those great gifts which hitherto they have been compelled to bring to fruition in countries which know not their language and belong not to their race.[17]

Gary Bauer remembers even as a young child being deeply offended when he heard the Lexington, Kentucky, locals make anti-Semitic slurs. Bauer explains his aversion to anti-Semitism by recalling that "my church made it very clear that Jesus Christ was a Jew. We were worshiping a Jewish carpenter."[18] Pat Robertson echoes the sentiment. "I love the Jewish people," says Robertson, "because...my Savior and my Lord Jesus is a Jew. It's our feeling that we're serving and worshiping the Jewish Messiah."[19] In discussing the motivation of Christian Zionists, Robertson has noted further that:

> The first thing we have to realize is that evangelical Christians take the Bible very seriously, so the Old Testament figures, who were all Jewish, are to them their heroes in faith.... The other point that we have to keep in mind is that Jesus was Jewish, and all of the early apostles were Jews. There was a distortion of that fact in the Middle Ages, when the Catholic Church got rather extreme against the Jews, and Martin Luther did the same thing in the early days of the Reformation. But in terms of American evangelical Christianity, we take it very seriously.[20]

Pastor John Hagee speaks often and passionately about the Christian debt to the Jews. According to Hagee:

> As Christians we support Israel because we have a debt of gratitude to the Jewish people. The Jewish people gave to us the patriarchs, Abraham, Isaac, and Jacob. The prophets, Elijah, Daniel, Zechariah, etc.—not a Baptist in the bunch. Every word in your Bible was written by Jewish hands. The first family of Christianity, Mary, Joseph, and Jesus, were Jewish. Jesus Christ, a Jewish rabbi from Nazareth, made this statement: "Salvation is of the Jews." The point is this: If you take away the Jewish contribution to Christianity, there would be no Christianity. The Jewish people do not need Christianity to explain their existence. But Christians cannot explain our existence without Judaism. The roots of Christianity are Jewish.[21]

The crucifixion of the Jews

It is impossible for a thoughtful Christian to feel such deep gratitude to the Jewish people and not be painfully aware of how poorly this debt to the Jews has been repaid over the centuries. The flip side of gratitude to the Jews is remorse over the long history of Christian anti-Semitism. Many of the most passionate Christian Zionists are quick to express regret and even fury over the record of Christian persecution of the Jews. For these Christian Zionists, the need to make amends for the past adds a sense of urgency to the task of supporting Israel today.

For centuries, Christians outraged by the crucifixion of Christ unleashed their fury upon the Jews. John Hagee turns this traditional view of crucifixion on its head. Hagee too is outraged by the crucifixion. But it is the "crucifixion of the Jews" about which Hagee rages. And he is clear about who is responsible for this crucifixion: the Christian church. With his linebacker's body and his lion's voice, Hagee throws his full emotion into the argument:

> Anti-Semitism has its origin and its complete root structure in Christianity! Until anti-Semitism is stopped in the Church, anti-Semitism will not be stopped on the face of the earth!
>
> Where are the Jews of Spain? They were murdered in cold blood by the Roman Church! Where are the Jews of Portugal? They were murdered in cold blood by the Roman Church! Where are the Jews of Italy and France? They were murdered in cold blood by the Roman

> Church! Where are the Jews of Austria and Hungary? A Godless theology of hate that no one dared try to stop for a thousand years produced a harvest of horror. When the Pale Rider of Death thrust in the sickle, the rivers of Europe turned red with the blood of the Jews. They were all killed in the name of a loving God.[22]

Hagee does not focus his outrage solely upon the Roman Catholic Church. He recognizes equally the sins of the Reformation. Hagee has written in detail about the ugly anti-Semitism of Martin Luther and the connection between his teachings and Nazi actions. Hagee concludes:

> Anti-Semitism is sin, and sin damns the soul. It is time for Christians to stop praising the dead Jews of the past—Abraham, Isaac, and Jacob, while slandering the Jews that live across the street. They are the same family.[23]

Gustav Scheller, a Christian Zionist from England, was active in funding and organizing the transport of Jews from the former Soviet Union to Israel in the 1990s. In explaining his devotion to the Zionist cause, Scheller wrote the following in his memoirs:

> I believe there will not be one reading this whose home country has not done harm to the Jewish people in some way. Many of us have repented; but in my understanding this is only the first step. The Lord has clearly shown us in His word that we should carry the Jews back home to Israel. What an opportunity to have to say to the nation of Israel how deeply we care and so turn past curses into blessings.[24]

Christian charities raising money to help poor Jews have invoked this theme of a debt of gratitude ill repaid to strengthen the punch of their appeals. One evangelical fund-raising letter noted:

> The Jewish people gave us our Bible, and our Messiah. Truly, they are our "royal family." And yet, for centuries they have known the judgment, disdain, and even hatred of many, sadly including many Christians. I believe that now is the time to show favor to Zion. Now is the time to show honor, love, and respect to the people who blessed us so

> much. Now is the time to allow God's light to shine again in the darkness of the world around us.[25]

THE COLD WAR AND THE CLASH OF CIVILIZATIONS

DURING THE COLD war, evangelical Christians typically supported a muscular policy against America's Communist adversaries. In their first modern foray as an organized political force, evangelical Christians gave Ronald Reagan his winning margin in 1980. It is no coincidence that when Reagan famously referred to the Soviet Union as an "evil empire," he did so before the annual convention of the National Association of Evangelicals. As people more attuned to viewing the world in the biblical absolutes of good and evil, evangelicals were inclined to agree with Reagan's assessment of the atheist and totalitarian Soviet regime.

In their enthusiasm for fighting the cold war, evangelicals found another reason to support Israel. During the decades of this conflict, Israel was a small but committed outpost of the Free World in the Middle East. Israel fostered a vibrant democracy at home while voting with the United States in the United Nations more than any other nation. Israel's largest Arab enemies, by contrast, were single-party dictatorships often aligned with the Soviet Union. After Israel's brilliant military victory over three Arab nations in the 1967 Six Days' War, many of Israel's supporters concluded that this tiny ideological ally was also an important strategic asset.

As Christian Zionists became more politically active in the 1980s, they often emphasized this strategic motive for supporting Israel. In discussing his support for Israel in 1984, for example, Jerry Falwell spoke in cold war terms:

> As a freedom-loving American, I am well aware that Israel is the sole democratic state in the Middle East, and the only real friend our country has there. Russia has made great inroads on occasion into practically every other nation over there except Israel. Thus, if for no other reason, I would be for strong support of Israel.[26]

Falwell also noted the strategic benefits that flowed to the United States from its alliance with Israel:

> Israel is America's defense line in the Middle East. Israel is a proven military force, supreme in the area, and a bulwark in defending the Middle East against a Soviet-inspired communist takeover.
>
> If the West had to maintain a force with equivalent capability in the area, it would cost many times what it costs her now and be not nearly as effective. Furthermore, the stationing of American troops in the area is a political impossibility.[27]

With the fall of the Soviet Union, this cold war motive for supporting Israel evaporated. For a brief period, talk of Israel as a strategic and ideological ally ceased to echo in the corridors of Washington. But it was not long before the cold war was replaced by a new paradigm of international relations in which Israel once again emerged as a crucial American ally.

IN A SEMINAL 1993 article in *Foreign Affairs* titled "The Clash of Civilizations?," Harvard professor Samuel P. Huntington set forth what he viewed as the emerging paradigm of international relations in the post–cold war world. Huntington argued that most world conflicts would no longer be between nations (as in the Napoleonic wars) or between ideologies (as in the cold war). Instead, Huntington argued, "The principal conflicts of global politics will occur between nations and groups of different civilizations. The clash of civilizations will be the battle lines of the future."[28]

Huntington divided the world into eight major civilizations: Western, Confucian, Japanese, Islamic, Hindu, Slavic-Orthodox, Latin American, and African. While he discussed a number of civilizational fault lines and tensions, Huntington was particularly concerned about the potential for conflict between two of these civilizations: Western and Islamic. Huntington predicted that, "The centuries-old military interaction between the West and Islam is unlikely to decline. It could become more virulent."[29]

WHILE EVANGELICAL CHRISTIANS are not always receptive to the latest pronouncements from the halls of academia, they have enthusiastically embraced Huntington's thesis. This is not surprising. Evangelical Christians were already predisposed to view foreign policy issues in broad moral and civilizational terms. To them, the cold war was not a value neutral struggle between two global powers but a civilizational clash between a Judeo-Christian America and an atheistic Soviet Union. With the end of the cold war, evangelical Christians naturally turned their attention to civilizational threats from other quarters. It was not long before leading evangelicals began warning of the great danger from radical Islam. In the words of Richard Cizik, vice president for governmental affairs at the National Association of Evangelicals, "The Muslims have become the modern-day equivalent of the Evil Empire."[30]

To people who believe that the major world conflict today is a clash of civilizations between Western society and radical Islam, Israel holds a special significance. Viewed from this perspective, Israel is once again a frontline ally, an outpost of Judeo-Christian civilization surrounded on all sides by Muslim nations and under siege from Muslim terror. This view of Israel as a lonely outpost of the West fits neatly into the space left vacant by the end of the cold war and provides a continuing strategic rationale for supporting Israel.

While evangelical Christians were concerned about the threat from radical Islam throughout most of the 1990s, this was hardly their primary focus. There were more immediate battles—mostly over domestic policy—to occupy their time. September 11 changed everything. September 11 was the Pearl Harbor of the clash of civilizations: it turned a looming civilizational threat into a hot civilizational war. And during wartime, domestic issues take a backseat to the dictates of fighting and winning. As a result, September 11 effected an instant reordering of the priorities of America's evangelical Christians along with those of most other Americans. Since 9/11, evangelicals have been focused on the clash of civilizations, and Israel's role in it, with far more intensity than ever before.

For many Christian Zionists, especially those who work in the Washington policy world, the clash of civilizations provides their most compelling rationale for supporting Israel. Conservative activist Gary Bauer exemplifies the Christian embrace of this new, civilizational paradigm. During the cold war, Gary Bauer was a cold warrior on the White House staff of President Reagan. Today, Bauer is a Christian soldier in the clash of civilizations.

In his speeches, letters, and articles Bauer sounds the constant theme that the United States and Israel are the twin "pillars" of the West, and any harm done to Israel would be a "disaster for Western civilization."[31] Bauer further emphasizes that these two pillars of Western civilization are now under attack from the same enemy. As Bauer notes in reference to radical Islam, this is an enemy with a global reach:

> It is the same philosophy that motivates the government of Sudan to kill 5 million Christians in the last decade. It inspires the gunmen with AK47's who run into churches in Pakistan and open fire on women and children. It inspires the kidnappers of Daniel Pearl who tormented him on video tape, forcing him to say over and over again "I am a Jew" before they decapitated him and sent the pictures of his severed head throughout the Middle East as a recruiting tool. This philosophy causes the Palestinian mother to leap with joy at the news her teenage son has blown himself up as long as she is assured he killed Jews in the process.[32]

Other Christian Zionists echo this central theme that the United States and Israel are fighting the same war against the same enemy. In the words of conservative commentator Alan Keyes:

> What is at stake in the Middle East is not just the survival of Israel, although the menace to Israel is real and immediate. If we learned anything on September 11th, then we should have learned that what is finally at stake in this confrontation is the survival of us all.[33]

Former House Majority Leader Tom DeLay has been outspoken in his view of Israel as a crucial ally in the war on terror. DeLay has repeatedly emphasized that, "Israel's fight is our fight. Israel's liberation from Palestinian terrorism is an essential component of the global war on terror."[34] DeLay has described the alliance in the following terms:

> America's victory in our war on terror relies on Israel's victory in its war on terror. The common destiny of our two nations is not an artificial alliance dictated by our leaders, or a partisan political calculation. It is a heartfelt friendship between the citizens of two democracies at war, bound by the solidarity of freedom.... It was perhaps best expressed in William Shakespeare's *Henry the Fifth*: "We happy few, we band of brothers; for he today that sheds his blood with me shall be my brother."[35]

The Special Relationship

Very often wartime alliances are little more than alliances of convenience. Facing a shared enemy, nations with very different, and sometimes competing, interests come together for a brief period and then go their separate ways once the immediate crisis is over. When it comes to the U.S.-Israel alliance, however, many Americans see something far more profound. Since Israel gained its independence in 1948, her American supporters have consistently invoked a "special relationship" between the United States and Israel characterized by shared founding principles, shared democratic government, and shared love of peace and freedom. Perhaps no other U.S. ally, with the possible exception of Great Britain, is spoken of in such glowing fraternal terms. This concept of a special relationship complements and reinforces the broader strategic considerations motivating U.S. support for Israel.

Today, Christian Zionists are among the most enthusiastic boosters of the special relationship. In a 2002 speech at John Hagee's San Antonio church, for instance, Tom DeLay went on at length on the topic:

> Americans and Israelis are allies in the historic battle between liberty and tyranny. Israel and the United States differ greatly in size, population, and natural resources. But in the things that truly matter, our countries are strikingly similar. The fundamental measures of our spirit, ideals, and aspirations show that Israel and America are kindred nations.
>
> Our founders were profoundly influenced by faith. Both countries practice religious tolerance.... We respect freedom and honor the rights of the individual. We tolerate a vigorous public debate through unfettered speech and a free press. We welcome the conflict of contested elections.... Since 1970, Israel changed its elected leader ten times. But regime change within Israel's neighbors is an accident of fate.
>
> We need to ask ourselves: Do we want the Middle East to look more like Israel, or do we want Israel to look more like the rest of the Middle East? In a land largely barren of freedom, we must preserve the lone fountain of liberty.[36]

Gary Bauer too emphasizes the shared values and founding principles of the United States and Israel:

> Israel and America are joined at the hip and joined at the heart. We are both democracies committed to the consent of the governed. We both believe in the dignity of each individual and in the sanctity of each life. Both of us understand that our liberty is not given to us by a prime minister or a president, or the Knesset, or the Congress, but comes instead from God.[37]

According to Pat Robertson:

> Of course, we [evangelicals], like all right-thinking people, support Israel because Israel is an island of democracy, an island of individual freedom, an island of the rule of law, and an island of modernity in the midst of a sea of dictatorial regimes, the suppression of individual liberty, and a fanatical religion intent on returning to the feudalism of eighth-century Arabia.[38]

It is often during difficult times when people learn who their true friends are. Likewise with nations, tragedy shines a light on true allies. Many Christian Zionists have noted that Israel's reaction to the attacks of 9/11 dramatically demonstrated the depth of the special relationship. In a letter he wrote to Israeli Prime Minister Ariel Sharon in July 2002, Gary Bauer emphasized this point:

> We want to remind the Israeli people that they are not alone in their hour of need. On September 11, 2001, the United States suffered a horrendous attack. As we mourned our losses we were shocked to see dancing in the streets, in celebration of our pain, in some parts of the Middle East. But in Israel you cried with us and lowered your flag and shared our grief. On September 11 many Americans came to understand for the first time what it is like to be an Israeli and to face barbaric terrorism that targets innocent civilians. We know that in the face of this evil the free people of the world who believe in human dignity, the sanctity of life and in free institutions must stand together.

ARMAGEDDON—THE MOTIVE THAT WASN'T

THIS CHAPTER HAS reviewed all of the major motives driving evangelical Christian support for Israel. Yet some readers, especially critics of Christian Zionism, will no doubt find this list incomplete. The media have conjured up a more sinister motive behind Christian Zionism, and this false motive has been mentioned so often that it has taken root in the popular understanding of the phenomenon. A thorough discussion of the motives for Christian Zionism must therefore address what *doesn't* motivate Christian support for Israel.

An October 2002 *60 Minutes* story on Christian Zionism reported by Bob Simon dramatically sets forth this alleged evil motive. Simon begins his piece by interviewing some Christian Zionists to demonstrate the depth of their support for Israel. Then Simon gets to the heart of the matter. "What propels them?" he asks. "Why do they love Israel so much?" Simon answers his own question:

> Because the return of the Jews to their ancient homeland is seen by evangelicals as a precondition for the Second Coming of Christ. Therefore, when the Jewish State was created in 1948, they saw it as a sign. Israel's conquest of Jerusalem and the West Bank in 1967 deepened their excitement, heightened their anticipation.
>
> The final battle in the history of the future will be fought on this ancient battleground in northern Israel called Armageddon. The blood will rise as high as a horse's bridle here at Armageddon, before Christ triumphs to begin his 1,000 year rule. And the Jews? Well, two-thirds of them will have been wiped out by now, and the survivors will accept Jesus at last.[39]

According to Simon and many others, the true motive behind Christian Zionism is a desire to speed the Second Coming of Christ. Far from dreading the tragedy that will befall the Jews when Christ returns, many commentators imply that the death or conversion of the Jews is actually one of the main attractions. From this perspective, Christian Zionism is not motivated by love for the Jews but may in fact be driven by the opposite sentiment. As writer Gershom Gorenberg noted, "The Jews die or convert. As a Jew, I can't feel very comfortable with the affections of somebody who looks forward to that scenario."[40]

THE GREAT THEOLOGICAL shift of the twentieth century took place largely under the radar of the mainstream media. Thus few secular commentators recognize the profound differences between the theology of a devout evangelical

Christian in America today and that of a devout Christian in the Europe of a prior era. To the secular pundit, these Christians read the same Bible, pray to the same Jesus, and likely share the same view of the Jews. Without an awareness of the changes that have taken place, such observers presume that the Christian anti-Semitism so prevalent in prior ages lives on in the hearts of today's committed Christians.

Such observers naturally tend to dismiss the assertion that Christian Zionism is a sincere outpouring of love for the Jewish people. Instead, they search for the true, dark motive that they know must lurk somewhere beneath the politically correct patina. These critics found the smoking gun they were looking for when they discovered that, according to dispensationalist eschatology, the birth of Israel is a milestone on the road to a Second Coming in which the Jews are ultimately killed or converted. To the skeptics, this belief confirmed that beneath the talk of love and reconciliation, Christian Zionism was nothing more than the continuation of the age-old quest to kill and convert the Jews by different means.

This myth about the true motives for Christian support for Israel ignores the great theological shift of the twentieth century. It ignores the powerful hold that Genesis 12:3 and its commandment to "bless Israel" have on the Christian Zionist imagination. It ignores the debt of gratitude that Christian Zionists feel toward the Jews for the Jewish roots of their faith. It ignores the U.S.-Israel alliance in the cold war and in the war on terror, as well as the special U.S.-Israel relationship. This argument that Christians support Israel only to speed the Second Coming presumes a Christianity still inimical to Jews at worst and indifferent to them at best. It is not an argument but a caricature.

Most Christian Zionists certainly do believe that the birth of Israel is the first in a chain of events that will culminate in the Second Coming, but it is a mistake to confuse this belief for a motive. While Christian Zionists have faith that the Second Coming will happen, they do not presume to speed it through their actions. Christian Zionists also believe that the sun will rise in the morning. They don't support Israel to speed the sunrise.

As we saw in chapter two, American Christians have not always believed themselves so helpless to alter God's timetable. Postmillennialism, the eschatology that dominated America during the seventeeth and eighteenth centuries, held that Christians *do* have the power to speed the coming of the

Millennium and the Second Coming through their own actions. Toward this end they worked to spread the gospel at home and abroad and to eliminate vice from American society. The Christian Zionists, however, are not postmillennialists; they are dispensational premillennialists. Dispensationalists have always believed that they are powerless to alter the timing of this Second Coming through their acts. The charge of intervention in international affairs to speed the Second Coming simply doesn't fit the theology of the particular Christians so accused. Those making this accusation have the wrong Christians in the dock.

In the words of Ed Dobson and Ed Hindson, two leading intellectuals of the Christian Right:

> A lot of talk about speeding up the apocalypse would be stopped if more people understood that prophecy cannot be altered. There are some conditional prophecies: in the Old Testament, for example, when people repented for their sins, God would abstain from sending down a divine punishment. But the prophecies about the end times are unconditional. They are written in God's book. It is arrogant and sinful to think that we can change them.[41]

All of the leading Christian Zionists share this dispensationalist belief that man cannot alter God's timetable for the Second Coming. According to Pastor John Hagee, "God has an exact timetable, and He is going to do what He wants to do when He wants to do it."[42] In Pat Robertson's words, "I think Israel is God's timepiece, and the clock is ticking along toward midnight. Nobody knows the day or the hour. It could be another hundred years or so. . . ."[43] According to Jerry Falwell:

> No human preparations are demanded by God to bring about the Second Coming of Christ. Whatever requirements may be involved are of His own making. God has set the time for that glorious event, and He will bring it to pass. And no man knows the day or the hour of His Second Coming.[44]

In making these statements, Falwell and Robertson are merely paraphrasing a much higher authority. In the Gospel of Matthew, Jesus Christ said of the end of days, "But of that day and hour no one knows, not even the angels of heaven, but My Father only."[45]

THE POSTMILLENNIALIST ZEAL for social activism was natural given their belief that their deeds would speed the Millennium and the Second Coming. If dispensationalists lack this belief, then what motivates their considerable political and social action in the world? Why do they join groups such as the Moral Majority and the Christian Coalition and through them work to eliminate sin from American society? This question goes to the heart of an early controversy in the dispensationalist camp.

Dispensationalists believe that there will be a number of "signs of the times" that indicate when the Second Coming is drawing near. The birth of Israel is one such sign of the times, but it is far from the only one. Dispensationalists also believe the days preceding the Second Coming will be characterized by the steep decline of society and the spread of vice and immorality. If such a decline is inevitable, then some dispensationalists have in fact argued that efforts to improve society are futile. In the earlier part of the century, many dispensationalists acted on this belief by withdrawing from political and social involvement to await the final days.[46] Even today, some dispensationalists argue that Christian involvement in social or political causes is foolish since no human action can prevent the inevitable social decay.[47]

Yet such doomsday dispensationalists are a very small minority these days. Today the great majority of dispensationalists reject withdrawal from the world and instead actively seek to improve society through social and political engagement. In explaining this activism despite their belief in an inevitable decline, dispensationalists stress the obvious: there is much more to Christianity than End-Times prophecy. The Bible is filled with positive commandments to be involved in the world, to help one's fellow man, to be the salt of the earth.[48] Evangelical Christians read the Sermon on the Mount as well as the Book of Revelation.

Because they reject the notion that social action is futile, dispensationalists created organizations such as the Moral Majority and the Christian Coalition and have led the fight to eliminate what they believe are America's greatest sins from abortion to pornography. Much to the chagrin of America's liberals, dispensationalists are not content to wait for the end of the world, but instead they seek its perfection.

This social activism is the greatest proof that dispensationalists are sincere when they disclaim any ability to alter God's apocalyptic time clock. As mentioned earlier, dispensationalists believe that along with the birth of Israel one of the preconditions to the Second Coming is widespread social and moral decay. If they believed that they could speed the Second Coming by helping to establish its preconditions, then dispensationalists should be busy opening up abortion clinics, brothels, and casinos. Instead, dispensationalists have been at the forefront of fighting to restore traditional morality to America. Jerry Falwell and Pat Robertson have galvanized millions of evangelical Christians into a powerful political force to fight against these indicia of the End Times.

Dispensationalists also believe that one of the signs of the approaching Second Coming will be increasing apostasy in the church. For the past century they have equated this apostasy with Christian liberalism and the movement to deny Christ's supernatural aspects (His deity, virgin birth, resurrection, and substitutionary atonement). Yet instead of hoping that liberalism will spread, or assisting in its rise, dispensationalists have led the fight against liberalism. It was the dispensationalists who galvanized fundamentalist Christians to fight liberalism in the early twentieth-century church, and they continue to lead the fight against liberalism today with the help of their enormous television ministries and network of Bible colleges.

Finally, the surest sign that the Second Coming is truly imminent will be the rise of the Antichrist. Dispensationalists believe that the Antichrist will be a slick, charismatic leader who will exercise dominion over the world by taking control of a large confederation of nations or world-governing body. The Antichrist's rise to power will start a seven-year countdown to Christ's return to earth. Throughout the twentieth century, dispensationalists believed that they saw the hand of the Antichrist in efforts to create international bodies such as the League of Nations and the United Nations. Yet dispensationalists have not cheered the creation of such bodies in fits of apocalyptic ecstasy. Instead, they have consistently warned of, and actively opposed, the rise of such international institutions.

Most recently, Pat Robertson loudly entered this fray with his 1991 book *The New World Order*. Robertson saw ominous signs, and the hand of the

Antichrist, in the rise of United Nations' authority and international cooperation that accompanied the 1991 Gulf War. His response was to write a book warning his country and the world of the great danger in these steps toward a world government. Robertson put the full weight of his media empire behind marketing the book, which rose to number four on the *New York Times'* best-seller list. In the face of this surest sign of Christ's imminent return, Robertson sounded an alarm of warning.

THUS EVANGELICAL CHRISTIANS have actively fought against almost every trend and development that they believe are preconditions to the Second Coming. Such behavior is completely inconsistent with a belief that through their actions they can somehow encourage these trends and accelerate Christ's return. This broader perspective clearly belies the assertion that Christians support Israel to speed the Second Coming. Evangelical Christians would have to be quite schizophrenic indeed to work against every sign of the End Times in the belief that their efforts will not alter God's timetable, but to somehow except Israel from this belief.

Even if dispensationalists did believe that they were capable of speeding the Second Coming, of course, it is not at all clear why they would act on this belief by supporting Israel instead of seeking to weaken her. Dispensationalists believe that the Second Coming will occur after a massive invasion of Israel by foreign powers. How does solidifying the U.S.-Israel alliance and securing greater U.S. military aid for Israel make such an invasion of Israel more likely? Short of Christ Himself descending from the heavens, a close alliance with the United States is the greatest deterrent to invasion that Israel could possibly hope for. It makes far more sense that someone wanting to speed the End-Times invasion of Israel would seek to undermine the U.S.-Israel alliance and remove from Israel its greatest benefactor and protector. A true doomsday Zionist would be no Zionist at all but a zealous ally of the anti-Israel Left.

Dogged critics of Christian Zionism make much of the apocalyptic implications of their support for West Bank settlements. Certainly Christian support for continued Israeli occupation of the West Bank, it is argued, is meant to escalate tensions in the region and invite an apocalyptic war. Such an assessment assumes that Christian Zionists share the critics' liberal conviction that Israel's occupation of the West Bank makes a Middle East conflict more likely. Yet, right or wrong, Christian Zionists are far more likely to share the view of Israeli hawks that retention of the West Bank is a strategic imperative that provides Israel with crucial strategic depth. To such thinkers, the surest way to invite aggression against Israel would be to relinquish control of these strategically vital territories.

This criticism of evangelical Christians—that they permit their end-of-days dreams to influence their policy—is not a new one. During the 1980s, for example, some critics accused evangelical Christians of supporting Ronald Reagan and his tough cold war policies to spark a nuclear war and thereby speed the Second Coming. Yet this critique, much like the West Bank critique discussed above, presupposed that evangelicals shared the liberal view that Reagan's policy made confrontation with the Soviet Union more likely. Most evangelicals, however, believed like Reagan himself that the Soviet Union respected strength and that weakness was the surest way to invite Soviet aggression. As fundamentalist scholars Ed Dobson and Ed Hindson noted in 1986:

> If we really wanted to accelerate the end, we would surely support the nuclear agenda of the American Left and Communist Party, because we firmly believe that unilateral disarmament is a sure way to send this country into the arms of its maker.[49]

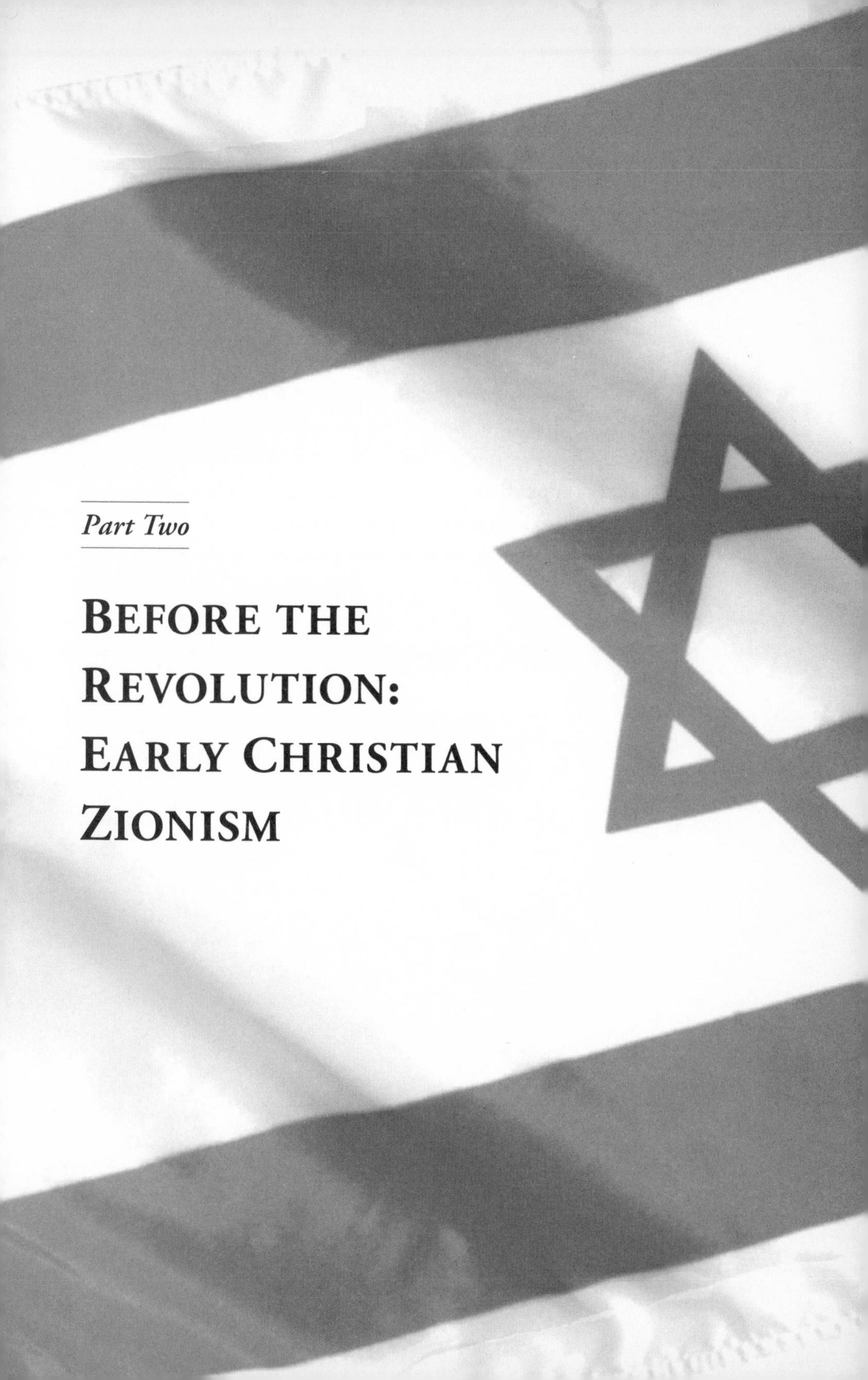

Part Two

Before the Revolution: Early Christian Zionism

We believe this is an appropriate time for all nations and especially the Christian nations of Europe to show kindness to Israel. A million of exiles, by their terrible suffering, are piteously appealing to our sympathy, justice, and humanity. Let us now restore to them the land of which they were so cruelly despoiled by our Roman ancestors.[1]

—William Blackstone, 1891

Chapter Four

THE DEEP ROOTS OF CHRISTIAN ZIONISM: HECHLER AND BLACKSTONE

CHRISTIAN ZIONISM IS not a new phenomenon. It is not the creation of Jerry Falwell and Pat Robertson. It did not suddenly materialize in the 1980s. In fact, Christian Zionism actually predates the Jewish Zionist movement.* For as long as there have been dissident Protestants who have rejected replacement theology, there have been Christian Zionists.

Today, the State of Israel is an important U.S. ally and major military power. America's Jewish Zionists are well connected, well funded, and highly influential. The pro-Israel organization AIPAC (American Israel Public Affairs Committee) is consistently rated one of the most powerful lobbies in Washington. But when the Zionist movement began, it was a movement of dreamers and their impoverished foot soldiers completely disconnected from power and influence. At crucial junctures during the early years of the Zionist enterprise, Christian Zionists provided diplomatic and political access to these marginal Jews. Two men in particular—William Hechler and William Blackstone—personify this early Christian Zionism.

* As used in this book, and throughout the relevant literature, the term *Zionism* refers to a Jewish movement started by Theodor Herzl at the close of the nineteenth century. The term *Christian Zionism* refers to Christians who support the creation of a Jewish home in Palestine both before and after the birth of Zionism.

WILLIAM HECHLER: HERZL'S FIRST ALLY

THE YEAR WAS 1896. As William Hechler tells the story, he arrived at Theodor Herzl's home uninvited and unannounced. Herzl opened the door.

"Here I am," said Hechler.

"That I can see," replied Herzl, "but who are you?"

"You are puzzled," Hechler observed. "But you see, as long ago as 1882, I predicted your arrival.... Now I am going to help you."[2]

As historian Paul Merkley notes, this conversation represents the first encounter between Zionism and Christian Zionism.[3] Who were these two men? What had brought them together?

OF THE TWO, Theodor Herzl is by far the better known. Herzl, a Jew, was the father of the modern Zionist movement. Herzl was a most unlikely prophet of the Jewish return to their biblical homeland. After the Enlightenment opened the gates of the Jewish ghettos throughout Europe, some Jews had emerged, shaved their beards, bought modern clothes, and sought to become full and equal citizens of the countries in which they lived. Theodor Herzl was both a product and a proponent of this assimilation. Herzl lived in Vienna and was a reporter for the prestigious *Neue Freie Press*. He preferred literary journals to the Bible and cafes to synagogues. Herzl was certain that the full assimilation of the Jews into European society would gradually end anti-Semitism. Events soon dashed these hopes.

The *Neue Freie Press* sent Herzl to Paris to cover the trial of Alfred Dreyfus, a Jewish captain in the French army charged with treason. As Captain Dreyfus was led to trial, angry mobs lined the streets chanting, "Death to the Jews!"* Herzl was not so much shocked by the behavior as by the *location* of the behavior. This was France—the very birthplace of the Enlightenment. It was the French, led by Napoleon, who had literally opened the doors of the Jewish ghettos throughout Europe and let the Jews out into the Western

* After being sentenced to the notorious French penal colony at Devil's Island, and serving four years there, Dreyfus was permitted to return to France and was eventually vindicated. As had been suspected, anti-Semitism had played a role not only in the French response to the accusations against Dreyfus but also in the very accusations themselves.

world. If the French could so easily revert to anti-Semitism, reasoned Herzl, "what are we to expect from other peoples, which have not even attained the level France attained a hundred years ago?"[4]

If the Enlightenment would not save the Jews from anti-Semitism, then what would? The Dreyfus affair immediately convinced Herzl that the only answer to anti-Semitism in Europe was for the Jews to build their own country in their ancient land of Palestine. Herzl reasoned that only by having a nation of their own, like every other people, could the Jews end their status as despised strangers everywhere. Within two weeks of witnessing the mobs of Paris, Herzl wrote a sixty-five-page pamphlet called *Der Judenstaat* [The Jewish State]. *Der Judenstaat* was published in Vienna in February 1896. Now that he found what he believed to be the answer to the Jewish problem, Herzl threw himself into his mission so completely that he would literally work himself to death over the course of the next eight years.

Herzl was hardly the first Jew to contemplate the return of his people to their ancestral land. Jews had been sporadically returning to Jerusalem and other holy cities in Palestine throughout the centuries of their exile, and Russian Jews had founded a number of agricultural colonies there prior to the publication of Herzl's book. What distinguished Herzl was the fact that he thought in grand, geopolitical terms. He saw no point in sending settlers to a land where they had no legal status or autonomy. Instead, Herzl proposed that the Zionists appeal directly to the great powers for political recognition. Since Palestine was at that time part of the Ottoman Empire, Herzl aspired to nothing less than securing a grant to Palestine from the Ottoman sultan. In return for such recognition, Herzl argued, the Jews could strengthen the economy of the entire region and help the Ottoman's pay down their large national debt.

Theodor Herzl thought big, but he was in no position to implement his grandiose scheme. Herzl was a Jewish journalist and patron of the arts who completely lacked political connections. Those Jews who did have political connections were almost universally hostile to the Zionist project, viewing it as a threat to their newly won status in Gentile society. How would Herzl secure an audience with the sultan of the Ottoman Empire?

ENTER WILLIAM HECHLER. Unlike Herzl, Hechler was motivated by a deep religious conviction that the Jewish return to Palestine was preordained by God. And unlike Herzl, Hechler was well connected with the ruling classes in both Germany and England. Ironically, it was this devout man of faith, not the secular man of letters, who would first introduce Zionism to Europe's elites.

William Hechler was born in India to missionary parents in 1845. His mother was English, his father German, and Hechler was raised to speak both of their native tongues. Hechler's father, Dietrich, was an evangelical Christian ordained as an Anglican preacher. The elder Hechler had a deep, biblically based love for the Jewish people. In 1854, Dietrich Hechler noted that:

> One of the wishes I had was that I might be a real descendant of Abraham. I entertained an almost superstitious reverence for Jews, and therefore disapproved of their being mocked or otherwise ill-treated by my schoolfellows.[5]

William Hechler drank in his father's religiosity and his philo-Semitism. Hechler added to this his own fascination with the biblical prophecies about the return of the Jews to their ancient homeland. Hechler was not a dispensationalist, but he embraced a broader English religious tradition dating back to the Puritans, which stressed biblical literalism and a belief in the eventual restoration of the Jews to their land. During the 1600s, Puritan leaders had actually lobbied to permit the Jews to return to England* in their belief that the exile of the Jews to all of the nations of earth must first be completed before the Jewish return to Palestine could begin. Oliver Cromwell, himself a Puritan, was likely influenced by these arguments when he welcomed the Jews back to England in 1655.[6] This Puritan passion for the restoration of the Jews to Palestine was given new life in the nineteeth century by the English evangelical revival.[7] William Hechler, like John Darby before him, took his views from this English restorationist tradition.

Like other Zionists of both the Christian and Jewish variety, Hechler was first spurred to act on his Zionist views by an outburst of anti-Semitism. In the

* The Jews had been expelled from England in 1290.

early 1880s, the Russian czar engineered a series of pogroms and forced relocations that left thousands of Russian Jews dead and great masses homeless. Living in England at the time, Hechler formed a committee with other Christian Zionists to raise money to resettle these Russian Jewish refugees in Palestine. On behalf of the committee, Hechler traveled to Russia in 1882 to meet with Jewish leaders, and he encouraged them to return to their ancient land.[8]

In 1884, Hechler authored a pamphlet entitled, "The Restoration of the Jews to Palestine According to the Prophets."[9] Here Hechler organized and explained the major biblical prophecies about the Jewish return to their land. He argued that this return was imminent and went so far as to predict that it would occur in 1897 or 1898.* Given his belief in the immediacy of the restoration, Hechler was naturally on high alert for any stirrings for Zion within the Jewish community.

In 1895, Hechler moved from England to Vienna to become chaplain at the British Embassy. So it happened that Hechler was living in Vienna when a new book by Theodor Herzl appeared in his neighborhood bookstore.

A FEW DAYS after their initial meeting, Hechler hosted Herzl in his home. Hechler showed Herzl his extensive Bible collection, charts of biblical history, and a large military map of Palestine that, when unfolded, covered the entire floor. With great enthusiasm, Hechler showed Herzl the jacket he would wear when the two of them would one day be "riding together around the Holy Land."[10]

When this show-and-tell was over, Herzl got down to business. Herzl later recounted the conversation in his diary:

> I said to him: I must put myself into direct and publicly known relations with a responsible or non-responsible ruler—that is, with a minister-of-state or a prince. Then the Jews will believe in me and follow me. The most suitable personage would be the German Kaiser. . . .[11]

* While Israel was not born until 1948, Hechler defenders have noted that the First Zionist Congress—which eventually led to the creation of the State of Israel—was held in 1897.

Hechler leapt into action. He went to see his old friend—and uncle to the kaiser—the Grand Duke of Baden. Hechler convinced the grand duke to meet with Herzl. Impressed by what he heard, the grand duke then arranged for Herzl to meet with a number of officials up the German chain of command. In September 1898, Herzl was informed that Kaiser Wilhelm II would receive him in person during the monarch's upcoming visit to the Ottoman Empire.[12]

On October 16, 1898, Herzl was granted the promised audience with the kaiser in Constantinople. The kaiser was enthusiastic about Herzl's plan, albeit for unfortunate reasons. The kaiser saw the Zionist enterprise as an easy way to rid his country of the "kikes." He told Herzl, "There are elements among your people whom it would be good to settle in Palestine" including the "socialists" and the "usurers."[13] The kaiser agreed to recommend Herzl's plan directly to the Ottoman sultan when the two met later in the week. Two years after publishing *Der Judenstaat*, Herzl's ideas were going to be presented to the man who could instantly make them a reality.

The kaiser promised that he would meet with Herzl again during the next stop of his tour, in Jerusalem, and brief him on his talks with the sultan. Herzl left for Jerusalem via ship, landing in the port of Jaffa. When he disembarked, William Hechler was waiting for him. History does not record what coat Hechler wore, but his prediction that he and Herzl would be "riding around the Holy Land together" had come to pass.

When the kaiser arrived in Jerusalem, Herzl and Hechler went to meet him in his lavish tent outside the walls of Jerusalem. Herzl detected a worrisome change in the kaiser's tone. Herzl later wrote in his diary that the kaiser had been less "obliging" than he had been in Constantinople. Herzl inferred that "a good deal has been happening behind the scenes," and that as a result the Zionist "stock" had somewhat "depreciated."[14]

This first Zionist diplomatic initiative ended in that Jerusalem tent. Yet these efforts were not made in vain. As Herzl had predicted, his well-publicized meetings with the German kaiser bestowed much needed legitimacy upon him and his young movement. And these meetings helped to alert leaders in England to the Jewish interest in returning to Palestine. In time, the English would more enthusiastically assume the role of Zionist benefactor with which Germany so briefly flirted.

After their return from Palestine, Hechler and Herzl remained close friends and collaborators. Hechler was the only nonfamily member permitted to sit by Herzl's bedside as Herzl lay dying in 1904. Disappointed by the failure of most Jews of that day to rally around Herzl and his Zionist movement, Hechler declared upon Herzl's death that, "God took Herzl from us, for the Jews were not worthy of him."[15]

Hechler returned to England in 1910. In accordance with Herzl's wishes, the Zionist Organization in London paid Hechler a pension for the remainder of his life. Hechler lived long enough to be among the spectators in Parliament on July 22, 1922, when the British formally accepted the Mandate for Palestine.[16]

Like that of other Zionist leaders after World War I, Hechler's Zionism became increasingly urgent as he saw storm clouds gathering over Europe. According to historian David Pileggi:

> Hechler repeatedly warned his Jewish friends that there would be an extensive massacre of Jews in Europe. It would make the Crusades and Spanish Inquisition look like "child's play," he predicted. His forewarnings grew into an obsession, and he made them with increasing frequency until his death in 1931. Tragically, Hechler's predictions were politely dismissed by everyone.[17]

William Blackstone: The Father of American Zionism

In its early years, the Zionist movement was bitterly split over the issue of where to build the proposed Jewish homeland. Most Zionists passionately believed that the Jewish State must be located in their ancestral land of Palestine. There were more pragmatic Zionists, however, who argued that the Jews should take the first land made available to them, even if it meant going to Argentina or Africa. Such Zionists did not view these other lands as an ultimate destination, but rather as a way station in which the Jews could safely ride out an impending storm. Theodor Herzl himself was open to these other territorial options.

Following this debate from Chicago, a man named William Blackstone was not at all pleased by Herzl's pragmatism. Blackstone sent Herzl a copy of the Old Testament in which he had carefully highlighted all the passages that state it is to Palestine that the Jews will return. Herzl must have been touched by this unsolicited advice from a Christian friend. He kept this marked-up Bible in his study for the remainder of his days. That Bible is now on display in the Herzl Museum in Jerusalem.[18]

This exchange was the only interaction between Theodor Herzl and William Blackstone. Unlike William Hechler, William Blackstone never met or collaborated with the founder of modern Zionism. Yet the parallels between Hechler and Blackstone are pronounced. Both predated Herzl in their Zionism. Both came to their Zionist beliefs from a deep Christian faith. And both provided political entrée to a young movement that lacked it.

WILLIAM BLACKSTONE WAS born in New York in 1841. Blackstone's youth coincided with one of the great periods of evangelical fervor in American history. While attending a revival meeting at the age of eleven, Blackstone was born again and remained a devout Christian for the rest of his life. He later married, moved to Chicago, and made a fortune in real estate. Blackstone then devoted his time and fortune to his religious mission.

Blackstone was an early and zealous convert to premillennial dispensationalism. In fact, Blackstone did more to spread and popularize dispensational theology than any other American with the exception of C. I. Scofield, author of the *Scofield Reference Bible*. In 1878, Blackstone wrote a best-selling book titled *Jesus Is Coming*. More than one million copies of the book have since been printed, and it has been translated into more than forty languages.[19] Here Blackstone sets forth the dispensationalist creed with great clarity and force. He devotes considerable space to a detailed review of the many prophecies that foretell the return of the Jews to their land. The rejection of replacement theology is a consistent theme. Toward the end of his analysis, Blackstone writes:

> It would seem that such overwhelming testimony would convince every fair-minded reader that there is a glorious future restoration in store for Israel. And yet, many say that we must interpret all this Scripture

> "spiritually," and they fritter away the point and the force of such explicit declarations, in attempting to apply them to the persecuted church. This is a great error....[20]

What distinguished Blackstone from so many other leading dispensationalists of the day was his decision to put his religious beliefs into political action. During the decade of the 1880s, Blackstone was distressed by the steady stream of reports detailing the murder and mass relocation of Russia's Jews. Like Hechler across the Atlantic Ocean, Blackstone was determined to find a solution for these long-suffering Jews. And, like Hechler, Blackstone saw a Jewish home in Palestine as the only real answer to this crisis.

In 1890, Blackstone organized a conference of Christian and Jewish leaders in Chicago to address the plight of Russia's Jews. The "Conference on the Past, Present, and Future of Israel" unanimously passed a resolution of sympathy for Russian Jewry. Here the delegates urged world leaders to intervene with the Russians to "stay the hand of cruelty from this time-honored people, which have given them as well as us our bible, our religion, and our knowledge of God."[21]

When Blackstone introduced a resolution in support of Zionism, however, the conference's consensus evaporated. Ironically, while Blackstone and the other Christians embraced the Zionist platform, the Jewish delegates rejected it.[22] These Jews, mostly Reform rabbis, objected to the idea that the Jews were a distinct nation—a concept that had been used to attack the Jews so often in the past. Much as Theodor Herzl still did at the time, these rabbis placed their hope for the future in assimilation, and they embraced America as their new Jerusalem.

The Blackstone Memorial

Despite such early opposition, Blackstone remained convinced that a Jewish homeland in Palestine was the only solution to the plight of Europe's Jews. Blackstone further believed, as Herzl would later conclude, that the most effective way to create such a Jewish homeland was to take the case directly to the world powers. Toward this end, Blackstone wrote a petition to the president of the United States, Benjamin Harrison, and his secretary of state, James Blaine, urging them to:

> ...secure the holding at an early date, of an international conference to consider the condition of Israelites and their claims to Palestine as their ancient home, and to promote, in all other just and proper ways, the alleviation of their suffering condition.[23]

In an impressive bit of coalition building, Blackstone secured the signatures of 413 prominent Americans on this petition. The signatories included the chief justice of the Supreme Court, the Speaker of the House of Representatives, the chairman of the House Foreign Relations Committee, and many other members of Congress. Outside of government, Blackstone procured the signatures of the most prominent Gilded Age industrialists, including J. P. Morgan, John D. and William Rockefeller, and Cyrus McCormick. Rounding out the list were editors and journalists from the leading newspapers, many Protestant and Catholic leaders, and even a handful of Jewish leaders.

This petition has come to be known as the Blackstone Memorial. It is an impressive document. As Justice Louis Brandeis, the leading American Zionist during the World War I era, would later remark:

> [T]he arguments which Mr. Blackstone used in that petition were in large part the arguments which the great Herzl presented five years later in setting forth to the world the needs and the hopes of the Jewish people.[24]

Blackstone opened the petition with the question driving him to action: "What shall be done for the Russian Jews?" In light of the organized and sustained campaign of persecution then underway, Blackstone concluded that Russia was determined to rid itself of its two million Jews. In determining where these Jewish refugees should go, he raised and then dismissed some alternatives. Allow the Jews into Europe? Europe is too crowded to take them. Take the Jews into America? Trans-Atlantic transport would be expensive and time consuming. In raising the specter of massive Jewish immigration into their countries, Blackstone no doubt sought to frighten Americans and Europeans into embracing Zionism.

Blackstone then arrived at his preferred solution for the Jews:

> Why not give Palestine back to them again? According to God's distribution of nations it is their home, an inalienable possession from which

> they were expelled by force. Under their civilization it was a remarkably fruitful land sustaining millions of Israelites....
>
> Why shall not the powers which under the treaty of Berlin, in 1878, gave Bulgaria to the Bulgarians and Serbia to the Serbians now give Palestine back to the Jews? These provinces, as well as Roumania, Montenegro and Greece, were wrested from the Turks and given to their natural owners. Does not Palestine rightfully belong to the Jews?...
>
> We believe this is an appropriate time for all nations and especially the Christian nations of Europe to show kindness to Israel. A million of exiles, by their terrible suffering, are piteously appealing to our sympathy, justice, and humanity. Let us now restore to them the land of which they were so cruelly despoiled by our Roman ancestors.[25]

In a personal letter to President Harrison and Secretary of State Blaine accompanying the petition, Blackstone added a biblical incentive that later generations of Christian Zionists would frequently echo. Blackstone wrote:

> May it be the high privilege of your Excellency, and the Honorable Secretary, to take a personal interest in this great matter, and secure through the Conference, a home for these wandering millions of Israel, and thereby receive to yourselves the promise of Him, who said to Abraham, "I will bless them that bless thee," Gen. 12:3.[26]

The Blackstone Memorial produced no immediate results. President Harrison promised to give it "careful attention," but there is no record of his taking any further action. Secretary of State Blaine sought feedback on the petition from foreign service officers in the Ottoman Empire. He was advised not to broach the topic with the Ottoman government, and he followed this advice. No call for an international conference to discuss the plight of Russia's Jews was ever issued.[27]

Yet, much like Hechler's efforts with the kaiser, Blackstone's work provided a long-term benefit to the Zionist cause by preparing the ground for what would follow later. Blackstone planted the idea of a Jewish return to Palestine, and an American role in that return, in the American political consciousness. He also provided an impressive example to future Christian Zionists of how to translate their Christian theology into political action. Unlike Hechler, however, Blackstone would later be called back into the service of the Zionist cause. As discussed in the next chapter, Blackstone would at that later date serve to greater immediate effect.

HECHLER, BLACKSTONE, AND CHRISTIAN ZIONISM

WILLIAM HECHLER AND William Blackstone were prototypical Christian Zionists. Although they predated the State of Israel and the Zionist movement itself, they foreshadowed most of the salient features of the Christian Zionist movement that emerged in the 1980s. Like present-day Christian Zionists, Hechler and Blackstone made their primary contributions to the Zionist cause by providing access to powerful people to whom the Jewish Zionists were not connected. Also like today's Christian Zionists, Hechler and Blackstone were philo-Semites whose broad agenda included the fight against anti-Semitism. For both Hechler and Blackstone, in fact, it was the plight of the Jews in Russia that galvanized them to go beyond predicting a Jewish return to actively working to engineer it.

The similarities between these early Christian Zionists and today's Christian Zionists extend to their motives. The Zionism of Hechler and Blackstone was primarily motivated by their Christian theology. They read their Bibles literally to conclude that it was God's will for the Jews to return to their homeland. Both also believed that this Jewish return was an important event on the road to the Second Coming. Yet like today's Christian Zionists, Hechler and Blackstone stressed that they merely sought to serve God's will, not to alter God's timing. Early on, in fact, Hechler's primary apprehension about collaborating with Herzl was his fear that Herzl presumed to engineer the fulfillment of prophecy. As Hechler wrote to the Grand Duke of Baden:

> After reading this book [Herzl's *Der Judenstaat*] I called to see Dr. Herzl, who was a perfect stranger to me, because I was wondering whether the doctor was trying to fulfill prophecy. This would be wrong, for God will in His own good time and in His own way bring about his wonderful purposes. This was however not Dr. Herzl's wish, for he knew nothing of the special prophecies on this subject.[28]

For his part, Blackstone wrote the following about the timing of the Second Coming in *Jesus Is Coming*:

> We conclude then that like the "day and hour," it is known to God only, and the church can have no definite sign in it. Therefore nothing is left for us to do but faithfully continue proclaiming the glad tidings of the coming kingdom while we watch momentarily for the Bridegroom.[29]

There was one topic on which Hechler and Blackstone did disagree: the importance of converting Jews to Christianity. In this difference, these men foreshadowed a difference of opinion that persists among Christian Zionists to the present day. For his part, Hechler did not believe in proselytizing the Jews. He noted that one of the conditions precedent to the Second Coming of Christ was the return of the children of Israel to their land in "unbelief." Christ would take care of the rest down the road. In Hechler's words:

> We are now entering, thanks to the Zionist Movement, into Israel's Messianic age. Thus, it is not a matter these days of opening all the doors of your churches to the Jews, but rather of opening the gates of their homeland, and of sustaining them in their work of clearing the land, and irrigating it, and bringing water to it. All of this is messianic work....[30]

Unlike William Hechler, William Blackstone did believe in proselytizing the Jews. For him, working to save Jewish lives in this world led logically to seeking to save Jewish souls in the next. In 1887, Blackstone helped to form the Chicago Committee for Hebrew Christian Work, an organization dedicated to "undertake Gospel work among the Jews of Chicago."[31] Blackstone even went so far as to preach the importance of accepting Christ to a large gathering of Jewish Zionists in Los Angeles. As a sign of the high esteem in which they held Blackstone, these Jews politely listened as Blackstone called for their conversion.[32]

THERE IS NO record of a debate within the Jewish community over how to react to Hechler's Christian Zionism. Hechler was welcomed at the early Zionist Congresses, and he was paid a pension by the Zionist movement until the day he died. When it came to Blackstone's efforts, however, the Jewish community had a decidedly mixed response, and this response foreshadowed well the current communal debate over how to respond to Christian Zionism. Many

Jews were suspicious of Blackstone. In commenting on the Blackstone Memorial, one Jewish paper, *The Jewish Messenger*, argued that:

> This petition will recoil against the Jews of Turkey.... Mr. Blackstone's ultimate aim is the evangelization of the Jews. His personality is charming, his zeal praiseworthy, but let him evangelize the Czar and his counselors.[33]

On the other side of the debate, *Ha Pisga*, a Hebrew-language daily, struck a more pragmatic tone when it said the following about Christian Zionists:

> It is not their intention to bring us under the wings of Christianity in our time... but rather in the days to come when peace returns and each of us sits under his fig tree and vine, and after the battle of Gog and Magog. Let the Christians do whatever they can to help us in the resettlement in Palestine. As to the question of our faith, let that rest until Elijah comes and then we shall see whether or not their dream materializes.[34]

IN 586 B.C., Babylonian King Nebuchadnezzar conquered Jerusalem and exiled the Jews to Babylonia. The Babylonian exile continued until 538 B.C., when Cyrus the Great of Persia defeated the Babylonians. Cyrus gave the Jews permission to return to Jerusalem and rebuild their temple. To Jews and Christians alike, Cyrus stands as a towering example of a Gentile liberating the Jews and restoring them to their land.

In A.D. 70, the Romans captured and destroyed Jerusalem and sent the Jews into a second, much longer exile. From that date, until the creation of Israel in 1948, the Jews and their Christian friends awaited a modern-day Cyrus.

In the personal letter he sent to President Harrison and Secretary of State Blaine together with his Memorial, William Blackstone sought to inspire these leaders to action by invoking the legacy of King Cyrus. Noting many signs that God was preparing to bring the Jews home to their land, Blackstone wrote:

> Not for twenty-four centuries, since the days of Cyrus, King of Persia, has there been offered to any mortal such a privileged opportunity to further the purposes of God concerning His ancient people.[35]

Neither Harrison nor Blaine is known to have had Christian Zionist leanings, and it is likely that Blackstone's biblical reference failed to capture their imaginations. Yet Blackstone was introducing a very powerful image into the public discourse on Zionism. This concept—playing the role of a modern Cyrus—would later captivate a future American president at a critical juncture in Zionist history.[36]

What do you mean helped to create [Israel]? I am Cyrus. I am Cyrus.[1]

—President Harry S. Truman, 1952

Chapter Five

THREE CHRISTIAN ZIONISTS WHO HELPED TO CREATE ISRAEL: BALFOUR, WILSON, AND TRUMAN

THEODOR HERZL WAS a man in a hurry. He had an obsessive sense that time was running out—both for him and for the Jews of Europe. He was correct on both counts.

When his overtures to the Germans and the Ottomans failed to bear fruit, Theodor Herzl recognized that he would probably have to wait for the teetering Ottoman Empire to fall before accomplishing his goals in Palestine. In the meantime, Herzl seized on a new idea: the creation of a Jewish colony in the Sinai Peninsula. The Sinai bordered on Palestine and could serve as a launching point for a future return. In addition, the Sinai had the advantage of being under British, not Ottoman, control. Herzl turned his attention to England.

In 1902, Theodor Herzl held a series of meetings with British Colonial Secretary Joseph Chamberlain. Chamberlain was quick to embrace Herzl's plans for Sinai. Chamberlain saw a strategic value in a colony of Jews beholden to Britain massed on the Ottoman border. But Chamberlain's support could not overcome determined opposition from other quarters in the British government, and the Sinai proposal quickly died.[2]

Despite the outcome, the Sinai episode convinced Chamberlain that Zionist manpower and enterprise should be employed in the service of British colonial policy. He quickly made Herzl a counter offer. Chamberlain suggested that Herzl create his Jewish home in another British colony in need of settlers: Uganda.

While the Sinai was not Palestine, it was at least in the right neighborhood and was bound up in Jewish history. Africa offered no such connections to home. Yet while Herzl resisted the idea at first, events quickly changed his mind. In April 1903, there was a series of large-scale pogroms in the Russian city of Kishinev, and scores of Jewish men, women, and children were brutally slaughtered. To Herzl and other pragmatists, the message was clear: this was no time to turn down a refuge anywhere in the world. In the words of Max Nordau, a Zionist who supported the Uganda plan, Uganda would be for the Jews a *nachtasyl*, a shelter for the night. Herzl decided to support the Uganda plan and brought the question before the Sixth Zionist Congress.

The Uganda plan sparked outraged opposition from the Zionist ranks. One delegate, shouting, "Death to the East African," tried to assassinate Max Nordau. What doomed the Uganda plan was the fact that most of the Russian Zionists—including the delegate from Kishinev—rejected it. The very Jews whom Herzl sought to save did not want a way station in the African mountains. They wanted their ancestral land in Palestine. Unable to overcome this opposition, the Zionists declined the offer of a colony in Uganda.[3]

ARTHUR BALFOUR AND THE BALFOUR DECLARATION

WHEN CHAMBERLAIN OFFERED Uganda to the Zionists in 1902, the prime minister of Britain was a man named Arthur Balfour. Balfour was an atypical politician whose intellectual curiosity extended well beyond elections and affairs of state. After the Uganda offer was rejected and Chamberlain and others had shifted their attention to other matters, Balfour continued to wrestle with the issue. He simply could not understand why a homeless people would turn down the offer of land anywhere in the world.

In 1906, Balfour's conservative government fell, and new elections were called. While campaigning in Manchester, Balfour learned that there was a young chemistry professor at Manchester's Victoria University who was emerging as a leader of the Zionist movement. Although in the midst of a frenetic reelection campaign, Balfour requested a meeting with the professor, Chaim Weizmann. He wanted to ask Weizmann about Uganda.[4]

Balfour set aside fifteen minutes for the meeting. The two men ended up talking for over an hour. Weizmann later recalled that he was having a difficult time explaining to Balfour why the Zionists rejected Uganda:

> I felt that I was sweating blood and I tried to find some less ponderous way of expressing myself....
>
> Then suddenly I said: "Mr. Balfour, supposing I were to offer you Paris instead of London, would you take it?"
>
> He sat up and looked at me and answered: "But Dr. Weizmann, we have London."
>
> "That is true," I said. "But we had Jerusalem when London was a marsh."
>
> He leaned back, continued to stare at me...[5]

Although Weizmann did not realize it at the time, his words had a profound impact on Balfour. Writing about the Uganda scheme years later, Balfour wrote:

> The scheme...had one serious defect. It was not Zionism. It attempted to find a home for men of Jewish religion and Jewish race in a region far removed from the country where that race was nurtured and that religion came into being. Conversations I held with Dr. Weizmann in January 1906, convinced me that history could not thus be ignored, and that if a home was to be found for the Jewish people, homeless now for nearly nineteen hundred years, it was vain to seek it anywhere but in Palestine.[6]

The election of 1906 went poorly for Balfour. His party lost power, and Balfour lost his seat in Parliament. But Balfour would later cross the path of power, and of Chaim Weizmann, once again.

World War I broke out in the summer of 1914. As the war dragged on, the British came close to exhausting their supply of acetone, a key component in the manufacture of explosives. Foreign sources of supply had already been tapped dry. Without a new source of acetone, Britain would lose the war in a matter of months.

Reenter Chaim Weizmann. Not only was Weizmann the leader of the Zionist movement, but he also had a day job. He was a chemistry professor who happened to specialize in the manufacture of synthetic compounds. At the request of Winston Churchill, then the First Lord of the Admiralty,

Weizmann oversaw the production of enough synthetic acetone to supply the British armed forces for the remainder of the war.

In 1916, a new First Lord of the Admiralty replaced Churchill. When Weizmann next reported to London, he was greeted by the familiar face of Arthur Balfour. Although ten years had passed, Balfour had not forgotten their prior meeting. Balfour welcomed Weizmann by stating, "You know, I was thinking of that conversation of ours, and I believe that when the guns stop firing you may get your Jerusalem."[7]

The Balfour Declaration

On November 2, 1917, Arthur Balfour, now serving as Britain's foreign secretary, wrote a letter to Lord Rothschild, the head of the British Zionist Federation. Balfour explained that he was writing to share with Rothschild and the Zionists a "declaration of sympathy with Jewish Zionist aspirations," which had been approved by the British Cabinet. Balfour then quoted the declaration, which read:

> His Majesty's Government view with favour the establishment in Palestine of a national home for the Jewish people, and will use their best endeavors to facilitate the achievement of this object, it being clearly understood that nothing shall be done which may prejudice the civil and religious rights of existing non-Jewish communities in Palestine, or the rights and political status enjoyed by Jews in any other country.

This paragraph has come to be known as the Balfour Declaration. It was, for the Zionists, a stunning victory. While billed as a "declaration of sympathy" with Zionist aspirations, it actually went further. With this brief paragraph, a leading world power had in effect committed itself to work toward the creation of a Jewish home in Palestine. Zionism was now an official goal of British foreign policy.

The Balfour Declaration very quickly gained an even greater significance. Five weeks after Balfour wrote his letter to Rothschild, British troops conquered Jerusalem from the crumbling Ottoman army. The nation that had formally endorsed the creation of a Jewish home in Palestine was now in control of Palestine.

In 1922, Zionist aspirations received yet another boost when the international community embraced the commitment to create a Jewish home in Palestine. That year the League of Nations ratified and conferred upon Britain an official mandate to administer Palestine. The mandate specifically obligated Britain to implement the terms of the Balfour Declaration and to "place the country under such political, administrative and economic conditions as will secure the establishment of the Jewish National Home." A mere quarter century after Herzl published *Der Judenstaat*, the Jewish State appeared to be a *fait accompli*.

Motives for the Balfour Declaration

According to popular lore, the Balfour Declaration was a reward to Chaim Weizmann for his contribution to the British war effort. While this explanation makes for an excellent story, there is little in the record to support it. Yet it turns out that the true motives for issuing this declaration were no less idealistic than this fabricated one. While not an expression of gratitude to Weizmann, the Balfour Declaration was to a surprising extent an expression of gratitude to the Jews.

While the Balfour Declaration was being debated, few of its supporters invoked altruistic rationales. Instead, the Jewish and Christian Zionists in Britain made a number of more pragmatic arguments in support of the creation of a Jewish homeland in Palestine. As is the case in the debate over support for Israel today, strategic arguments figured prominently. During the early twentieth century, the Suez Canal was the lifeline of the British Empire, linking Britain to India and points east. Supporters of the Balfour Declaration argued that planting a friendly power—the Jews—so close to the canal would help ensure its security. Chaim Weizmann noted that, "A strong Jewish community on the Egyptian flank is an efficient barrier for any danger likely to come from the north."[8] Sir Herbert Samuel, the first Jewish cabinet minister in Britain, echoed this point, arguing that a Jewish settlement in Palestine would block other powers from gaining control of this strategic strip of land.[9]

Others asserted diplomatic rationales. While the Balfour Declaration was under consideration, England was working to secure the entry of the United States into World War I and to prevent the withdrawal from the war of its ally Russia. Toward this end, it was argued that a formal British embrace of Zionism would win the support of influential Jews in both countries for these British war aims. In his *War Memoirs*, the prime minister at the time of the Balfour Declaration, David Lloyd George, noted that he supported the initiative in order to win the sympathies of the Russian Jews, who "wielded considerable influence in Bolshevik circles," and to secure "the aid of Jewish financial interests in the United States."[10] Intelligence reports that the German government was close to striking a deal of their own with the Zionists added a sense of urgency to this diplomatic rationale.[11]

While such pragmatic motives certainly played a role in the issuance of the Balfour Declaration, their significance may well be exaggerated. On the strategic side, the British successfully maintained colonies around the globe with the cooperation of the indigenous populations. It is not at all clear why the successful administration of Palestine would demand the importation of a new people. As for diplomacy, support for Zionism was hardly a key to Jewish sympathies. In fact, prominent Jews involved in finance and politics, the very groups that the British most wanted to influence, were at that time typically hostile to Zionism. Finally, by the time the Balfour Declaration was actually issued in November 1917, it was too late to influence either the Americans or the Russians: the United States was already in the war, and the Soviets had already embarked on a precipitous exit.

Although Prime Minister Lloyd George stressed pragmatic rationales in his *War Memoirs*, there is reason to believe that he was not being completely forthcoming in so doing. According to historian Barbara Tuchman, whose book *Bible and Sword* is perhaps the definitive study of the British role in Palestine, Lloyd George "unquestionably... doctored the picture." In her words:

> My own feeling is that he knew that his own motivation, as well as Balfour's, was in large part a sentimental (that is, a Biblical) one, but he could not admit it. He was writing his Memoirs in the 1930s, when the Palestine trouble was acute, and he could hardly confess to nostalgia for the Old Testament or to a guilty Christian conscience toward the Jews as a reason for an action that had committed Britain to the painful, expensive and seemingly insoluble problem of the Mandate.[12]

According to Tuchman, the true motive underlying the Balfour Declaration was a tradition of British Christian Zionism dating back to the Puritans. During the 1600s, the Puritans set a compelling example of religious piety, biblical literalism, and enthusiastic support for the restoration of the Jews to their ancient homeland. During a widespread evangelical revival in the 1800s, many in Britain's ruling class embraced the Puritans' religious fervor and, along with it, their Christian Zionism. In nineteenth-century England, these evangelicals accomplished what the dispensationalists would later achieve in twentieth-century America: they planted Zionism firmly in the broader Christian culture. Both Balfour and Lloyd George were products of this culture.

Tuchman's assertion is bolstered by statements made by the people most directly involved in securing the Balfour Declaration. Referring to the argument that the Balfour Declaration was undertaken as part of a "British imperialistic scheme," Weizmann wrote that:

> The truth is that British statesmen were by no means anxious for such a bargain. . . . England's connection with Palestine rested on the idea of a Jewish Homeland in Palestine; but for the idea of a Jewish Homeland, England would not have entertained the thought of a protectorate—or later of a mandate—over Palestine. England felt she had no business in Palestine except as part of the plan for the creation of a Jewish Homeland. . . . They understood as a reality the concept of the Return. It appealed to their tradition and their faith.[13]

While Lloyd George may have referred later in life to strategic motives for the Balfour Declaration, he also acknowledged that:

> It was undoubtedly inspired by natural sympathy, admiration and also by the fact that, as you must remember, we had been trained even more in Hebrew history than in the history of our own country. I could tell you all the kings of Israel. But I doubt whether I could have named half a dozen of the kings of England![14]

Balfour was more explicit about his motivation. In 1922, the English House of Lords was debating whether to accept the Mandate for Palestine from the League of Nations. A motion to reject the mandate had been introduced and received great support. Balfour rose in opposition to the motion and at this time made his only public defense of the Declaration that bore his name. Balfour stated:

> I hold that from a purely material point of view that policy that we initiated is likely to prove a successful policy. But we have never pretended—certainly I have never pretended—that it was purely from

> these materialistic considerations that the Declaration of November 1917 originally sprung....
>
> Surely, it is in order that we may send a message to every land where the Jewish race has been scattered, a message that will tell them that Christendom is not oblivious of their faith, is not unmindful of the service they have rendered to the great religions of the world, and most of all to the religion that the majority of Your Lordships' house profess, and that we desire to the best of our ability to give them the opportunity of developing in peace and quietness under British rule, those great gifts which hitherto they have been compelled to bring to fruition in countries which know not their language and belong not to their race. That is the ideal which I desire to see accomplished, that is the aim which lay at the root of the policy I am trying to defend; and though it be defensible indeed on every ground, that is the ground which chiefly moves me.[15]

BALFOUR'S STATEMENT BEFORE the House of Lords was an expression of a lifelong conviction. Like William Hechler before him, Balfour was raised within the English evangelical tradition, which embraced the restoration of the Jews to their homeland. According to Blanche Dugdale, Balfour's biographer, niece, and frequent companion, Balfour's philo-Semitism was deeply rooted in his personality:

> Balfour's interest in the Jews and their history was lifelong. It originated in the Old Testament training of his mother, and in his Scottish upbringing. As he grew up, his intellectual admiration and sympathy for certain aspects of Jewish philosophy and culture grew also, and the problem of the Jews in the modern world seemed to him of immense importance. He always talked eagerly of this, and I remember in childhood imbibing from him the idea that Christian religion and civilization owes to Judaism an immeasurable debt, shamefully ill repaid.[16]

Given Balfour's background, his Bible-based feelings for the Jews were natural. Balfour had always been an observant Christian. Every Sunday, he would gather his family and guests in his large dining room. There, by the flicker of candlelight, Balfour would lead the group in prayer. He would follow this by reading, out loud, a chapter of the Bible. He favored the Old Testament prophets, especially Isaiah. According to Blanche Dugdale, Balfour read the Bible slowly, bringing out every "shade of beauty and meaning" so that "it was impossible for attention to wander from it for a minute."[17]

Balfour's faith was so profound that he wrote a book about it. In 1877, Balfour wrote a discourse on religion with the misleading title, *Defense of Philosophic Doubt*. The doubt that Balfour defended was not doubt about the existence of God. Rather, Balfour defended his doubt in the modern creed that man should believe only those things that can be proven by scientific means. Balfour, a thoroughly modern man, refused to subject his faith in God to rational proofs.[18]

Other key British leaders at the time sprang from this same evangelical tradition. By all accounts Prime Minister Lloyd George shared Balfour's Christian Zionism. Lloyd George was raised by a poor but pious family in Wales. Growing up, religious instruction was integral to his education. Lloyd George was taught a love for the Bible and, through it, an appreciation for the Jewish people and their eventual restoration to their homeland. According to Lloyd George, "I was taught more about the history of the Jews than about the history of my own people."[19] Of his meetings with Chaim Weizmann, Lloyd George would later recall:

> When Dr. Weizmann was talking of Palestine he kept bringing up place names which were more familiar to me than those on the Western Front.[20]

ARTHUR BALFOUR HAD a long, distinguished career as a British statesman. He had reached the towering heights of power, serving as prime minister of Britain during a time when the sun never set on the British Empire and as foreign minister of Britain during a world war. Yet, near the end of his days, Balfour confessed to Blanche Dugdale that "what he had been able to do for the Jews had been the thing he looked back upon as the most worth his doing."[21]

WOODROW WILSON AND THE BALFOUR DECLARATION

IN APRIL 1917, the United States entered World War I on the side of the British. The Americans were crucial allies, supplying a massive infusion of armaments and troops that turned the tide of the war. Determined to keep the Americans by their side, the British Cabinet was unwilling to approve any postwar commitments that might alienate them. The Zionists and their allies recognized that an American green light would have to precede any British endorsement of Zionism.

Both Weizmann and Balfour approached Louis Brandeis, a man uniquely situated to help them secure the approval they needed. Brandeis was the leading American Zionist of his day. Brandeis was also a close confidant of President Woodrow Wilson. Brandeis had campaigned for Wilson during his 1912 presidential campaign, and then served as an influential advisor during Wilson's subsequent first term. In 1916, Wilson rewarded Brandeis by nominating him for the U.S. Supreme Court, where Brandeis served as the first Jewish justice. Yet unlike most Supreme Court justices before and after, Brandeis remained deeply involved in public policy, especially relating to Palestine, even after his ascent to the Court.

Brandeis agreed to seek from President Wilson an expression of support for creating a Jewish home in Palestine. In so doing, Brandeis' entrée would certainly play a crucial role. Equally important, however, was Brandeis' familiarity with Woodrow Wilson and how best to motivate this man.

IN THE NATIONAL memory, and even during his own lifetime, Woodrow Wilson has been thought of as a northeastern intellectual. Prior to entering politics, Wilson had spent decades at Princeton University, first as a professor and later as the university's president. Wilson then served as the governor of New Jersey. Yet these positions, and the stereotypes associated with them, obscured some of the core elements of Wilson's personality.

Throughout his life, Woodrow Wilson was a deeply religious Christian. As the son of a Presbyterian minister, Wilson was raised in a devout home. In adulthood, Wilson continued to actively participate in his church and read the Bible daily. At Princeton, Wilson regularly attended chapel and led the services twice a week. Wilson once wrote a friend:

> My life would not be worth living if it were not for the driving power of religion, for faith, pure and simple. I have seen all my life the arguments against it without having ever been moved by them....[22]

Wilson himself frequently asserted that the key to understanding him was to know that he was a son of the "manse"—colloquial for the home of a Presbyterian minister.[23]

Wilson was also a son of the South. He was raised in Virginia, Georgia, and South Carolina as his father moved between various congregations and seminaries. During the Civil War, Wilson's father served as a chaplain in the Confederate army. This southern upbringing likely reinforced the centrality of religion and the Bible to his life.

In seeking to persuade President Wilson to support the creation of a Jewish home in Palestine, Brandeis had a number of solid political and policy rationales from which to choose. Wilson's support would arguably help Democrats win the Jewish vote in the large eastern cities. An embrace of Zionism would also please the labor movement, which was wary of an influx of Jewish immigrants into the American labor market. Zionism also fit well into Wilson's global vision.[24] Wilson believed deeply that all peoples were entitled to self-determination, and he did not exclude the Jews from this basic right.

Yet Brandeis believed it was important to appeal to President Wilson's Christian faith. Brandeis had learned of William Blackstone and the petition he had sent to President Harrison in 1891. Brandeis was impressed with the cogent argument made therein for a Jewish State in Palestine and was more impressed still by the fact that it was written by a believing Christian.[25] While the Memorial may have been ahead of its time in 1891, Brandeis felt that Blackstone's work could now be pivotal in persuading Wilson.

Brandeis contacted Blackstone and urged him to resuscitate and recirculate his Memorial. Blackstone readily agreed. Although time was short, Blackstone secured eighty-two new signatures on the old petition. Among those endorsing the petition were the leadership bodies of the Methodists,

Baptists, and Presbyterians (Wilson's own denomination), thus demonstrating broad Christian support for this Zionist manifesto.[26] Writing of this success to a Zionist colleague, Brandeis noted that:

> As to the non-Jewish sentiment, we have every assurance... that the vast mass of Christian opinion in this country, particularly of course the Protestant Churches, supports our idea. A petition has been prepared on that head, signed by very many distinguished Christians, and which will be presented to the President at the right moment, which emphasizes this favorable attitude.[27]

On June 30, 1917, the Blackstone Memorial was presented to Wilson. On October 13, 1917, Wilson permitted Brandeis to convey to Lord Balfour and the British cabinet President Wilson's "entire sympathy" with the proposal to create a homeland for the Jews. The Balfour Declaration followed in November. Brandeis later attributed his success in winning Wilson over to the Zionist cause to his ability to appeal to Wilson's deep Christian faith.[28]

Without Wilson's assent, it is unlikely that the British Cabinet would have approved the Balfour Declaration. Although involved only indirectly, Woodrow Wilson played a crucial role in securing the Balfour Declaration and all that followed. As Wilson himself later marveled, "To think that I, the son of the manse, should be able to help restore the Holy Land to its people."[29]

HARRY TRUMAN AND U.S. RECOGNITION OF THE STATE OF ISRAEL

HARRY TRUMAN WAS a relatively inexperienced politician when the Democrats nominated him to be Franklin Roosevelt's running mate in the 1944 presidential election. Truman had been a county judge in Missouri and then a low-profile U.S. senator for one and a half terms. Truman would serve as vice president for a mere eighty-two days.

President Roosevelt died on the afternoon of April 12, 1945. Harry Truman was sworn in as president of the United States that evening. After the brief ceremony, Harry Truman fervently kissed the Bible upon which his hand had rested.[30]

Such a rapid ascent to the presidency of the United States would be a shock under any circumstance. Under the particular circumstances—World War II was still raging—the burden was crushing. On his first day as president, Truman summed up his feelings with rare candor to a group of reporters:

> Boys, if you ever pray, pray for me now. I don't know whether you fellows ever had a load of hay fall on you, but when they told me yesterday what had happened, I felt like the moon, the stars, and all the planets had fallen on me.[31]

Among the burdens falling on Truman was the thorny issue of Palestine. Within months, the war in Europe would be over, and the full horrors of the Nazi genocide of the Jews would be revealed. Thousands of survivors of the Holocaust—the so-called displaced persons—would languish in European camps with no home to which to return. The Zionists, with a new determination fueled by communal grief and humanitarian emergency, would take the offensive once again.

THE FACT THAT these survivors of the Holocaust had nowhere to go reflected just how poorly things had gone for the Zionists in the years following their victory in securing the Balfour Declaration. With some notable and bloody exceptions, the Arabs had remained largely quiescent during the early years of the British Mandate, when Jewish immigration remained relatively low. But when Jewish immigration to Palestine increased dramatically following Hitler's rise to power in 1933, Arab passivity gave way to open revolt. From 1936 until 1939, the Palestinian Arabs maintained a general strike, shut down municipal governments, refused to pay taxes, and engaged in a string of attacks against both British and Jewish targets. The leaders of the Arab Revolt demanded the abandonment of the commitments made in the Balfour Declaration through imposition of a ban on Jewish immigration and land sales to Jews.

The Arab Revolt ended with British capitulation to almost all of the Arabs' demands. In 1939, the British issued the notorious White Paper, which effectively canceled further Jewish immigration and land purchases in Palestine. Upon issuance of the White Paper, Winston Churchill declared, "This is the breach, this is the violation of the pledge, this is the abandonment of the Balfour Declaration, this is the end of the vision, of the hope, of the dream."[32] The British had closed the doors of Palestine to Jewish immigration just as Hitler was opening the door of Auschwitz.

The generation of British leaders that walked away from the Balfour Declaration was different from the generation that had promulgated it. By and large, this new generation was raised outside of the British evangelical tradition that had so captivated earlier generations and therefore lacked their Christian affinity for the Jews and their dreams of a homeland. Without a Christian Zionist motive, and now without any convincing strategic motive, there remained little to bind Britain to its earlier embrace of Zionism.

As Britain turned its back, the Zionists looked increasingly toward the United States to be their new champion and protector. After World War II, they would find support from a new president who shared the Bible-based sympathy for their cause that had animated the prior generation of British leaders. The seat of Christian Zionism would cross the Atlantic.

AS SOON AS the war in Europe was over, the Zionists mobilized to enlist American assistance in opening Palestine to the displaced Jews of Europe. Had history followed a different course, Chaim Weizmann would have been a retired statesman basking in the appreciation of his new nation and the warm Mediterranean sun. Instead, he packed his bags and flew to Washington. Thirty years after he helped to secure the Balfour Declaration, Weizmann was still pounding the pavement with his diplomatic wares.

President Truman agreed to meet Weizmann for the first time on December 4, 1945. The meeting was brief and unsuccessful. Weizmann argued that the problem of the displaced persons must be settled through the creation of a Jewish State in Palestine. Having come freshly briefed from a meeting with anti-Zionist Jews, Truman disagreed and suggested alternative solutions for the refugee problem. Adding to the insult, Truman kept mispronouncing Weizmann's first name. According to Truman aide Sam Rosenman, despite repeated reminders that the "C" in *Chaim* was silent, Truman kept calling his guest "Cham." The meeting ended with no clear commitments from the president.[33]

Although he refused his request and mangled his name, Truman took an instant liking to Weizmann. Like the leaders of Britain a generation earlier, Truman found Weizmann to be an unusually intelligent and engaging personality. This favorable impression would prove to be of enormous value at a later date.

UNABLE TO RESOLVE the competing claims over Palestine, the British decided to punt. On February 25, 1947, the British announced that they would relinquish their Mandate and submit the issue of Palestine to the United Nations. After twenty-five years of British vacillation, the international community took quick action. In August 1947, a majority report of the UN Special Committee on Palestine recommended partitioning the country into a Jewish state and an Arab state. A UN General Assembly vote on this partition plan was scheduled for November 1947.

The UN Special Committee was tasked with finalizing the proposed borders of the two new states prior to the vote. As these deliberations neared their conclusion, the U.S. delegation came out in support of placing the Negev Desert—representing over half of the territory of the present State of Israel—within the Arab state. Had this taken place, the Jews would have been left with little more than a city-state comprised of Tel Aviv and its suburbs. The Zionists mobilized.

On November 19, 1947, President Truman met with Chaim Weizmann for the second time. At this meeting, Weizmann worked his old magic. Weizmann spread a map of Palestine on Truman's desk. Truman sat enthralled as Weizmann spoke of the economic potential of Palestine and how Jewish pioneers were making the Negev Desert bloom. Truman decided on the spot that that the Jews should have the Negev. At the end of the meeting, Truman personally phoned his UN delegation and instructed them to support inclusion of the Negev in the Jewish State.[34]

ON NOVEMBER 29, 1947, the United Nations General Assembly voted in favor of the plan to partition Palestine. The Jews of Palestine danced in the streets in celebration. Partition meant a Jewish state, even if that state was far smaller than originally hoped. The Arabs of Palestine had the opposite reaction. The same leaders who had started a revolt to stop Jewish immigration and land purchases were by no means willing to accept losing half of Palestine to a

Jewish state. The Palestinian Arabs responded to the UN vote by launching a series of armed attacks against the Jewish communities in Palestine.

Partition had always been a controversial solution to the question of Palestine. Critics of partition had warned from the start that, given Arab rejectionism, a vote for partition would mean war. Now that blood was being shed, those opposed to partition gained the upper hand. Central players, including the United States, began to back away from the partition plan they had voted for only a few months earlier. In its place they now proposed to maintain the status quo by replacing the British Mandate for Palestine with a UN trusteeship for Palestine. It appeared, for a time, that the UN vote for partition would suffer the fate of the Balfour Declaration before it—a stunning Zionist victory would be unceremoniously reversed.

The Zionists again sought an audience with Truman. Yet at this crucial juncture, with the fate of the Jewish State hanging in the balance, President Truman refused to meet with the Zionists. With the exception of Weizmann, Truman never liked most Zionist leaders. He found them to be demanding, self-righteous, and condescending. Zionist emissaries too often lectured Truman on the basics of an issue with which he was deeply familiar. The situation reached its nadir when the leader of the American Zionists, Rabbi Abba Hillel Silver, got so angry during a meeting that he pounded his fist on Truman's desk and shouted at the president. This outburst was more than Truman could abide. The ban on Zionists would be a total one.[35]

Into this moment fate thrust a most unlikely hero. One of Harry Truman's closest personal friends was Eddie Jacobson, a Jew from Kansas City. Truman met Jacobson in the army, where together they managed the canteen at their army base. After the war, Truman and Jacobson continued their business collaboration by opening a men's clothing store in Kansas City. Although Truman & Jacobson Gents Furnishings quickly went out of business, the two remained close friends for the rest of their lives. While Truman was president, Jacobson frequently flew to Washington to spend time with his old friend.

While neither intellectual nor political, Jacobson identified viscerally with Zionism and agreed to place his fortuitous entrée to power in the service of this cause. At the behest of the Zionist leadership, Jacobson sent Truman a telegram asking that he meet with Chaim Weizmann, the one Zionist leader he seemed to like. When Truman rebuffed this request, Jacobson flew to Washington. Upon entering the Oval Office, Jacobson made an emotional plea to his old friend that he agree to see Weizmann. Jacobson later recalled what happened next:

> Just as I finished I noticed that the President began drumming on the desk with his fingers and as I stopped talking, he abruptly turned around while still sitting in his swivel chair and started looking out the window into what in the summer is a beautiful rose garden, gazing just over the pictures of his mother, wife and daughter. I knew the sign. I knew that he was changing his mind. I don't know how many seconds passed in silence but it seemed like centuries. All of a sudden he swiveled around again, faced his desk, and looked me straight in the eye and said the most endearing words I ever heard: "You win, you bald-headed... I will see him."[36]

On March 18, 1948, Chaim Weizmann was ushered into the White House through a back door for a secret meeting with President Truman. As Jacobson and the Zionists had hoped, Weizmann's power of persuasion, and the great mutual affection that had developed between Weizmann and Truman, won the president over. Truman assured Weizmann that the United States would abandon the trusteeship idea and continue to support the partition of Palestine into two independent states.[37]

At midnight on May 14, 1948, the British Mandate over Palestine formally expired. Minutes later, David Ben-Gurion, leader of the Jewish community in Palestine, read Israel's Declaration of Independence to a gathering in Tel Aviv. Once again, Israelis danced in the streets, and once again, the dancing was quickly followed by fighting. The armies of five Arab states—Egypt, Iraq, Lebanon, Syria, and Jordan—invaded the new State of Israel. Israel's war of independence had begun.

While Israel's military victory would take months, diplomatic victory came almost instantly. This time there was no need for secret meetings or last-minute supplication. A mere eleven minutes after Israel declared her independence, President Truman recognized the new Jewish State by signing the following statement:

> This government has been informed that a Jewish State has been proclaimed in Palestine, and recognition has been requested by the provisional government thereof.
>
> The United States recognizes the provisional government as the de facto authority of the State of Israel.

The United States was the first country to recognize Israel. President Truman had acted so quickly, in fact, that he had to write the name *Israel* by hand on his statement. The document had been typed before anyone even knew the name of the new Jewish State.[38]

Truman's motives

On matters of foreign policy, President Truman enjoyed the counsel of an unusually experienced and talented brain trust. This group, later remembered as the "Wise Men," has been credited with successfully ending World War II and then recognizing and responding to the emerging cold war. When it came to recognizing Israel, this legendary assemblage was unanimously opposed. Among those who lobbied Truman against recognition were Secretary of State George Marshall, Undersecretary of State Robert Lovett, Lovett's predecessor Dean Acheson, Secretary of Defense James Forrestal, Director of the Office of UN Affairs Dean Rusk, and Chief of the Policy Planning Staff George Kennan.[39]

This opposition to recognizing Israel was heartfelt and boldly asserted. At one point, in the heat of debate, Secretary of State Marshall informed President Truman that if he recognized the Jewish State, he, Marshall, would vote against him in the next election.[40] Marshall and the others believed that U.S. recognition would endanger U.S. security by alienating millions of Arabs in control of vast territory containing underneath it enormous oil wealth. They also argued that U.S. recognition would harm the Jews themselves by encouraging them down a path that would result in their slaughter at the hands of the militarily and numerically superior Arabs.

What caused Truman to ignore the unanimous advice of his foreign policy team and recognize the Jewish State? Some observers both during and after the event have provided a cynical response: politics. Truman was facing an uphill battle for reelection. He needed campaign contributions and votes, and the Jewish community was an important source of both. The conventional political wisdom of the time held that the Jewish vote could be decisive in winning the crucial swing states of New York, Pennsylvania, and Illinois. As Truman biographer David McCullough noted, "Support for a Jewish homeland was, of course, extremely good politics in 1948."[41]

While certainly a factor in Truman's decision to recognize Israel, domestic politics was by all accounts a secondary consideration at best. One of Truman's most intimate advisors during his presidency was a young St. Louis attorney named Clark Clifford. Clifford was a key player in the debate leading up to recognition of Israel and was perhaps the most vocal proponent of the Zionist position within the Truman White House. In his 1991 autobiography, *Counsel to the President*, Clifford asserts that the Jewish vote was "in no way the central factor" in President Truman's decision to recognize Israel.[42]

Even decades after the fact, of course, Clifford had a clear interest in portraying his behavior and that of his boss in the noblest possible light. Yet Clifford invokes convincing contemporaneous support for his assertion. In November 1947, Clifford presented Truman with a forty-three-page memorandum setting forth a grand strategy for winning the 1948 presidential election. Truman was so impressed by the memo that he kept it in his desk drawer for easy reference throughout the campaign, and the memo subsequently became somewhat of a classic of political strategy. This document downplayed the importance of the Jewish vote and stressed instead the need to appeal to other crucial voting blocs including labor, blacks, and farmers. When it came to competing for the Jewish vote, the memorandum stressed that the key was not the issue of Palestine, but a "continued commitment to liberal political and economic policies." The memo noted, accurately, the fact that the Jewish community was still divided over Zionism, with many Jews opposed to a Jewish state. Clifford concluded, "In the long run, there is likely to be greater gain if the Palestine problem is approached on the basis of reaching a decision founded upon intrinsic merit."[43]

Truman followed Clifford's advice. While he recognized Israel, he rarely mentioned this act on the campaign trail. He also turned down additional Zionist requests with which he did not agree. Most notably, even after recognizing Israel Truman refused to lift the U.S. embargo on the shipment of arms to the region. Israel would fight its war of independence without American weapons. In the end, Truman would go on to win reelection while losing all three states that contained significant Jewish votes: New York, Pennsylvania, and Illinois.[44]

IF TRUMAN'S SUPPORT for Israel was not driven by political considerations, then what was behind it? Biographer David McCullough concluded that when it came to Palestine, "for Truman, unquestionably, humanitarian concerns mattered foremost."[45] Where Truman's advisors saw Arab oil wealth and numerical might, Truman saw Jewish underdogs and sympathized with them.

Clark Clifford's account largely supports the view that moral and humanitarian concerns were foremost in Truman's mind. In his autobiography, Clifford listed a number of factors that he thought "dominated" Truman's thinking regarding Israel. These included Truman's hatred of discrimination and sympathy for the underdog, his horror at the Holocaust, and his fidelity to the obligations undertaken by Britain in the Balfour Declaration. Clifford then notes one final factor:

> [H]e was a student and believer in the Bible since his youth. From his reading of the Old Testament he felt the Jews derived a legitimate historical right to Palestine, and he sometimes cited such Biblical lines as Deuteronomy 1:8: "Behold, I have given up the land before you; go in and take possession of the land which the Lord has sworn unto your fathers, to Abraham, to Isaac and to Jacob."[46]

Truman's familiarity with the Bible apparently led him to identify with the Zionist devotion to Palestine in a way that even Balfour had not. As Clifford elsewhere noted of Truman:

> His own reading of ancient history and the Bible made him a supporter of the idea of a Jewish homeland in Palestine, even when others who were sympathetic to the plight of the Jews were talking of sending them to places like Brazil. He did not need to be convinced by Zionists.[47]

Given Truman's background, the existence of this biblical motive is hardly surprising. While he is remembered more for his blunt talk than his reverence for Scripture, Harry Truman was in fact a student of the Bible his entire life. Truman had poor eyesight as a child and had to wear glasses from a very early age. His glasses prevented him from participating in sports as a youth, and he instead devoted his attention to books. Among Truman's favorite books was the Bible. By the age of fourteen, Truman had read the Bible cover to cover four or five times.[48]

Truman maintained a love for the Bible the remainder of his life and continued to read it over and over. According to one Truman biographer, he "maintained an almost Fundamentalist reverence for the Bible and liked to read and quote it...."[49] In Truman's words, "The stories in the Bible...were to me stories about real people, and I felt I knew some of them better than actual people I knew."[50]

To Truman, the Bible was far more than a good read. It was his moral compass, and he clung to it throughout his life. Truman constantly quoted the Bible in his writing and in his speeches. On more than one occasion, Truman declared that the Sermon on the Mount was the basis of his political philosophy. Truman believed that "every problem in the world would be solved if only men followed the Beatitudes."[51]

Like President Wilson before him, and Presidents Reagan and George W. Bush after him, Truman saw a religious purpose to American power:

> Divine Providence has played a great part in our history. I have the feeling that God has created us and brought us to our present position of power and strength for some great purpose....It is given to us to defend the spiritual values—the moral code—against the vast forces of evil that seek to destroy them.
>
> This is a hard task. It is not one that we have asked for. At times we would like to lay it down, and, as we go on with it, we see it is full of uncertainties and sacrifices, but we need not be afraid, if we have faith.[52]

HARRY TRUMAN WAS not bashful about citing the Bible as a general moral guide. When it came to discussing the factors that led him to recognize the State of Israel, however, Truman was more reticent. Like Britain's Prime Minister Lloyd George before him, perhaps, Truman recognized the perils of defending a controversial foreign policy decision by reference to one's religious sentiments. Yet in a series of dramatic moments that followed Truman's recognition of Israel, his emotions opened a portal into his motives.

Like most men of his generation, Harry Truman avoided public displays of emotion. Truman made a series of tough decisions—including ordering American warplanes to drop atomic bombs on two Japanese cities—without shedding public tears of sorrow. Likewise, Truman won the wars in Europe and in the Pacific and brought the troops triumphantly home without shedding public tears of joy. Yet there were a handful of occasions on which Truman was so overcome with emotion that he was unable to contain himself. According to Truman biographer David McCullough:

> I have about three instances where Truman cried in public. They are very few and they are always real.[53]

Although McCullough doesn't discuss these three instances, other accounts go into greater detail. In fact, other observers describe no less than four instances in which Truman shed public tears. All four occasions were in response to expressions of appreciation for his decision to recognize Israel.

IN EARLY 1949, the chief rabbi of the newly independent Israel came to visit President Truman in the White House. The rabbi thanked the president for recognizing Israel and placed the president's action among the high points of Jewish history. Israel's chief rabbi concluded by telling Truman that:

> God put you in your mother's womb so that you could be the instrument to bring about the rebirth of Israel after two thousand years.[54]

As tears started welling up in Truman's eyes, the rabbi continued, opening up his Bible and reading aloud the words of King Cyrus from the Book of Ezra:

> The Lord God of heaven hath given me all the kindness of the earth; and he hath charged me to build Him a house at Jerusalem, which is in Judah.[55]

An observer noted Truman's reaction:

> On hearing these words Truman rose from his chair and with great emotion, tears glistening in his eyes, he turned to the Chief Rabbi and asked him if his actions for the sake of the Jewish people were indeed to be interpreted thus and the hand of the Almighty was in the matter. The Chief Rabbi reassured him that he had been given the task once fulfilled by the mighty King of Persia, and that he too, like Cyrus, would occupy a place of honor in the annals of the Jewish people.[56]

Subsequent to the chief rabbi's visit, Israel's first prime minister, David Ben-Gurion, came to the White House to pay his respects to President Truman. Recalling Truman's bravery in recognizing the State of Israel against the wishes of his State Department, Ben-Gurion said to the president:

> I don't know what the Americans are saying about you . . . but in the eyes of the Jewish people you will live forever!

As Ben-Gurion spoke these words, Truman listened intently, and then broke into tears.[57]

Years later, in 1961, Ben-Gurion returned to America for what would be his final visit. Ben-Gurion met with former President Truman in a New York hotel suite. Ben-Gurion relates what transpired:

> At our last meeting . . . I told him that as a foreigner I could not judge what would be his place in American history; but his helpfulness to us, his constant sympathy with our aims in Israel, his courageous decision to recognize our new State so quickly and his steadfast support since then had given him an immortal place in Jewish history. As I said this, tears suddenly sprang to his eyes. And his eyes were still wet when he bade me good-bye. I had rarely seen anyone so moved.
>
> I tried to hold him for a few minutes until he had become more composed, for I recalled that the hotel corridors were full of waiting journalists and photographers. He left. A little while later, I too had to go out, and a correspondent came up to me to ask, "Why was President Truman in tears when he left you?"[58]

In May 1952, President Truman attended a dinner in Washington to commemorate the founding of a village in Israel named "Kfar Truman" in the president's honor. The Israeli ambassador to the United States, Abba

Eban, served as the keynote speaker and told the crowd the following about his country:

> We do not have orders or decorations. Our material strength is small and greatly strained. We have no tradition of formality or chivalry. One thing, however, is within the power of Israel to confer. It is the gift of immortality. Those whose names are bound up with Israel's history never become forgotten. We are, therefore, now writing the name of President Truman upon the map of our country. In a village of farmers near the airport of Lydda at the gateway to Israel, we establish a monument not of dead stone but of living hope.[59]

Eban recalls what happened next:

> As I left the rostrum I saw the tough-minded President burying his face in a handkerchief without any effort to restrain his emotion. The next day he sent me a letter asking me for the text of my address: "You spoke so flatteringly about me that for a moment I had the impression that I was dead."[60]

A FEW MONTHS after the end of his presidency, Harry Truman made a visit to the Jewish Theological Seminary in New York together with his friend Eddie Jacobson. Jacobson introduced Truman to the crowd as "the man who helped create the State of Israel." Upon taking his place at the podium, Truman promptly corrected his old friend: "What do you mean 'helped to create'? I am Cyrus. I am Cyrus."[61]

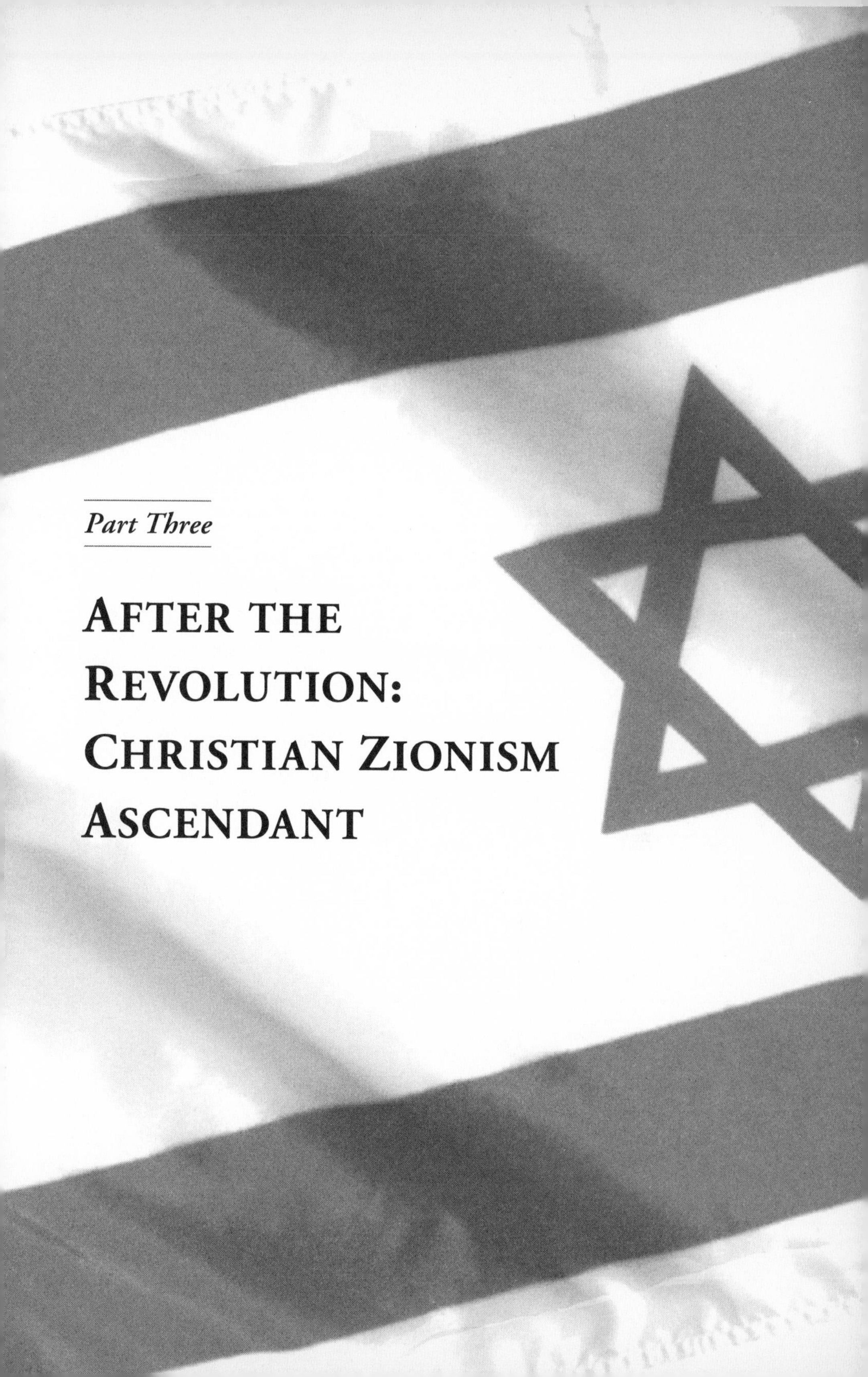

Part Three

After the Revolution: Christian Zionism Ascendant

There's nothing that would bring the wrath of the Christian public in this country down on this government like abandoning or opposing Israel in a critical matter.[1]

—Jerry Falwell, 2002

Chapter Six

CHRISTIAN ZIONISM IN WASHINGTON

THE YEAR IS 1992. The Soviet Union has imploded. As the iron curtain lifts, hundreds of thousands of Jews from the former Soviet Union stream into Israel. Israel turns to the United States for assistance in absorbing this historic wave of immigration, requesting $10 billion in loan guarantees. While sympathetic, President George H. W. Bush has a broader agenda: he wants to pressure Israel to stop building Jewish settlements in the West Bank. Bush rejects Israel's request for loan guarantees until Israel promises to freeze its settlement activity.

The American Jewish community erupts in protest over the Bush administration's use of humanitarian assistance as a lever on the settlements. When a White House aide expresses concern over this mounting opposition, Secretary of State James Baker reportedly responds with the infamous political hardball to forget the Jews since "they don't vote for us anyway." The loan guarantees are withheld for almost a year, until a new Israeli government, headed by Yitzhak Rabin, agrees to curtail settlement activity.

Fast-forward ten years. Israel has sent its troops into the West Bank to seek and destroy terrorist cells responsible for a wave of suicide bombings that have killed hundreds of Israeli civilians. While sympathetic to Israel's need to fight terrorism, President George W. Bush wants to stop Israel from conducting too long and deep a raid. A few days after the incursion begins, Bush starts pressuring Israel to pull its soldiers out of the West Bank.

This time, protest comes not only from the Jewish community but also from the evangelical Christian community. The White House is flooded with hundreds of thousands of e-mails and phone calls from the heartland in support of Israel. Evangelical Christians organize a nationwide day of prayer for Israel with the participation of an estimated sixteen thousand churches and five million parishioners. The Christian Coalition holds a large rally in Washington to demonstrate its solidarity with Israel.

While George W. Bush received no more Jewish support than did his father, evangelical Christians formed the core of his political base. This time, the administration could not afford to ignore the protests. And this time, due to his own evangelical leanings, President Bush was, by all accounts, predisposed to listen. When Israel kept its tanks in the West Bank for many months thereafter, the U.S. administration was silent.

THIS TIDAL WAVE of Christian Zionism that descended upon President George W. Bush in the spring of 2002 had been quietly building momentum for decades. For most of the twentieth century, evangelical Christians were largely politically passive, and Christian Zionists were no exception. As Harry Truman was agonizing over his decision to recognize Israel, there were no Christian Zionists in Washington seeking to lobby the president. They were at home, waiting by their radios for news of his decision. Even when a Christian Zionist such as William Blackstone sought to rally fellow believers to action, he received minimal grassroots support.

With the emergence of the Religious Right in the late 1970s, evangelical Christians reclaimed their political voice. Yet for most of the next two decades, these Christians used this voice to speak mostly about abortion and their other trademark social issues. When it came to Israel, evangelical Christian activism was heartfelt but sporadic. Christian Zionists rose to Israel's defense when called upon to do so by Israeli leaders, but they typically did not engage in any sustained political activism of their own.

September 11, 2001, shuffled the priorities of the Christian Right. While evangelical activists remained devoted to their established domestic agenda, the war on terrorism in general, and support for Israel in particular, took on a much higher priority. After 9/11, many leading evangelical Christians began to argue on behalf of Israel with a passion and consistency that they had previously reserved for the abortion debate. While the first Bush administration could still view Israel as a Jewish issue, and thus dismiss the domestic political repercussions of its policies, the second Bush administration viewed

Israel, first and foremost, as an evangelical issue. This Bush administration disregarded the Israel lobby at its political peril.

THE RETURN OF THE EVANGELICALS

AFTER THE SCOPES trial in 1925 and the wave of criticism and ridicule that followed, fundamentalist Christians confronted a grim reality. They abhorred the modernist teachings of evolution and higher biblical criticism that cast doubt on the absolute truth of the Bible and threatened, in their view, to corrupt the Christian faith. Yet the fundamentalists had failed to purge modernism from the public schools and, in many cases, from their own denominations. Fundamentalists now faced a choice between accommodating modernism and separating from those institutions that embraced it. For most fundamentalists, this was no choice at all: they withdrew into their own network of churches and schools.

During their decades of separatism, fundamentalists eschewed politics. Early in his career, for instance, Jerry Falwell preached to his church that clergy should shun politics since the "government could be trusted to correct its own ills."[2] When Pat Robertson's father was running for reelection to the U.S. Senate in Virginia in 1966, Robertson refused to participate in the campaign. He believed that God wanted him to devote his full energies to his ministry.[3] His father lost his race.

Separation, however, was not hibernation. During their decades in the wilderness, fundamentalists built their own institutions and grew their movement. They started churches, schools, institutions of higher learning, and popular radio and television ministries. The fundamentalists engaged in energetic outreach and won converts to their version of the faith. When the fundamentalists later reentered politics, they did so with a great reservoir of numbers, power, and confidence.

AS JERRY FALWELL tells it, January 23, 1973, started out like any other day for him. He rose early, showered, and descended the stairs to a large southern breakfast. He talked about the coming day with his wife and three children. And then he opened the *Lynchburg News*.

A banner headline about the death of former President Lyndon Johnson and a long presidential obituary dominated the front page. But it was not the loss of this one life that upset the reverend. A smaller headline lower down on the page read, "Supreme Court Legalizes Abortion." The day before, the Supreme Court had handed down its decision in the case of *Roe v. Wade* and ruled unconstitutional all state laws that prohibited voluntary abortions in the first trimester of pregnancy. Reading his newspaper that morning, Jerry Falwell was seized by "growing horror and disbelief."[4]

According to Falwell, the *Roe v. Wade* decision was the catalyst that launched him on a new mission in life culminating in the creation of the Moral Majority in 1979.[5] In the face of such alarming government action, Falwell decided that an otherworldly abstention from politics was no longer justifiable. Evangelicals would have to act to correct the government's ills.

When Falwell opened the door to a fundamentalist return to politics, he found millions of ready collaborators. Conservative Christians had held their tongues while hippies and war protesters danced across their television screens throughout the 1960s and early 1970s. After *Roe v. Wade*, however, they could no longer sit silently by. As Ralph Reed has noted of Falwell's movement, "Like a spark tossed into a dry haystack, it swept the nation like wildfire."[6] The Moral Majority grew rapidly, reaching approximately two million members by the 1980 elections and six and a half million members by the 1984 elections.[7]

The Moral Majority mobilized conservative Christians to register to vote and to vote for socially conservative candidates. Due to the success of these efforts, Falwell's organization was widely credited with providing the winning margin to Ronald Reagan and a number of Republican senatorial candidates in the 1980 elections. According to pollster Lou Harris, "Reagan would have lost the election by one percentage point without the help of the Moral Majority."[8]

In 1989, Jerry Falwell abruptly disbanded the Moral Majority, claiming that it had fulfilled its original mission of bringing Christian conservatives back into American politics. Yet although he relinquished his formal political position, Falwell remains an influential national personality through his television ministry and his public appearances. And the political force Falwell built lives on as well, albeit in a different form. In 1989, the same year that Falwell turned out the lights at the Moral Majority, Pat Robertson opened the doors of the Christian Coalition. To this day, the Christian Coalition remains the largest grassroots organization of the Christian Right. Falwell had led the fundamentalists back from the political wilderness and passed his staff to a new leader.

MOST WASHINGTON INSIDERS gain power and influence because they can deliver large campaign contributions to candidates who use them to purchase airtime and print space for political advertisements. These advertisements, in turn, help win votes on Election Day. The leaders of the Christian Right cut out the middleman and deliver the votes directly. The great political power of the Moral Majority, the Christian Coalition, and other evangelical political organizations rests upon the large numbers of voters they can mobilize. According to estimates, there are anywhere from 40 to 80 million evangelical Christians in America today. These evangelicals are overwhelmingly Republican. According to polls, a full 28 percent of Republicans fit the category "Religious Right," making this the largest single voting bloc in the party.[9]

While conservative evangelicals are not likely to vote Democratic, GOP operatives dare not take their votes for granted. Uninspired or disgruntled evangelicals may simply choose to stay home on Election Day. A healthy evangelical turnout was central to George W. Bush's election strategy in 2000. Bush's chief political strategist, Karl Rove, has stated that the only reason the 2000 presidential election was so close was because the evangelicals failed to turn out in the numbers he had expected. From day one of the Bush administration, Rove was determined to secure better evangelical turnout for the 2004 presidential election.[10]

Beyond delivering votes, there is a second way in which evangelicals wield influence in Washington: they get elected to office. Ever since their reentry into politics in the 1970s, evangelical Christians have been running for and winning public office with increasing frequency. With the 2000 elections, this trend reached an historical apex. President Bush is himself an evangelical Christian, and he has appointed other evangelicals to key positions in his administration. In Congress, evangelical Christians rose to key positions in the leadership of the House and Senate.

Friends of Israel from the start

Throughout the closing decades of the twentieth century, Jerry Falwell and Pat Robertson personified the political arm of the Religious Right more than any other individuals in America. Both men organized Christian conservatives into powerful political blocs. Both men sat atop large Christian television ministries reaching into millions of American homes. And both men were staunch friends of Israel from the very beginning of their political careers.

When Jerry Falwell created the Moral Majority in 1979, he announced a fourfold platform for the movement that would become the voice of the Religious Right:

1. Pro-life—opposition to abortion and euthanasia
2. Pro-traditional family—"one man for one woman in one lifetime"
3. Pro-moral—opposition to pornography and illegal drugs
4. Pro-American—favoring a strong national defense *and support for Israel and Jewish people everywhere*[11]

Support for Israel and "Jewish people everywhere" was not an afterthought for the Moral Majority. It was a central organizing principle.

In 1980, shortly after he became a household name, Falwell published a political manifesto titled *Listen, America!* Here Falwell discusses his views on all of his trademark social issues: abortion, pornography, and homosexuality. And in this little book is a chapter titled "That Miracle Called Israel," where Falwell sets forth his rationale for supporting the Jewish State. Falwell writes that Israel is a bastion of democracy in a region of despots and a cold war ally that has vanquished Soviet surrogates. He details how Israel's existence is the fulfillment of a series of biblical prophecies about the triumphant return of the Jews to their land. Finally, Falwell invokes Genesis 12:3 to remind his readers that those nations that bless Israel will be blessed, while those nations that curse Israel will be cursed. In Falwell's words:

> I firmly believe God has blessed America because America has blessed the Jew. If this nation wants her fields to remain white with grain, her

> scientific achievements to remain notable, and her freedom to remain intact, America must continue to stand with Israel.[12]

Falwell has continued to consistently support Israel, and to invoke these same rationales for doing so, throughout his long public career.

Pat Robertson has also made Israel central to his mission since the earliest days of his ministry. In Robertson's case, this commitment had a more dramatic genesis.

On October 6, 1973, the armies of Syria and Egypt launched a coordinated surprise attack on Israel. Almost all Israelis were at home on that day, observing Yom Kippur, the most holy day of the Jewish calendar. By the time Israel could mobilize its citizen army and send them to the northern and southern fronts, it had suffered serious losses. For a time, it looked as if Israel might actually be overrun.

In the weeks that followed, Israel eventually turned the tide and regained the territory it had lost in those first perilous days. Yet despite the ultimate victory, the Yom Kippur War left Israel in a deep national depression. Israel's lightning victory in the 1967 Six Days' War held out the promise of peace through overwhelming military might. After the 1973 Yom Kippur War, Israelis buried thousands of her fallen and confronted the dark prospect of interminable struggle.

Into this sullen postwar Israel flew a young Christian television personality named Pat Robertson. Robertson interviewed Prime Minister Yitzhak Rabin and other leaders for his television show and spoke with Israelis in the street. The despair was palpable. When he returned to his hotel that evening, Robertson stared out at his view of the Old City of Jerusalem. Robertson relates what happened next:

> I made a solemn vow to the Lord that whatever happens, however unpopular it would be, whatever the consequences, that I personally, and those organizations that I was in charge of, would stand for Israel. And we have not deviated.[13]

CHRISTIAN ZIONISTS PRE-9/11: FLEXING THEIR MUSCLES AT CRITICAL JUNCTURES

FALWELL'S EARLY PRONOUNCEMENTS on Israel, and Robertson's solemn promise, were not empty words. Although Israel would not become a top priority of Christian conservatives until later, these two men and their allies repeatedly acted on their Zionist talk when called upon by their friends in Israel.

The beginning: Falwell, Begin, and Reagan

Shortly after becoming prime minister of Israel in 1977, Menachem Begin visited the office of Dr. Larry Samuels, a nuclear medicine specialist at Jerusalem's Hadassah Hospital. To Begin's surprise, the American-accented Samuels was not a Jewish immigrant to Israel, but a Christian from Illinois who had heard a call from God to bring his medical skills to Jerusalem. As Samuels recounts the story, he said to Begin, "You know, I think you have more supporters among evangelical Christians in North America than you have Jews supporting Israel."[14] When Begin left the hospital that day, he had both a clean bill of health and millions of new allies in the struggle for Israel's survival.

Menachem Begin immediately set out to tap this new reservoir of support for his country. He quickly developed a special relationship with the evangelicals' emerging political leader, Jerry Falwell. Despite enormous differences of culture and life experience, Begin and Falwell were kindred spirits, sharing a reverence for the Bible and for the Jewish State they believed was predicted in and justified by it. In 1980, at Begin's initiative, Reverend Falwell was one of a select group to be honored with a Jabotinsky Medal on the 100th anniversary of the birth of Vladimir Jabotinsky.[15] Jabotinsky, a fiery Zionist and territorial maximalist, was Begin's political mentor and hero. For Begin, there was no higher honor he could bestow.

IN JUNE 1981, Prime Minister Begin sent Israeli warplanes on a daring mission to bomb the Osirak nuclear reactor outside of Baghdad. Israeli intelligence had discovered that the Iraqis had initiated a program at the reactor to produce enriched uranium for a nuclear bomb—a bomb that Saddam Hussein had threatened to use against Israel. Begin decided to act, and to do so before the Iraqi project progressed to the point that an Israeli strike would unleash nuclear fallout upon Baghdad. Begin and Israel were universally condemned for this action. The United States joined the loud chorus of criticism.

Shortly after the attack was made public, Prime Minister Begin telephoned his friend Jerry Falwell. Begin explained his reasons for bombing the reactor and requested Falwell's help in sharing Israel's side of the story with the American public.[16] Jerry Falwell immediately took to the airwaves in Israel's defense. He urged his grassroots supporters to phone and write President Reagan to express their support for Israel's action.*

That September, on a visit to Washington, Begin invited Jerry Falwell to meet with him at Blair House. This meeting, held directly across the street from the White House, was a strong reminder to the Reagan administration that Begin could reach over their heads to one of their major constituencies. According to Falwell, Begin told him:

> There are those who are working very hard to separate us. But we are not going to be separated. There is a special relationship between Christians and Jews that is very dear to me.[17]

Begin emerged from the meeting and commented:

> They [evangelical Christians] are sincere and devoted friends. We are very grateful to them. They have proved it. There are some who object to this. But if a man or group will stretch out his hand and say "I am a friend of Israel," I will say, "Israel has very strong enemies and needs friends." Reverend Falwell is a very strong friend.[18]

The Oslo Accords: Falwell, Netanyahu, and Clinton

In January 1998, Israeli Prime Minister Benjamin Netanyahu arrived in the United States during a tense time in U.S.-Israel relations. Netanyahu was elected prime minister shortly after the assassination of Yitzhak Rabin. Rabin, a lifelong soldier and general, had in his final years aggressively pursued peace with the Palestinians through the framework of the Oslo Accords. President Clinton had been Rabin's enthusiastic partner in the peace process, and he

---

* Even with Falwell's help, Begin was condemned by the Reagan administration and most of the civilized world for this attack. It would take another decade, until the Gulf War, for public opinion in the United States to catch up with Begin and Falwell.

still had a deep personal commitment to move this process forward. Netanyahu, who opposed Oslo and the Israeli territorial concessions it prescribed, was perceived in Washington to be dragging his feet on implementation. The prime minister was in for a rough visit.

Despite the long flight from Israel, Prime Minister Netanyahu went directly to an important meeting upon landing in Washington. His limo took him to neither the White House nor the State Department. Nor did Netanyahu stop at a synagogue or Jewish community center. Instead, the Israeli prime minister went directly to a rally of Christian Zionists. Here Jerry Falwell was waiting to welcome him and introduce him to the enthusiastic crowd as the "Ronald Reagan of Israel."[19] Falwell pledged to mobilize 200,000 evangelical pastors in support of Netanyahu's position on the peace process.[20] The next day, Netanyahu met with Pat Robertson, who conducted a sympathetic interview with the Israeli prime minister on his television program *The 700 Club*.[21]

In openly embracing Falwell and Robertson, Netanyahu was following the lead of the founder of his own party, Menachem Begin. Like Begin, Netanyahu believed that Israel should retain all of the West Bank and was comfortable invoking the Bible in support of this claim. And like Begin, Netanyahu was willing to circumvent a recalcitrant administration to muster domestic political support for his position. By meeting with these evangelical leaders, Netanyahu reminded the Clinton administration that there would be a political price to pay for pressuring Israel.

PERHAPS THE MOST significant political action undertaken by Christian Zionists in the pre-9/11 decades was not to lobby Washington but to build up a powerful network in the heartland. During these years the leaders of the Religious Right brought increasing numbers of evangelicals into the political process and gave them a Christian Zionist education. This army of activists would be in place and ready to answer the call when Israel would later become a more immediate priority of the movement.

Most of these new Christian activists were, due to their dispensationalism, already inclined to support Israel. But it was the leaders of the Christian Right who converted this latent sympathy into political activism. During these years, Jerry Falwell, Pat Robertson, and other leaders regularly shared their pro-Israel interpretation of current events through their television shows, lectures, books, and direct mail. In addition, Falwell and Robertson each founded a Christian university: Liberty University and Regent University, respectively. Through these institutions they trained future generations of Christian leaders to love and support Israel.

Jerry Falwell, for example, has visited Israel more than thirty times since 1960.[22] On almost all of his visits to Israel, Falwell has brought student groups with him. In 1999, Falwell brought a group of three thousand students from Liberty University to tour Israel, meet its leaders, and develop a bond with the Jewish State. As Falwell commented during that visit, "In every situation the pilgrims have returned literally enraptured through the experience. What we are talking about is three thousand young people who will return forever lovers of Israel."[23]

Those whom Falwell cannot bring to Israel, he reaches on campus:

> I personally feel a heavy responsibility to educate the American people on the importance of supporting the State of Israel and Jewish people everywhere. I am training thousands of pastors to do the same. At Liberty Baptist College, where I am Chancellor, and its schools, we are teaching 6,000 students the importance of this issue and how they can do their part in the future to stamp out anti-Semitism.[24]

The educational efforts of Falwell and Robertson were reinforced at the grassroots level by pastors and teachers across the country who spread the Christian Zionist gospel to an ever-expanding following.

Christian Zionists Post-9/11: A New Priority

After 9/11, the priorities of the Christian Right shifted. While the movement remained devoted to its trademark social issues, the war on terror in general, and support for Israel in particular, became a leading priority. The Christian Right was now prepared to spend its hard-earned political capital on Israel's defense.

During the early years of the war on terror, the White House was occupied by an extraordinarily pro-Israel president in the person of George W. Bush. President Bush consistently supported Israeli policy, even as dictated by the right-wing government of Prime Minister Ariel Sharon. Yet on those limited occasions when the president appeared to pressure or criticize Israel, a newly energized and focused Christian Right leapt to Israel's defense.

Israel's 2002 West Bank incursion

On the evening of March 27, 2002, hundreds of Israelis gathered in the ballroom of the Park Hotel in Netanya, a seaside city north of Tel Aviv. The Jewish holiday of Passover was beginning, and the crowd had come to celebrate with the traditional Passover dinner and service. Passover is a family holiday, and, much like Thanksgiving, you had better have a good excuse if you're not joining your family for dinner.

In the midst of the large groups entering the hotel, a man carrying a bag slipped by the armed guard posted outside. He walked straight to the dining room. Before he could be stopped, he detonated a bomb packed with powerful explosives. The force of the blast gutted the room, blowing sections of walls and windows into the street outside. Thirty people were killed, and one hundred forty people were injured. Hamas claimed responsibility for the attack.

This bombing was not an isolated incident—it was the third terrorist attack against Israeli civilians that week. But it was the largest single incident over the course of a Palestinian uprising that had begun over a year earlier. Israel had threatened on numerous prior occasions to send its own troops into the West Bank to root out the terrorists if Yasser Arafat's Palestinian Authority failed to do so. Now Israel let the tanks roll.

AFTER A GRACE period of a few days, President Bush weighed in on the tense situation in the Middle East. In language that seemed to equate the Israeli raid with Palestinian terror, Bush called on each side to refrain from violence and started to pressure Israel to withdraw its troops from the West Bank.

The Christian Zionists responded with a quick and powerful barrage. On April 11, 2002, Gary Bauer sent President Bush a letter signed by him and other leading Christian Zionists, including Jerry Falwell, Ed McAteer, and the Reverend John Hagee. Bauer sharply protested the president's position:

> It is because we so strongly support the moral case you have made against terrorism that we write you today with heavy hearts.... We believe it is imperative for the United States to stand with our friend and ally Israel

> as they attempt to defeat the same forces of terrorism that we have been battling since September 11, 2001. We would ask you to end pressure on Israeli Prime Minister Ariel Sharon so that he has the time necessary to complete the mission he has undertaken—the elimination of terrorist cells and infrastructure from the West Bank territories.[25]

Bauer, Robertson, Falwell, and others added the weight of their grassroots networks to the power of their pens, flooding the White House with hundreds of thousands of calls and e-mails. In their regular conference call with White House officials, Falwell and other evangelical leaders strongly reiterated their critique.[26] The Bush administration stopped pressuring Sharon, and Israeli forces remained in the West Bank.

As Israel's West Bank incursion continued into the following months, so did the pressure from the Christian Zionists to let Israel continue the operation for as long as it deemed necessary. In June 2002, Ralph Reed, the former executive director of the Christian Coalition, joined with a Chicago rabbi named Yechiel Eckstein to launch a new organization called Stand for Israel. Their ambitious goal was to organize the masses of unaffiliated Christian Zionists into a powerful grassroots movement on the model of the Christian Coalition. That October, Stand for Israel held its first event—a nationwide day of prayer for Israel with the participation of an estimated 16,000 churches and 5 million parishioners.[27]

Also in October, the Christian Coalition organized a "Christian Solidarity With Israel Rally" at the Washington Convention Center. Thousands of grassroots Christian activists waved Israeli flags and listened to speeches from Pat Robertson, Tom DeLay, and the Coalition's new president, Roberta Combs. At the end of the event, the Christian crowd diligently stumbled its way through the Hebrew of Israel's national anthem, "Hatikva."[28]

Appearing on the October 6, 2002, edition of *60 Minutes*, the Reverend Jerry Falwell sent a clear message that Israel is not just a priority of the Christian Right, but *the* priority of the Christian Right. According to Falwell:

> There are 70 million of us, and if there is one thing that brings us together quickly, it's whenever we begin to detect our government becoming a little anti-Israel. There's nothing that would bring the

> wrath of the Christian public in this country down on this government like abandoning or opposing Israel in a critical matter.[29]

Pat Robertson too was outspoken in his support for Israel during this crisis. In an October interview, Robertson rose to Israel's defense:

> Israelis can't allow a group of suicide bombers to continue to go to universities and kill innocent young people. To go to a pizza parlor and kill people. To go to a bar mitzvah and kill people. They have to stop it. And if the Palestinian Authority won't stop it and Hamas won't stop it...the Israelis have to come in with military force and suppress that kind of activity.[30]

As the fall of 2002 wore on, more suicide bombings occurred in Israel. The Christian Zionists continued to demonstrate their solidarity with the Jewish State. Israeli troops stayed in the West Bank. And the Bush administration remained silent.

ON THE MORNING of November 21, 2002, the number 20 bus was making its way through the Kiryat Menachem neighborhood of Jerusalem. The bus was filled with passengers, including many schoolchildren, making their way downtown in the morning rush hour. Near Mexico Street, a strange man boarded the bus. He was tense and unusually sweaty for having emerged out of the November morning chill. Before observation could lead to action, he detonated his bomb. Eleven people were killed and some fifty were wounded, many seriously. Hamas claimed responsibility for the attack.

A few hours later, as another number 20 bus made its way past Mexico Street, the bus was again boarded by some unusual passengers. Roberta Combs, president of the Christian Coalition, and a delegation of Coalition activists paid their fares and took their seats. The group was touring Israel, and when they heard what had happened that morning, they wanted to show their solidarity with the victims. "We cannot let the terrorists win," said Combs. "We hope to take a stand, because once they [the terrorists] inject fear into your heart they win."[31] Following their bus ride, the Christian

Coalition delegation traveled to Hadassah Hospital, where they visited many of the wounded from the morning attack.[32]

Later that same day, Ms. Combs and her group stopped for lunch in the Jerusalem branch of the American pizza chain Sbarro's.[33] This too was an act of solidarity. A little over a year earlier, a suicide bomber had entered that same Sbarro's during the lunchtime rush and detonated his bomb. Fifteen people, including eight children, were killed. More than one hundred twenty-five people were injured. Hamas and Islamic Jihad claimed responsibility for the attack.

The Roadmap tug of war

In March 2003, as the violence in Israel continued unabated, President Bush announced that he would support a new Middle East peace initiative developed by the United States in concert with the European Union, Russia, and the United Nations. The new plan, called the "Roadmap for Peace," set an aggressive timetable to be met over the course of the following three years, culminating in the creation of a Palestinian state in 2005. On June 3, 2003, President Bush traveled to Aqaba, Jordan, to formally launch the Roadmap at a summit with Israeli Prime Minister Sharon and the new Palestinian Prime Minister Mahmoud Abbas.

The president's embrace of the Roadmap was widely viewed as a victory for British Prime Minister Tony Blair and Secretary of State Colin Powell. President Bush had initially been sympathetic to the Israeli position that peace talks should not resume until the Palestinians ended all terror attacks against Israel. Yet Blair and Powell pressed for an immediate resumption of negotiations despite the ongoing violence. With the United States and Britain about to undertake a war in Iraq that was deeply unpopular in the Arab world, both men felt that the United States needed to demonstrate its willingness to push Israel toward a resolution of its conflict with the Palestinians. Bush publicly announced his support for the Roadmap on the eve of the Iraq war.

While Blair and Powell pulled Bush toward the Roadmap, supporters of the Israeli position on negotiations began to push back. The Christian Zionists quickly emerged as the most outspoken and influential of those opposing the Roadmap. They embraced the position that Israel should not be pressured to make concessions while still under the fire of Palestinian terror. They also stressed that the Palestinian Authority, which allowed such acts of terror to continue, was not a credible partner for peace. To the Christian

Zionists, the Roadmap sent a dangerous message by rewarding Palestinian terror with the promise of an accelerated path to statehood.

A Christian Zionist in a very high place assumed leadership of the Roadmap opposition: then House Majority Leader Tom DeLay. Although members of Congress are typically reluctant to criticize publicly a president from their own party on important foreign policy initiatives, DeLay waded carefully but doggedly into the opposition camp. Addressing a crowd of Christian and Jewish Zionists on April 2, 2003, Tom DeLay predicted the path ahead:

> After Operation Iraqi Freedom is won... there will be, as we know, calls on Israel to set aside decades of experience and once again trust the words and paper of a terrorist entity bent on her destruction.... Voices will call on the United States to serve as an "honest broker" on negotiations between the Palestinian Authority and the Israeli government. They will call on Israel to "take risks for peace." As a friend of Israel, and a lover of liberty for all God's children, we must reject any suggestion that its government negotiate from weakness, stand on an even moral footing with suicide bombers, or trust the promises of terrorists.[34]

On April 24, 2003, DeLay denounced the Roadmap more pointedly as "a confluence of deluded thinking between European elites, elements within the State Department bureaucracy and a significant segment of the American intellectual community."[35] On May 19, 2003, Gary Bauer and a group of twenty-three other evangelical leaders, including Jerry Falwell and John Hagee, sent a letter to President Bush sharing their "deep concerns" about the Roadmap. They wrote that it would be "morally reprehensible" for the United States to be "evenhanded" between Israel and "the terrorist infested Palestinian infrastructure that refuses to accept the right of Israel to exist at all."[36]

Christian Zionist opposition to the Roadmap came as a surprise to no one. This anticipated dissent was not a sufficient deterrent to prevent President Bush from embarking on the Roadmap process in the first place. But the Christian Zionists were able to influence the way in which the Roadmap was implemented, limiting pressure on Israel and blunting criticism of her at crucial junctures.

A WEEK AFTER President Bush had traveled to Aqaba, Jordan, to officially launch the Roadmap, Israeli helicopter gunships fired missiles at a car carrying Dr. Abd Al-Aziz al-Rantisi, a prominent leader of the militant Palestinian group Hamas. Although al-Rantisi escaped with his life, many Roadmap supporters viewed the Israeli attack as a blow to the peace process in its fragile infancy. President Bush issued a measured yet uncharacteristic critique of the Israeli action. Bush told reporters that he was "troubled" by the Israeli action and that "I don't believe the attack helped Israeli security."[37]

The Christian Zionists leapt into action. Tom DeLay held a private meeting with Bush aides and threatened to introduce a congressional resolution in support of Israel's actions if Bush continued to criticize Israel.[38] Christians ginned up their grassroots network and flooded the White House with e-mails asking President Bush to support Israel in its war on terror.[39] The Bush administration voiced no further criticism of the operation against al-Rantisi. When the Israelis eventually did kill al-Rantisi in April 2004, the only White House response was a restrained critique issued by the president's press secretary.

At the end of June 2003, DeLay, together with Democrat Tom Lantos, introduced a congressional resolution in support of Israel in the House of Representatives. While this resolution was less provocative than the one DeLay had threatened earlier in the month, it clearly reiterated DeLay's message that Israel must be free to fight its war on terror as it sees fit. The resolution noted that despite the Roadmap's call for an end to terrorism against Israel, "22 innocent Israelis nevertheless were murdered and scores wounded in three separate suicide bombings within less than a week after the Aqaba summit." The resolution then affirmed that President Bush's vision of a two-state solution "can be fully realized only once terrorism is defeated. . . ."[40] Greased by DeLay and House Minority Leader Nancy Pelosi, the resolution passed the House within a day of its introduction by an impressive vote of 399 to 5.

In July, Tom DeLay upped the ante even further by embarking on a high-profile visit to Israel and the Middle East. The weight of tradition and loyalty prevents members of Congress from criticizing a president's foreign policy while abroad, especially if that congressman is from the same party as the president. Thus Tom DeLay made his strongest statement on the evening prior to his departure, criticizing the Roadmap's ultimate goal:

> I'm sure there are some in the administration who are smarter than me, but I can't imagine in the very near future that a Palestinian state could ever happen. I can't imagine this president supporting a state of terrorists, a sovereign state of terrorists. You'd have to change almost an entire generation's culture.[41]

Upon arriving in Israel, DeLay addressed a gathering of Israeli legislators in the Israeli Knesset—an honor bestowed upon few visiting officials. Here, DeLay proclaimed himself an "Israeli at heart." While he did not criticize the Roadmap directly, he reiterated his belief that that no peace plan would succeed unless the Palestinians renounced terrorism and stopped letting violent men "speak for them." Arguing that a temporary cease-fire by Palestinian terrorist groups did not comply with the Roadmap's call for an unconditional cessation of violence, DeLay noted that "murderers who take 90-day vacations are still murderers."[42]

IN AUGUST 2003, President Bush left Washington for a summer vacation at his ranch in Crawford, Texas. He escaped the oppressive humidity of the Washington summer and much of the political pressure. But President Bush could not escape the Christian Zionists. On August 17, a group of approximately two hundred Christian supporters of Israel marched from downtown Crawford to the gates of President Bush's ranch, where they held an outdoor rally. For a full day, speakers loudly protested the Roadmap, the creation of a Palestinian state, and American pressure on Israel to curtail its war on terror.[43]

On the drive to his ranch that August, President Bush likely passed by an unusual billboard. Printed in large, bold letters was a quote from Genesis, "And the Lord said to Jacob... Unto thy offspring will I give this land!" The text beneath the quote urged readers to call the White House and tell President Bush not to violate "God's covenant with Israel." Over the course of the summer, more than one hundred such billboards appeared in Texas and other states throughout the South, West, and Midwest. The billboards were designed and paid for by a coalition of Christian and Jewish Zionists opposed to the

Roadmap. The same group distributed thousands of bumper stickers exhorting the public to "Pray Pres. Bush Honors God's Covenant with Israel."[44]

EVANGELICALS IN POWER

As President Bush has sought to navigate the dangerous shoals of the Israeli-Palestinian conflict, he has faced pressure at every turn from his right flank. Christian Zionists have been a powerful and consistent force pushing his hand toward greater deference to Israeli concerns. Given a reelection strategy that required an enthusiastic evangelical turnout, President Bush has certainly taken this constituency very seriously.

Yet external pressure and election year calculations alone do not explain Bush's Mideast policy. President Bush is himself an evangelical Christian. Like Woodrow Wilson and Harry Truman before him, George Bush assumed the presidency with certain deeply held Christian ideals that influence his worldview. Unlike Wilson and Truman, however, George Bush's faith is neither understated nor compartmentalized. Bush's Christianity is a salient component of his personality and an admitted influence on his policy. To a certain extent, therefore, evangelical Christians are preaching to the converted when they speak to George Bush about Israel. As Frank Gaffney of the Center for Security Policy noted in regard to Christian Zionist efforts to lobby the Bush administration:

> It's the old issue of pushing on an open door. You are seeing American government policy being profoundly influenced by beliefs that are shared by the pushers outside and the people on the inside.[45]

President Bush has been candid about his own evangelical faith. He described his conversion experience in detail in his autobiography, *A Charge to Keep*. While Bush's father was president, the Reverend Billy Graham visited Bush's family for a summer weekend in Maine. Over the course of the weekend, Bush and Graham went for a long walk on the beach. Bush found Graham to be "like a magnet" and he felt "drawn to seek something different." According to Bush:

> Over the course of that weekend, Reverend Graham planted a mustard seed in my soul, a seed that grew over the next year. He led me to the

> path, and I began walking. And it was the beginning of a change in my life. I had always been a religious person, had regularly attended church, even taught Sunday school and served as an altar boy. But that weekend my faith took on a new meaning. It was the beginning of a new walk where I would recommit my heart to Jesus Christ.[46]

During the 2000 presidential campaign, Bush was asked to name the philosopher who had the greatest influence on his life. Without skipping a beat, Bush responded, "Jesus Christ." Bush begins each day by kneeling in prayer, and then he studies a daily Bible lesson. The president believes in the power of prayer and acknowledges that he often prays for guidance.[47]

GEORGE W. BUSH is by no means the only religious man to have occupied the White House. One need go back no further than Jimmy Carter to find another evangelical Christian who served as president. While Abraham Lincoln was the only president who did not belong to a church, his deep personal faith in God helped him weather the death of a son and the darkest days of the Civil War. Throughout the history of the Republic, American presidents have invoked God for both inspiration and rhetorical flourish. Yet in one important way George W. Bush's actions as president are more deeply influenced by religion than those of his predecessors: President Bush sees policy implications to his faith.

When it comes to domestic policy, President Bush has been explicit about this link between faith and policy. The president credits his Christianity with saving him from a drinking problem and enabling his rise to the White House. Given his own experience, Bush believes that faith-based institutions can help others escape alcoholism, drug abuse, and wasted lives. Both as governor of Texas and as president of the United States, one of Bush's top legislative priorities has been to multiply such faith-based programs through government funding.

This overt link between faith and policy ends at America's borders. When it comes to issues of defense and foreign affairs, President Bush has explained his actions in terms of America's security and its international responsibilities. Much like Britain's Prime Minister Lloyd George and President Truman before him, President Bush may well be reticent to acknowledge a sentimental or religious motive behind such policies.

Yet there are indications that Bush's Christian faith does in fact influence his perception and actions well beyond the domestic arena. According to evangelist James Robison, Bush's decision to run for president in the first place was motivated, at least in part, by a religious call to serve in a time of international crisis. Robison first met Bush shortly before he launched his 2000 campaign for president. Robison recalls that in this meeting Bush eerily foreshadowed the events of September 11 when he told Robison that:

> I feel like God wants me to run for president. I can't explain it, but I sense my country is going to need me. Something is going to happen, and, at that time, my country is going to need me. I know it won't be easy, on me or my family, but God wants me to do it.[48]

Beyond this general sense of mission, Bush's evangelical Christianity clearly influenced his response to the tragedy once it had occurred. According to his closest friend, former Commerce Secretary Don Evans, Bush's faith "gives him . . . a very clear sense of what is good and what is evil."[49] Indeed, Bush's biblical division of actors and actions into "good" and "evil" has been evidenced repeatedly by the language he chooses to discuss world affairs. The day after the 9/11 terror attacks, the president described the nascent war on terror as a "monumental struggle between good and evil." In his first official press conference after 9/11, President Bush referred to the terrorists as "evil-doers" and used the word *evil* a dozen times. In his 2002 State of the Union address, Bush famously noted that the rogue states of Iraq, Iran, and North Korea and their terrorist allies constitute an "axis of evil."

Such stark language is not mere rhetoric. President Reagan's reference to the Soviet Union as an "evil empire" was part and parcel of a policy of actively confronting this evil. Likewise, Bush's language both flows from and contributes to a policy of confronting the evil that he now sees in the world. Both the war in Afghanistan and the war in Iraq are the products of this worldview. As Gary Bauer has said of Bush:

> Many people will point to his faith-based initiative as evidence of how faith has influenced policy, but I would point to the war on terrorism

> and the fact that he's most comfortable talking about the war in terms of good and evil.[50]

TO THE EXTENT that President Bush's evangelical Christianity motivates his foreign policy in general, it likely exercises a similar influence on his policy toward Israel. By any measure, President Bush has been an extremely pro-Israel president. Yet as with other components of his foreign policy, Bush has never explained his support for Israel in the religious terms of biblical promises or divine will. The depth of Bush's Christian Zionism thus remains difficult to plumb.

Bush made his first visit to Israel in 1998, when he was governor of Texas. In *A Charge to Keep*, Bush discusses the trip in strictly personal terms. According to Bush, it was "an incredible experience." Bush visited the Western Wall and the Church of the Holy Sepulcher, which is believed to have been built on the spot of Christ's crucifixion. Bush then traveled to the Sea of Galilee and stood atop the hill where Jesus is thought to have delivered the Sermon on the Mount. Bush shares his thoughts upon visiting this site:

> It was an overwhelming feeling to stand in the spot where the most famous speech in the history of the world was delivered, the spot where Jesus outlined the character and conduct of a believer and gave his disciples and the world the beatitudes, the golden rule, and the Lord's prayer.[51]

The closest Bush has come to acknowledging a connection between his Christian faith and his support for Israel was, ironically, in a speech to a Jewish audience. Here he noted that:

> I am a Christian, but I believe with the psalmist that the Lord God of Israel neither slumbers nor sleeps. Understanding my administration should not be difficult. We will speak up for our principles; we will stand up for our friends in the world. And one of the most important friends is the State of Israel.[52]

Yet despite Bush's reticence on the topic, many observers see a clear link between Bush's devout evangelical Christianity and his support for Israel. As former White House speechwriter David Frum has noted:

> The widespread view that Bush's intense Christianity somehow biased him against non-Christians was both unjust and unintelligent. It was precisely the most religious members of the Bush administration who tended to be the friendliest to Jews as individuals and most sympathetic to Israel as a Jewish state.... Those who believed most strongly in the Bible naturally felt the strongest affinity to the people of the Bible.[53]

PRESIDENT BUSH IS not the only evangelical Christian shaping United States foreign policy from the inside. While less public about her faith, Secretary of State Condoleezza Rice is also an evangelical Christian. Rice, who comes from a devout Presbyterian background, has described herself as a "pro-choice evangelical."[54] She is the granddaughter of a Presbyterian minister who founded a church in her hometown of Birmingham, Alabama, and she is the daughter of a popular reverend who ran a youth fellowship there. Rice told an interviewer from a religious publication, "I have a very, very powerful faith in God. I'm a really religious person."[55]

Rice has a very close personal and working relationship with President Bush and is considered the most influential Secretary of State since Henry Kissinger. Commentators have attributed Rice's success to the fact that Rice and Bush share similar personalities and interests, including their "deep religious faith."[56]

Other influential administration officials also share the president's deep Christian faith. White House Chief of Staff Andrew Card Jr. is married to a Methodist minister. Bush's top speechwriter, Michael Gerson, is a graduate of Wheaton College, known as the "Evangelical Harvard." Many White House staffers meet weekly at hour-long prayer and Bible study sessions. Presidential speechwriter David Frum remembers that the first words he heard in the Bush White House were, "Missed you at Bible study."[57]

Beyond the White House, Christian Zionists hold powerful positions in the legislative branch. As noted earlier, Tom DeLay, the former House

Majority Leader, is an outspoken Christian Zionist.* DeLay is joined in the House by a number of rank-and-file members who share his evangelical support for Israel.

Christian Zionists also populate the Senate. Sam Brownback of Kansas has been an outspoken supporter of Israel who has regularly sponsored important pro-Israel legislation and once chaired the subcommittee on Near Eastern and South Asian Affairs of the Senate Committee on Foreign Relations.** Lindsey Graham of South Carolina is an evangelical who has helped the Christian Coalition implement its pro-Israel agenda on Capitol Hill.

No senator has been more direct about the link between the Bible and his Middle East policy than Senator James Inhofe of Oklahoma. Senator Inhofe is no political neophyte. He was elected to the Oklahoma House in 1966 and has served the people of Oklahoma ever since through a series of elective offices including stints in the Oklahoma Senate and the U.S. House of Representatives, and six years as mayor of Tulsa. He was elected to the U.S. Senate in 1994.

Senator Inhofe is also a believing Christian who is proud of the connection between his religion and his politics. As he announced on the Senate floor:

> I am a born-again Christian. I have accepted Jesus Christ as my personal Lord and Savior. I believe that it is through him that we will reach the Father.[58]

In a March 2002 speech on the Senate floor, Senator Inhofe detailed seven reasons why Israel is entitled to the land currently under its control, including the West Bank. The seven reasons included many typically voiced by Israel's secular supporters. Inhofe noted that Israel has had an historical presence in the land since Roman times, that persecuted Jews need a homeland, and that

---

* DeLay was forced to step down as House Majority Leader in 2005 following a Texas indictment on charges of money laundering in connection with campaign finance. DeLay has denied any wrongdoing and is fighting the charge. At the time of this writing, DeLay remains one of the most powerful Republicans in the House of Representatives.

** Brownback, an evangelical Protestant most of his life, converted to Catholicism in 2002. Another leading Christian Zionist in the Senate, Pennsylvania's Rick Santorum, is also Catholic.

Israel is a strategic ally of the United States. Then Senator Inhofe arrived at the final reason why, in his view, Israel is entitled to the land:

> This is the most important reason: Because God said so.... In Genesis 13:14–17, the Bible says: The Lord said to Abram, "Lift up now your eyes, and look from the place where you are northward, and southward, and eastward and westward: for all the land which you see, to you will I give it, and to your seed forever.... Arise, walk through the length of it and the breadth of it; for I will give it to thee."
>
> That is God talking.
>
> The Bible says that Abram removed his tent and came and dwelt in the plain of Mamre, which is in Hebron, and built there an altar before the Lord. Hebron is in the West Bank. It is at this place where God appeared to Abram and said, "I am giving you this land"—the West Bank.
>
> This is not a political battle at all. It is a contest over whether or not the Word of God is true.[59]

Such an unabashed expression of biblical literalism did not win Senator Inhofe many kudos in the *New York Times* or the *Washington Post.* Nor are there many Jews back in Oklahoma to appreciate Inhofe's words of support. There is a Muslim community in Tulsa, however, and they did take note of their senator's floor speech. A few weeks later, approximately two hundred Muslims marched outside of Inhofe's Tulsa office in protest.[60]

If the Gentiles have shared in the Jews' spiritual blessings, they owe it to the Jews to share with them their material blessings.

—Romans 15:27, NIV

Chapter Seven

CHRISTIAN ZIONISM'S GOOD WORKS

THE PITCH SOUNDS familiar, just like so many seen in magazines or heard on late-night television. "Can you please help?" "Your gift will literally change their lives." "Your one-year commitment will provide generous food parcels, urgently needed assistance, much needed hope, and encouragement." And then, of course, the obligatory personal touch:

> Upon receipt of your first gift, you will be sent the name and profile of your adoptee, including a photograph (if available). We encourage the exchange of letters between you and your adoptee, and we will assist in translation.[1]

While the script may be standard, the money raised by this appeal did not make its way to any of the typical third world recipients. This fund-raising letter—sent to evangelical Christians—raised money for poor Jews living in Israel.

MOST STORIES ABOUT Christian Zionists in the popular media focus on their political activism. Quoting Jerry Falwell or Tom DeLay, these stories describe the efforts of Christian Zionists to influence American policy in the Middle East. Yet most Christian Zionists live well beyond the Beltway, and when they act on their theology, they tend to do so outside the political realm.

Christian Zionists donate large sums of money to support Israel and the Zionist mission. The most popular charities are those that help pay the costs of bringing Jews from the former Soviet Union and other poor countries to

Israel in fulfillment of biblical prophecy. Yet Christian Zionists also contribute to the Jewish people in ways that have little to do with prophecy. Christians give generously, for example, to support poor Jews living abroad who have no intention of immigrating to Israel.

Beyond contributing money, Christian Zionists contribute their time. Evangelical volunteers can be found fixing the plumbing of poor Jews in Jerusalem and teaching young Jews in Ukraine about the better life that awaits them in Israel. When Israel's tourism industry suffered from the greatest downturn in its history in 2002 and 2003, Christians started visiting Israel in numbers that rivaled, and sometimes even surpassed, tourism from the Jewish community. Christian Zionists also donate their time in the form of prayer. They pray for Israel and the Jewish people both alone and in organized round-the-clock vigils.

When it comes to politics, Christian Zionists may well be more influential than the Jewish community, at least when there is a Republican in the White House. In the realm of charity, however, Christian Zionists have not yet begun to rival the Jewish community. Jewish donations to Israel still far surpass those of Christian Zionists. The true significance of the Christian giving lies not in the absolute amounts raised—although these amounts are quite large and growing—but in the symbolism of the act. The fact that Christian Zionists work extra jobs or save a portion of their social security checks to have money to share with poor Jews around the world is an eloquent testimony to how a new theology has changed Christian hearts.

SUPPORTING THE MODERN EXODUS

THE HEBREW PROPHETS warned that the Jewish people would one day disobey God and that God would punish them for their sins by exiling them from their land to the "four corners of the earth." The same prophets who predicted the tragic exile also predicted a triumphant return. Moses, Isaiah, Jeremiah, and Ezekiel all spoke of a day when God would gather His people from the four corners of the earth and lead them back to their Promised Land. In the words of the prophet Isaiah:

> Thus says the LORD . . . I will bring your descendants from the east, and gather you from the west; I will say to the north, "Give them up!" And

> to the south, "Do not keep them back!" Bring My sons from afar, and My daughters from the ends of the earth.
>
> —Isaiah 43:1, 5–6

With the creation of Israel in 1948, many Christian and Jewish Zionists were certain that the long promised return of Israel to their homeland had begun. Yet this miracle stopped short. The prophecies of the return suggest that the great majority of Jews will return to their ancestral home from every region of the globe. In 1948 and for decades thereafter, however, a majority of the Jewish people continued to live outside of the State of Israel, and certain regions offered no immigrants at all. To many observers, it was only a matter of time until another massive migration of Jews to Israel took place.

For many Christians, this expected future exodus has been a topic of particular fascination. When the biblical exodus of the Jews from Egypt took place, Gentiles were the villains of the piece. The Christian Zionists believe that when this second exodus takes place, however, the Gentiles will play a central supporting role. According to the prophet Isaiah:

> Thus says the Lord God: "Behold, I will lift My hand in an oath to the nations, and set My standard for the peoples; they shall bring your sons in *their* arms, and your daughters shall be carried on *their* shoulders.
>
> —Isaiah 49:22, emphasis added

To Christian Zionists, this prophecy makes clear that when the great exodus occurs, it will be the "nations"—that is, the Gentiles—who carry the wind-tossed Jewish refugees home to their ancient land. In the second exodus, the Christians have been assigned the role of Moses.

Of all the prophets who foretold of this great future exodus, the prophet Jeremiah provided the greatest detail. In Jeremiah's day, people referred to God by His most famous miracle, the exodus of the Jews from Egypt. Jeremiah prophesied, however, that a day would come when people no longer referred to God as the Lord "who brought up the children of Israel from the land of Egypt" (Jer. 23:7). Instead, Jeremiah spoke of a future era when people would refer to God as the Lord "who brought up and led back the descendants of the household of Israel from the north land" (v. 8, NAS). In a number of other passages, Jeremiah repeated his prediction of a great exodus of the Jews from these "lands of the north." The only lands to the north of Israel with a large Jewish population are Russia and the other nations of the former Soviet Union.

In the 1970s and 1980s, many Christian Zionists invoked Jeremiah's words to predict that there would be a great exodus of Jews from the Soviet Union. Yet in those days no such Jewish exodus was possible. The Soviet Union did not permit Jews or any other of its citizens to emigrate. Any Jews who requested permission to leave the Soviet Union were fired from their jobs, harassed by the KGB, and, if they persisted, sent to prison camps in Siberia. These Jewish "refuseniks" were celebrated victims of Communism and a cause célèbre of Jewish and many Christian activists of the time.

Then in 1990, in its dying days, the Soviet Union opened its gates, and thousands of Jews began to leave for Israel. To many Christian Zionists, biblical prophecy was once again being fulfilled before their eyes: first the birth of Israel in 1948, then the conquest of the Temple Mount in 1967, and now the great exodus of the Jews from the lands of the north. While they were mere spectators for the first two events, these Christians now saw an opportunity to play their assigned role in the greatest human drama since the Exodus from Egypt.

TO LATE-NIGHT CHANNEL surfers, Rabbi Yechiel Eckstein is likely a familiar face. Throughout the night, Rabbi Eckstein can be seen on various Christian cable channels. He addresses the viewer from Ukraine, or Russia, or Israel. He speaks with great emotion, sometimes on the verge of tears. He pleads for contributions from his Christian viewers to help fund the transport of Jews from the former Soviet Union to Israel in accordance with biblical prophecy, and contribute they do. Over the past decade, Rabbi Eckstein has raised over $100 million for Jewish immigration and poor Jews around the world, almost entirely from a base of more than 300,000 evangelical Christian donors.[2]

Rabbi Yechiel Eckstein has a most unfortunate first name for a man who has devoted his life to outreach to evangelical Christians. Yet he is on a first-name basis with his thousands of supporters. Unable to pronounce the guttural "ch" sound (as in *Chanukah* or *chutzpah*), these evangelicals refer to their rabbi as "Yekiel," and these Christian Zionists love their "Yekiel." Instead of questioning their motives, Rabbi Eckstein has graciously welcomed their support. In fact, Eckstein was a pioneer, building bridges to evangelicals when most in his community scoffed at the idea. Rabbi Eckstein founded his organization, the International Fellowship of Christians and Jews (IFCJ), back in 1983. This organization has become the base for his fund-raising and other charitable efforts.

When the Jewish emigration from the Soviet Union began in 1990, Rabbi Eckstein was approached by evangelicals in his fellowship who believed they were witnessing the long-awaited exodus from the "lands of the north." They wanted to help. Eckstein responded by creating a new program, called "On Wings of Eagles," to raise money to fund flights to Israel.

To raise seed funds for this new initiative, Rabbi Eckstein produced a television special for Christian cable stations. Pat Boone, country singer turned Christian activist and Christian Zionist, agreed to host the show. The special documented the nascent Jewish emigration from the former Soviet Union and offered viewers an opportunity to make financial contributions to pay for flights to bring these immigrants to Israel. According to Eckstein, the response was so tremendous they aired the special a second time.[3] In time, On Wings of Eagles became the Fellowship's leading activity. Television appeals are aired nightly on Christian television. Fund-raising appeals are sent through the mail. The money continues to pour in.

In its first years, On Wings of Eagles focused on bringing Jews from the former Soviet Union to Israel. The program quickly expanded to assist Jews from other poor countries who wanted to immigrate to Israel. After the 2001 economic crisis in Argentina, On Wings of Eagles began to fund flights from Buenos Aires to Israel. When Israel resumed the rescue of Jews from Ethiopia in early 2004, Eckstein's group began raising money for these flights as well.

ONE OF THE oldest and most venerable of the Christian Zionist organizations is an Oklahoma-based group named Bridges for Peace. According to its literature, Bridges was founded in 1976 to give Christians the opportunity to "actively express their biblical responsibility before God to be faithful to

Israel and the Jewish community."[4] One of the ways that Bridges expresses its faithfulness to Israel is by supporting Jewish immigration.

While Eckstein's fellowship focuses on the cost of the airplane flight, Bridges for Peace is more focused on getting people to the plane in the first place. Large numbers of Jews in the former Soviet Union have never contemplated moving to Israel. After a lifetime under the Communist regime, which forbade the teaching and practice of Judaism, many adult Jews are too distant from their Jewish identity to feel a connection to Israel. Others may feel Jewish but are unaware of the assistance available to them to make the trip.

To overcome these barriers, Bridges for Peace maintains a staff of 250 Christian representatives in the former Soviet Union to teach Jews about their identity and recruit them to immigrate to Israel.[5] Bridges calls these representatives "fishers," a name taken, not surprisingly, from biblical prophecy. Not only did Jeremiah speak of an exodus of Jews from the "lands of the north," but he also added an important detail about how the exodus would occur: "'I will send for many fishermen,' says the LORD, 'and they shall fish them'" (Jer. 16:16).

Beyond education, Bridges for Peace also provides financial assistance. For many impoverished residents of the former Soviet Union, the various expenses involved in emigrating can be prohibitive. A potential immigrant must pay for a visa and passport, and must often pay off all debts prior to receiving these documents. Money from Bridges eliminates these financial hurdles.

To date, Bridges for Peace has helped more than thirty-five thousand Jews immigrate to Israel.[6]

IN 1991, AN English businessman and Christian Zionist of Swiss extraction named Gustav Scheller traveled to Jerusalem to meet with representatives of the Jewish Agency, the authority responsible for helping Jews immigrate to Israel. When the meeting began, Scheller pulled out his Bible and read a quote from the prophet Isaiah: "The ships of Tarshish will come first, to bring your sons from afar, their silver and their gold with them" (Isa. 60:9). Scheller then turned to his Jewish hosts and said:

> This is your Bible, the word of the living God. And the prophet Isaiah says here that your people will return...by ships. We'd like to work with you on opening a sea route to Israel.[7]

The professional bureaucrats at the Jewish Agency were not impressed by Isaiah's prophecies. The Jewish Agency had organized regular flights to bring immigrants from the former Soviet Union to Israel, and these flights were running smoothly. There was no apparent need for a sea route to Israel. Yet Scheller was not easily deterred. He went ahead and chartered a ship for three sailings to Israel before he had even raised the hundreds of thousands of dollars needed to pay for it, offering his own home as collateral. In December 1991, 550 Jews from the former Soviet Union boarded a ship in Odessa and sailed to Haifa. By December 1999, Scheller's organization, Operation Exodus, had conducted 100 sailings and had brought more than 21,000 Jews to Israel by boat.[8]

Operation Exodus later developed a second specialty in the Jewish emigration business. Most Jews in the former Soviet Union live in and around the major urban centers. These Jews were quickly provided with opportunities to learn about their Jewish heritage and Israel, and they were close to the major transportation hubs from which they could fly or sail to their ancestral home. Yet there were still hundreds of thousands of Jews in remote regions of the former Soviet empire who were far removed from this network and thus far less likely to emigrate.

Operation Exodus assumed responsibility for reaching these distant Jews. It established an on-the-ground presence in Armenia, Georgia, Kazakhstan, Turkmenistan, Tajikistan, and the vast frozen expanse of Siberia. To all of these places, Operation Exodus, like Bridges for Peace, sent teams of volunteers to "fish" for Jews and teach them about their heritage and the opportunity to return to Israel. Operation Exodus also paid for their paperwork and their transportation to the major transit points. From Siberia alone Operation Exodus has sent thousands of immigrants to Israel in recent years.[9]

Since 1991, Operation Exodus has helped approximately 100,000 Jews return to Israel by ship and by plane.[10]

As the great "exodus from the north" got underway in 1990, another group of English evangelicals found a unique way they could help shoulder the burden of bringing home the sons and daughters of Israel. These evangelicals learned, much as Gustav Scheller did, that there were Jews in the remote villages of the former Soviet Union who were too poor to afford transportation to the airports from which the Jewish Agency would fly them to Israel. Conveniently, these Christians happened to know a great deal about organizing ground transport—their day job was running an English bus company. They answered the call by starting the "Exobus Project," which transports Jews from the hinterlands to the major cities for their flights to Israel.

From 1991 until the present, Exobus has helped transport approximately eighty thousand Jews to their flights to Israel. Exobus maintains a staff of over forty representatives in Ukraine and Russia to set up the transport and to "fish" for Jews to make the journey. Exobus is funded entirely by private donations from Christians in England and the United States.[11]

INSTEAD OF FUNDING Christian organizations, some Christian Zionists have preferred to help Jews immigrate to Israel by making contributions to Jewish charities. Pastor John Hagee, for example, has raised more than $4.7 million for the Exodus II project of the United Jewish Communities, a fund dedicated to supporting Jewish immigration to Israel. This amount covers the cost of transporting approximately 7,500 Jews from the former Soviet Union to Israel.[12] Pat Robertson's Christian Broadcasting Network has also donated hundreds of thousands of dollars to the United Jewish Communities for this purpose.[13]

AS IS THE case with their political efforts, Christian Zionist philanthropy to help Jews immigrate to Israel is sometimes viewed skeptically by the Jewish community and others. Critics are often quick to wave the red flag of eschatology. Christians help transport Jews to Israel not out of love for the Jews, it is alleged, but merely to fulfill a precondition of the Second Coming.

If the Second Coming is the real motive for such generosity, then someone should inform the people who write the fund-raising literature for these charities. Fund-raising appeals are not a subtle form of communication—they presume a message that will move people to send money and then shout it at high volume. Yet the literature for these Christian charities is devoid of references to the Second Coming of Christ. The only second coming mentioned, in fact, is the "second coming" of the Jews to their homeland. Over and over, these appeals invoke the prophecies of the Jewish return and offer potential donors an opportunity to play a role in their fulfillment.

Likewise, if conversion of the Jews is the true motive behind this Christian generosity, then the employees of these charities did not get the memo. When they "fish" for Jews in the former Soviet Union, evangelical Christians instruct a very vulnerable group of Jews who know next to nothing about their religion. Yet there have been no reports of Christian fishers trying to convert Jews or teach Christianity under the guise of Judaism. Quite to the contrary, these Christians help to rebuild Jewish identities on the verge of being extinguished. Through their desire to play their role in the biblical prophecy of the Jewish return, these devout Christians have morphed into Jewish missionaries.

Helping Poor Jews

The Christian tradition has always stressed charity to the poor and disadvantaged, those whom Jesus called "the least of these." In Romans 15:27, the apostle Paul gets more specific. He exhorts his fellow Christians to give charity to the Jews in particular, reasoning that if the Gentiles have shared in the Jews' spiritual blessings, they owe it to the Jews to share with them their material blessings. Christians, it turns out, are obligated to give charity to Jews.

For centuries, Christians more focused on persecuting Jews than supporting them largely ignored this particular form of Christian charity. But Paul's exhortation has recently been dusted off by Christian Zionists who share Paul's appreciation for the Jewish roots of their Christian faith. Thus, in addition to their efforts to help Jews immigrate to Israel, Christian Zionists also contribute generously to charities that care for needy Jews both in Israel and in poor countries around the globe.

Echoing the words of the apostle Paul, the fund-raising literature for such humanitarian appeals typically stresses the need to repay a debt to the Jewish people for their spiritual gifts. According to one evangelical fund-raising letter:

> The Jewish people gave us our Bible, and our Messiah. Truly, they are our "royal family." And yet, for centuries they have known the judgment, disdain and even hatred of many, sadly including many Christians. I believe that now is the time to show favor to Zion. Now is the time to show honor, love and respect to the people who blessed us so much.[14]

"WE NEED A Miracle!" shouted the headline from the Bridges for Peace pamphlet. The text proceeded to describe a most dire situation:

> Hunger is a problem in Israel. 281,000 people are unemployed. More than one million people, 25% of the population, live beneath the poverty line. A significant number of them worry about what they will eat for their next meal.[15]

Bridges for Peace, the organization that helps bring Jews to Israel, is also one of the organizations at the forefront of the effort to help poor Jews. For years, Bridges has run a food bank for the elderly and homeless of Jerusalem. As economic conditions in Israel declined after the start of the second Palestinian *intifada* in 2000, Bridges had to expand its program to accommodate requests for assistance from the newly unemployed across Israel. By August 2003, over 16,000 Israelis a month received food from Bridges.[16]

Beyond seeking financial contributions, Bridges runs a mini peace corps for Christian volunteers. Bridges' "Repairers of the Breach" program flies skilled Christian craftsmen from America and Canada to live in Israel for months at a time. While in residence, they do repair work free of charge for people who could not otherwise afford it. So far, Bridges has brought a series of carpenters, plumbers, electricians, bricklayers, and painters to serve Jerusalem's poor.[17]

Rabbi Eckstein's International Fellowship of Christians and Jews also provides humanitarian relief for Israel's poor. Through the Fellowship's "Guardians of Israel" program, American Christians support Israel's poor with food, clothing, job training, and medical care. Just like Bridges for Peace, Eckstein's program has been forced by recent events to expand its operations beyond an original focus on the elderly and homeless. In Eckstein's case, the new emphasis has been on helping poor Israelis meet the financial burdens created by the recent wave of terror attacks. Guardians of Israel provides financial assistance to families that have lost breadwinners to terror, and it also helps to fund the expensive physical rehabilitation of Israelis injured in these attacks. Guardians of Israel also helps communities buy armor-plated buses for their schools and bulletproof windows for their kindergartens.[18]

DURING HIS FREQUENT visits to the former Soviet Union, Rabbi Eckstein was appalled to see the conditions in which many Jews lived, especially elderly Jews living on starvation pensions. Yet many of these older Jews lacked the will or physical strength to start new lives in Israel. In an effort to help those who would be left behind, Eckstein started a program called "Isaiah 58," invoking the prophet Isaiah's call to, "Divide your bread with the hungry, and bring the homeless poor into the house; when you see the naked, cover him . . . and do not hide your eye from your own flesh."[19]

Eckstein's literature points out that seven decades of Communist rule in Russia and other former Soviet republics and the subsequent collapse of the region's economy have left a "tragic legacy" of hundreds of thousands of elderly Jews trapped in poverty. "These destitute men and women," he notes, "are the forgotten victims of both Communism and the Nazi's murderous rampage." According to Eckstein:

> Two out of three of these needy Jews are completely alone, with no families to help them. And over 80 percent of elderly Soviet Jews must survive on meager government pensions of as little as $10 a month. These pension checks are often months late in arriving.[20]

Isaiah 58 provides these elderly Jews with food packages, hot "meals-on-wheels," in-home medical care, and heating fuel.

Originally intended to cover the elderly in the former Soviet Union, Isaiah 58 has expanded in recent years to meet new needs. When other sources of funding disappeared, Isaiah 58 started to support a number of struggling Jewish orphanages. As Argentina's economy collapsed in 2001, Isaiah 58 began to provide food to needy Argentinean Jews. Isaiah 58 currently provides food and other essentials to more than 200,000 people in the former Soviet Union and Argentina.[21]

THESE EFFORTS TO help poor Jews outside of Israel through Isaiah 58 and other charities contradict some of the negative stereotypes of Christian Zionists.

As mentioned earlier, Christian efforts to help transport Jews to Israel—a humanitarian cause to which the Jewish community is itself devoted—are sometimes dismissed as merely an attempt to meet a precondition for Christ's Second Coming. What makes this allegation so believable is the fact that the return of the Jews to Israel is a central event in Christian prophecies about the end of days. But there is nothing in Christian prophecy about feeding elderly Jews in Minsk or Vladivostok. Such charity is completely devoid of prophetic significance. The donations pour in nonetheless.

Rabbi Eckstein highlights the point with an anecdote. One of his donors, he notes, is a woman from Oklahoma who contributes 10 percent of her monthly social security check to help an elderly Jew in Uzbekistan buy clothes and heating oil. According to Eckstein, "That woman in Uzbekistan is not going anywhere either literally or figuratively. She's not emigrating to Israel, and she's not converting to Christianity. The donation is a genuine act of love, comfort, and solidarity."[22]

IN ADDITION TO helping poor Jews through the larger, national charities, many Christian Zionists help Jews on a one-to-one basis or through hundreds of smaller organizations and church-based efforts. In Memphis, Tennessee, for example, the local chapter of a group called Christian Friends of Israel raised $100,000 from local Christians to purchase an ambulance for Israel.[23] In Texas, a group of Christian Zionist women calling themselves the Battalion of Deborah raises money to support some of the friends they have made over the course of numerous solidarity missions to Israel. On one such visit, for example, Battalion members met a group of Jews in Safed (*Tsfat* in Hebrew), a Jewish town in Galilee. As Passover 2003 approached, the Battalion of Deborah sent out an urgent e-mail to its members and friends:

> Passover Seder Food Needed! Passover is very near, and we have an urgent situation in the area of Tsfat, an Orthodox area north of the Galilee. Due to the economy and the bad weather, income for these families has been drastically reduced.... We would like to help out now to see that many will have a Blessed Passover.[24]

The Battalion ended up raising $6,000 to help the people of Safed celebrate Passover.[25]

Five months later, Rosh Hashanah was approaching, and the economy in Israel had not recovered. The Battalion sent out another e-mail, this time asking for contributions to "bless the people of Tsfat again" on this important Jewish holiday.[26]

While the amount of money raised by grassroots group such as the Battalion is small in absolute terms, it is quite large relative to the incomes and discretionary dollars of the donors. Most of the Battalion members, for example, are working women on tight budgets. To raise money for their organization, they work extra jobs, including regular weekend shifts running a concession stand at the NASCAR stock car races. To help poor Jews in Israel, these women sacrifice time with family, weekend outings, and new wardrobes.[27]

Pilgrimage to Israel

One of the most important ways that Christian Zionists support the State of Israel is by visiting the country. When the second Palestinian *intifada* began in 2000, tourism to Israel plummeted. In 2001, the number of visitors to Israel dropped by 54 percent compared to the previous year. In 2002, that figure slid a further 29 percent below the 2001 level.[28] In the wake of this plunge, scores of Israeli hotels had to close their doors, and those that remained in business had to lay off more than 50 percent of their workers.[29] Since tourism is the second largest industry in Israel, this plunge in visitors was a major factor in Israel's overall economic downturn.

Christian Zionists responded to the crisis by making a concerted effort to encourage more Christians to visit Israel. The leading Christian Zionists set a personal example by visiting the country themselves. Pat Robertson, for instance, visited Israel in July 2001 and again in December 2003. Both times he conducted numerous broadcasts on location for his Christian Broadcasting Network, sharing his visit with millions of viewers back home. Robertson noted that the fact that he and his wife were visiting Israel should be "a statement to the American Christian community that it is safe to come and visit the holy sites in Israel, and to travel in this nation."[30] Benny Hinn, another televangelist with a massive television audience, also broadcast live from Israel during this period. Gary Bauer visited Israel in 2002 and again in 2003, and each time he shared detailed reports of his visit with his 100,000-strong e-mail list.

Since 2000, most of the leading Christian Zionist organizations have sponsored annual or biannual solidarity missions to Israel. The Christian Coalition, for example, conducted two well-publicized missions to Israel in 2002 and 2003. Over the same period, the Christians' Israel Public Action Campaign, a Washington-based group, sponsored four missions to Israel.[31] Hundreds of Christian Zionist churches, both large and small, have organized trips of their own. These Christians ignored advice from worried friends and even their own government* to board planes and show their support for Israel in a very concrete way.

Many Christians, especially first-time visitors, choose to visit Israel for personal reasons, namely to see the land where Jesus once walked. But in marketing Israel trips in recent years, Christian Zionists have made support for Israel a major selling point. In promoting its 2003 Solidarity Mission to Jerusalem, for example, Bridges for Peace stressed that:

> Israel needs all her friends at this time, when UN votes castigate her actions, the US threatens to slash much needed loan guarantees, the economy is in recession, and the security situation remains tenuous. Israelis often feel all alone. Let's show just how much Christians love them.[32]

These efforts have borne fruit. In some recent years, more Christians have visited Israel than Jews.[33]

Christians who are unable to travel to Israel support the Israeli economy from home. Many Christians have begun to join the Jewish community in sponsoring and attending "Shop Israel" days, where Israeli craftsmen, artisans, and merchants hurt by the drop in tourism travel to America to sell their wares. Many Christian Web sites and churches urge their members to "buy Israeli," and offer for sale a variety of products from Dead Sea face creams to Israeli foods and flowers.

---

* For much of the period since the outbreak of the violence in 2000, the United States government has urged its citizens to defer travel to Israel.

PRAYERS FOR ISRAEL

PSALM 122:6 EXHORTS the reader to "pray for the peace of Jerusalem." Christian Zionists take this charge seriously. Most evangelical Christians believe that, through God's intervention, their prayers have the power to change the course of human events. Many further believe that the power of their prayers can be multiplied by the numbers of people praying together at sustained intervals. Having one church pray for Israel helps. Having national groups that organize hundreds of churches to pray for Israel at the same time helps a great deal.

Across the street from the Israeli embassy in Washington DC sits a nondescript house that blends nicely into the upscale neighborhood. Yet unlike the other homes on the block, this one is not a residence. This house is the Washington headquarters of the American Christian Trust, a Christian Zionist organization. One of the main activities of the trust is to organize prayer vigils for Israel. Here, across the street from what is technically Israeli soil, Christians often pray around the clock for God to bless and protect the State of Israel.

Other organizations have sought to build national networks of Christians praying for Israel. An organization called the Jerusalem Prayer Team is working toward a goal of "having one million people praying daily and 100,000 houses of worship praying weekly for the peace and protection of the Jewish people."[34] Their Web site boasts a list of hundreds of prominent supporters and participating institutions. In addition to organizing prayers for Israel, the Jerusalem Prayer Team's founder, Mike Evans, has raised funds to aid Israeli victims of terror through massive church rallies.

Rabbi Eckstein and Ralph Reed have also organized an annual nationwide day of prayer for Israel. Their first "Day of Prayer and Solidarity for Israel" was held in October 2002. More than 5 million Christians in some 16,000 churches across the country prayed for peace and security in Israel. When the event was held for a second time the following October, participation grew to include approximately 17,000 churches and more than 7 million Christians.[35]

Whether or not these prayers are heard in heaven, they are most certainly heard in Washington. An organization that can mobilize millions of Christians to pray can also mobilize these Christians to vote. Ralph Reed and Rabbi Eckstein have effectively used the success of their Day of Prayer and Solidarity with Israel to send a message to the White House and Congress about the size and devotion of the Christian Zionist ranks. These prayers also demonstrate the sincerity of Christian talk. Whatever its efficacy, hours spent at prayer is a concrete demonstration of solidarity and concern.

SPREADING THE CHRISTIAN ZIONIST GOSPEL

LIKE ALL EVANGELICALS, Christian Zionists seek to spread their version of the gospel. A particular focus of many Christian Zionists has been to spread their beliefs about Israel and the Jews to fellow Christians who don't yet share them. Although replacement theology has been disavowed by most of the major Christian denominations, it persists in rank-and-file churches throughout America. Such churches are apathetic toward Israel at best, inimical at worst. While Christian Zionism may be ascendant, there remain pockets of resistance.

Every time a televangelist takes to the airwaves to talk about Israel—which, as of late, has been often—they spread their Christian Zionist teachings to millions of viewers who are not yet committed to them. Pat Robertson, Jerry Falwell, John Hagee, and many others constantly bombard the Christian airwaves with a staunchly pro-Israel message. Much as these charismatic men are successful in getting Christians to "come to Christ," they are also successful in getting Christians to embrace Israel.

Some Christian Zionist groups such as Bridges for Peace and the International Christian Embassy engage in grassroots missionary work among their fellow Christians. Volunteers from these organizations travel to hundreds of churches and present them with their message that the Jewish people are the "Israel" of biblical promise and prophecy. These field representatives come back with plenty of stories of apathy and even hostility from Christians who still embrace replacement theology. But they also report frequent success in winning zealous "converts" to Christian Zionism.

Many leading Christian Zionist churches hold outreach and education programs to solidify support for Israel in their congregations and communities. Annual tributes to Israel have become popular in churches across the country. Pastor John Hagee, for example, holds an annual "Night to Honor Israel" in his 5,000-seat megachurch in San Antonio, Texas, and broadcasts the event over cable and satellite to millions worldwide. Starting from humble beginnings in 1980, this event has grown into a sophisticated, choreographed production. The 2002 "Night to Honor Israel" featured a keynote address from Tom DeLay and video appearances by Ariel Sharon and Benjamin Netanyahu. As the event drew to a close, massive Israel and American flags fell from the ceiling to form the backdrop as the church choir sang the national anthems of both nations.

Faith Bible Chapel outside of Denver, Colorado, holds an annual Israel Awareness Day that rivals Hagee's event. In 2003, Faith Bible Chapel's twenty-fifth Israel Awareness Day featured a multimedia march through Jewish history from Abraham's trek to the Promised Land through mournful Holocaust scenes to the triumphant birth of the State of Israel. The church's high school students practice all year to put on the show, perfecting their Hebrew singing and complex Israeli dance routines. After performing at their church, these Christian students board planes for an annual tour of Israel. There they visit army bases across the country to entertain the Israeli troops.

Some of the leading Christian Zionists have made their most significant contributions to Israel by preaching Zionism to their fellow Christians. For example, the name Derek Prince is not well known in Washington policy circles or on the evening news. Yet Prince, who died in 2003, was an extremely popular evangelical leader who helped to build the Charismatic movement in America. Prince wrote more than forty books and for many years had a daily radio program that was broadcast to millions around the globe. In addition, Prince preached in person throughout the world, and his semons were routinely recorded on audiocassettes and videotapes for broader distribution. In all of these forums, Prince repeatedly emphasized the fundamentals of Christian Zionism, especially the error of replacement theology, the importance of blessing the Jews, and the debt of gratitude owed by Christians to the Jews.* Many of today's better-known Christian Zionists, including Pastor John Hagee, author Stephen Mansfield, and publisher Stephen Strang, recognize Derek Prince as a formative influence on their attitudes toward Israel and the Jews.

---

* So central was Israel to Prince's theology that toward the end of his life he moved to Jeruslaem in order to "identify with the Jews and encourage their return to the land." (Stephen Mansfield, *Derek Prince: A Biography* [Lake Mary, Florida: Charisma House, 2005], 270.)

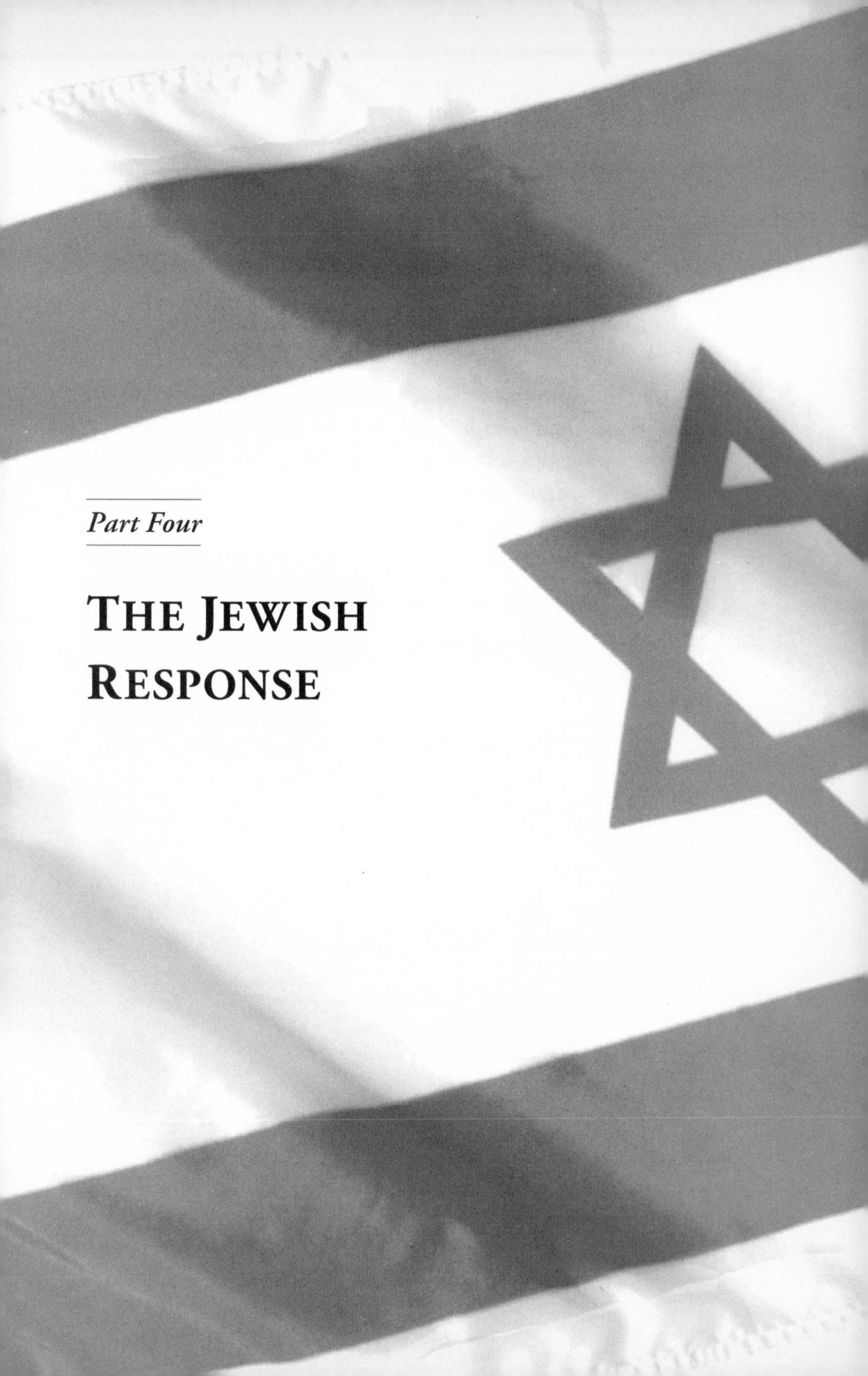

Part Four

The Jewish Response

Men like the opinions to which they have become accustomed from their youth; they defend them and shun contrary views: and this is one of the things that prevent men from finding the truth, for they cling to the opinions of habit.

—Moses Maimonides
The Guide for the Perplexed

Chapter Eight

THE RESPONSE FROM THE JEWISH MAINSTREAM

THE RESPONSE OF the American Jewish community to the outpouring of philo-Semitic and pro-Israel sentiment from evangelical Christians has been mixed and largely unenthusiastic. Certainly, a minority of Jewish leaders have warmly welcomed evangelical support, but such unreserved support is the exception. What is far more common is a discomfort, a wariness, an absence of trust.

Why has the Jewish community largely withheld its embrace from the Christian Zionists? Community leaders and commentators have expressed a handful of concerns that are detailed in this chapter. Many Jews are suspicious of the true intent of the Christian Zionists. They believe that Christian support for Israel is driven by dark theological motives that belie professions of love for the Jews. Others express concerns of a more pragmatic and partisan nature. When it comes to domestic policy, many Jews view the Christian Right as a threat to the religious pluralism that has allowed Jews to thrive in America, and they do not wish to confer legitimacy upon such opponents. As for foreign policy, a segment of the Jewish community is troubled by the fact that Christian Zionists tend to support the policies of the Israeli Right. Jews who believe that Israel must trade land for peace see these Christians as a force that will tip the scales toward extremism and war.

As we will see, these concerns are largely exaggerated. Some of these suspicions happen to be pure fantasy and can be easily dismissed. Other complaints are based on fact, but these facts are then applied too broadly or inconsistently to support the conclusions that are reached. When it comes to the Jewish critique of Christian Zionism, presumption, not detached analysis, is typically the hallmark of the review. This failure of the Jewish community to objectively confront evangelical support for Israel is a strong indication that something deeper than policy is driving this Jewish hesitation.

Beneath the political arguments, Jewish discomfort with Christian Zionism flows largely from Jewish discomfort with robust Christianity. The Jewish experience in Christian Europe has left deep scars. Over the centuries, Jewish communities in Europe enjoyed some periods of relative peace and prosperity. But these episodes were typically brief, and they were punctuated by persecution, forced conversions, crusades, inquisitions, pogroms, massacres, and, finally, genocide. Many of these tragedies, such as the Spanish Inquisition and the countless Easter Day pogroms, were directly linked to church-based anti-Semitism. Other tragedies—such as the Holocaust—were perpetrated by secular regimes, but they flourished in a soil that had been richly fertilized over the centuries by church-based anti-Semitism.

These persecutions are hardly ancient history. The Holocaust occurred barely sixty years ago. Most American Jews know that if their grandparents or great-grandparents had not immigrated to America when they did, the family line would have ended in a Nazi gas chamber. Given this history, the Jewish fear of robust Christianity is eminently understandable. It is programmed into Jewish genes. It is Pavlovian. When Christian soldiers are on the march, Jews get nervous.

This communal posttraumatic stress clouds a new reality. Today, in America, the loudest Christian soldiers are marching to fight for Israel, not against it. These Christians want to defend the Jews, not harm them. While justified, the Jewish community's mistrust is interfering with something even more important than history: the future.

THE MARTIN LUTHER SYNDROME

THE PROBLEM IS not that the Jewish community is unaware of what the Christian Zionists are saying. They know that with few exceptions the words have been right. Unlike Christians in prior generations, these Christians do appear to come in peace. Yet the suspicion is so deep that words, and even deeds, are discounted. There is a fear that even if sincere, this Christian enthusiasm for Israel could instantly morph into the hostility of the past. Even for so paranoid a scenario, Jewish history provides ample precedent.

In the early 1500s, a priest named Martin Luther wrote a manifesto entitled *95 Theses* in which he boldly challenged certain policies of the Roman Catholic Church. Legend holds that Luther nailed this document to the door of a church in his hometown of Wittenberg. Whether or not the revolution began in such a dramatic fashion, Luther's *95 Theses* did indeed spark a revolution. Out of Luther's critique of the church grew the Reformation and Protestantism.

When Luther rejected Catholic doctrine, he also rejected the anti-Semitism that had characterized the Catholic Church since its earliest days. In a tract bearing the sympathetic title *That Jesus Christ Was Born a Jew*, Luther criticized the prevailing anti-Semitism of the Catholic Church and the way in which every Easter "Passion preachers do nothing else but enormously exaggerate the Jews' misdeeds against Christ and thus embitter the hearts of the faithful against them."[1] Luther asked his fellow Christians:

> What good can we do the Jews when we constrain them, malign them, and hate them as dogs? When we deny them work and force them to usury, how can that help? We should use toward the Jews not the pope's but Christ's law of love.[2]

Since Luther felt that the church had perverted Christ's message, he blamed the church, not the Jews, for the fact that the Jews continued to reject Christianity. Now that Luther was preaching the true gospel, he was certain that the Jews would see the light. In Luther's words:

> I hope that if one deals with the Jews in a kindly way and instructs them carefully from Holy Scripture, many of them will become genuine Christians and turn to the faith of their fathers, the prophets and patriarchs.[3]

And what if they did not become genuine Christians? Luther seemed quite open to the possibility. "If some of them prove stiff-necked, what of it?" remarked Luther. "After all, we ourselves are not all good Christians either."[4]

Given the anti-Semitism of the times, Luther's words were revolutionary in their tolerance. Jews excitedly read and circulated Luther's writings. According to one Jewish historian, "The Jews of Antwerp sent them to Spain, their former homeland, and even as far away as Palestine."[5] Luther created great hope among Jews that there could be a new beginning in relations with their Christian neighbors. But while the Jews welcomed Luther and his tolerance, they did not convert. Despite Luther's innovations, almost all of the Jews proved to be, in Luther's borrowed biblical words, "stiff-necked."

When the Jews failed to respond to his teachings, Luther's attitude changed. Tolerance and understanding gave way to rage. As we saw in chapter one, Luther penned some of the most anti-Semitic writings in the history of the Christian church. In his bluntly titled *The Jews and Their Lies*, Luther advised his readers to deal with the Jews by burning their synagogues, destroying their homes, and expelling them from their villages. Elsewhere in this tract, Luther noted of the Jews:

> [T]hey are thirsty bloodhounds and murderers of all Christendom, with full intent, now for more than fourteen hundred years, and indeed they were often burned to death upon the accusation that they had poisoned water and wells, stolen children, and torn and hacked them apart, in order to cool their temper secretly with Christian blood.[6]

WHILE MANY JEWS may not be familiar with Martin Luther's metamorphosis, they may still fear its replication. This cautionary tale, like so many others, has been absorbed into the Jewish psyche and passed down from generation to generation. Thus within the Jewish community there is an oft-expressed suspicion that Christian love can quickly turn to Christian hate if the Jews don't perform as expected. Yes, these Christians support Israel today. But what will happen when their theological hopes are dashed? What if Israel bucks its last-days script? What if Jesus doesn't return as hoped? From this perspective the very zeal with which Christian Zionists support Israel is merely an ominous indication of the rage that will fall upon Jewish heads if prophecy goes unfulfilled. When they look at Jerry Falwell and Pat Robertson, many Jews cannot help but see the face of Martin Luther before his anti-Semitic vitriol burst to the fore.

FEAR OF CONVERSION

ONE IMMUTABLE FEATURE of Christian persecution of the Jews throughout the ages was forced conversion. Generation after generation of Jews was offered the Hobbesian choice of death or conversion to Christianity. Even when Christians stopped forcing Jews to convert at the point of a knife, they continued to seek their conversion through heavy social and economic pressure. Given this context, it is not surprising that some of the most frequently voiced complaints about Christian Zionists center on the theme of conversion.

Conversion at the end of days

Perhaps the most common critique of Christian Zionism focuses on Christian theology. As discussed in chapter three, many evangelical Christians believe that the birth of Israel is one of the preconditions to the Second Coming of Christ. They further believe that in the final days before Christ's return a majority of Jews will die, and those who survive will eventually accept Christ as their Savior. Thus, the faulty syllogism holds, Christians support Israel only to speed the Second Coming and the concomitant death and conversion of the Jews. Referring to this belief, for example, author Gershom Gorenberg has noted:

> The Jews die or convert. As a Jew, I can't feel very comfortable with the affections of somebody who looks forward to that scenario.
>
> They [the evangelical Christians] don't love real Jewish people. They love us as characters in their story, in their play, and that's not who we are. And we never auditioned for that part, and the play is not one that ends up good for us....If you listen to the drama that they are describing, essentially, it's a five-act play in which the Jews disappear in the fourth act.[7]

Abraham Foxman, national director of the Anti-Defamation League (ADL), expressed a similar concern in 1998. He stated that evangelical support for Israel was "troubling" because:

> This is not support without strings. They would like to see us at the end of the day be Christians, so what good is it to have a strong Jewish state if at the end of whatever millennia we are to disappear as a people?[8]

It is difficult to have a conversation about Christian Zionism without hearing some variation of this argument. The belief that Christians support Israel to speed the Second Coming has entered the conventional wisdom and is now as widely accepted as any urban myth. But like most urban myths, this story does not hold up under closer scrutiny. This dark motive behind

Christian Zionism, it turns out, is as apocryphal as the packs of alligators said to roam the sewers of New York.

THERE IS A wonderful irony in secular critics of Christian Zionism, typically Jewish, complaining about the great disasters that will befall them upon Christ's Second Coming. These critics, of course, don't actually believe that there will be a Second Coming of Christ. If there will be no Second Coming, then there will be no mass conversion or death. So what exactly are these critics worried about? It's as if a man who does not believe in voodoo nevertheless cowers under his bed when he learns that an enemy has made a voodoo doll in his image. This is not logic; it is paranoia.

What really disturbs such critics is not a fear that this end-of-days scenario will actually happen, but a belief that evangelicals *want* it to happen. For people who are suspicious of robust Christianity, this eschatology is the smoking gun that confirms their darkest fears about Christian motives. It is proof that Christian Zionism is merely the latest in a long line of Christian plots to kill and convert Jews. In modern, liberal society, Christians are no longer able to impose upon Jews the grim choice of death or conversion. It is, therefore, presumed that these Christian soldiers work to speed the day when Christ will return to accomplish what they no longer can.

This allegation reads into Christian Zionism an agenda that simply does not exist. As discussed in chapter three, evangelical Christians do not support Israel to speed the Second Coming because they do not believe that they have the ability to speed the Second Coming. In their theology, man is powerless to change God's timetable. Evangelical support for Israel flows instead from a series of more positive motives that reflect respect for the Jews and a recognition of their centrality to God's plan.

While unable to speed the Second Coming, however, evangelical Christians definitely do wish for it. Given what will happen to the Jews upon Jesus' return, such aspirations strike some as profoundly disturbing. Yet prayers for Christ's return have nothing to do with killing and converting Jews. Christians pray for the Second Coming for the same reasons that Orthodox Jews pray for the first coming of their Messiah—they long for the promised reign of God on earth that will follow. Both the Christian and the Jewish tradition hold that there will be great violence and death prior to the messianic era.* Neither tradition looks forward to the bloodshed—this is simply the ugly business that must be endured prior to the Golden Age.

The Jews refer to the tribulations preceding the messianic era as the "birth pangs" of the Messiah. This analogy to childbirth is instructive. Both religious traditions hold that only knowledge of the great joy to come will enable someone to endure the excruciating pain of the process by which that joy is brought. Christians and Jews do not look forward to the birth pangs of the Messiah any more than a pregnant woman looks forward to the pain of her labor. All concerned look past the pain toward the prize that awaits them afterward.

Armageddon, furthermore, is not just about the Jews. To evangelicals, the final days will be a tragedy for all humanity. The blood that they believe will "rise as high as a horse's bridle" at Armageddon is not Jewish blood but the blood of the foreign armies that invade Israel. And the expected destruction will spread far beyond Israel, leaving all of Earth's major cities in ruins. While two-thirds of the Jews will be killed, it is believed that as many as three-fourths of Earth's population will be wiped out in the final days. Seven months will be spent burying the dead. Perhaps this is why they call it the Apocalypse. Someone who actually looks forward to the bloodshed, and not beyond it to the glory that will follow, may very well be a sociopath, but he is no anti-Semite.

The Old Testament contains many passages about death and destruction that are troubling to modern, post-Enlightenment thinkers. The Bible documents the indiscriminate killing of entire villages, tribes, and, on one occasion, all humanity minus one family. The Bible also predicts more bloodshed of such biblical proportions in the future. The theological debate over whether a just and loving God would so destroy innocent humanity has been underway for centuries and will no doubt continue. It is simply unfair, however, to isolate one instance of biblical violence and hold it up to ridicule as if the remainder of the Judeo-Christian tradition fits perfectly into the ethos of the twenty-first century. The issue is a far deeper one.

* The Jewish tradition does not emphasize the final days as much as the Christian tradition, much as Judaism does not emphasize the afterlife to the extent that Christianity does. Yet both concepts derive, originally, from the Jewish tradition.

Jews and Christians who work together in support of Israel have worked out an excellent solution to their different beliefs about the Messiah and the end of days. When the Messiah appears in Jerusalem, they will ask Him, "Is this Your first or second visit?" Until then, they've agreed to suspend their disagreement on this one issue and cooperate on a shared agenda of great importance to both parties.

THIS HAND-WRINGING OVER Christian end-of-days theology becomes more persuasive when another step is added to the argument. What if the Christians aren't content to wait patiently for Armageddon and the Second Coming of Christ? What if they actively seek to unleash a war in Israel in the psychotic hope that this will speed Christ's return? In this scenario, a theological difference takes on very real, and very dangerous, this-world implications.

As discussed in chapter three, the fear that mainstream Christian Zionists would engage in such behavior is misplaced. They do not believe that they can speed the Second Coming, and there is nothing in their actions that contradicts this belief. But what about less responsible individuals? Will Christian fanatics undertake what their leaders will not?

Author Gershom Gorenberg has written at length about such doomsday scenarios. As he notes, such plots to unleash Armageddon almost always involve the Temple Mount. The Temple Mount is the holiest site in Judaism, the site where the biblical temple once stood. Under a popular reading of the Book of Revelation, the Jews must rebuild their temple at this site prior to Christ's return.

Even if the Jews wanted to rebuild the temple—and the vast majority do not—there remains an enormous obstacle to the project. Two obstacles, actually. The Temple Mount compound is today the site of two mosques built late in the seventh century: the Dome of the Rock and the Al-Aqsa Mosque. These mosques and the Temple Mount on which they rest comprise the third holiest site in Islam. The only way to build the temple is to destroy the mosques, a move that would be certain to unleash an instant and massive jihad against Israel. To certain unstable minds, destroying these mosques would thus set up the perfect end-of-days scenario—both clearing the ground for a new temple and launching a massive war that will bring Armageddon.

The fear of fanatics acting out such a scenario is not far-fetched. They have already tried. In the 1980s, a group of religious extremists made extensive plans to blow up the Dome of the Rock to clear the way for a Jewish temple and the Messianic Age. The Israeli police caught them before they could follow through on their plans, and the plotters were sentenced to jail. These particular extremists happened to be Orthodox Jews, not Christians.

But Christian extremists have also taken their shot. In 1969, a Christian from Australia named Dennis Rohan set fire to the Al-Aqsa Mosque to hasten Jesus' return. While the fire was put out in time to save the structure, significant damage was done. This was the act of a crazy man. Literally. Rohan had spent time in a mental institution prior to coming to Israel. The Israeli judges that tried him concluded that he was a paranoid schizophrenic and returned him to a mental institution.[9]

The threat of insane people seeking to start World War III is a serious one, and it demands the constant vigilance of the Israeli police. But the existence of such a lunatic fringe is hardly an indictment of mainstream religious movements. The Jews who plotted to blow up the mosques are not representative of the vast majority of Orthodox Jews. The existence of these fanatics does not disqualify Orthodox Jews from participating in the Israeli government or Zionist coalitions. Likewise, the psychotic Dennis Rohan is hardly representative of evangelical Christians. His existence does not delegitimize the Christian Zionist movement.

Conversion here and now

Jewish discomfort with Christian Zionism is often driven by concerns more immediate than what will happen at the end of days. Many American Jews are more worried about efforts to convert them here and now. Such individuals suspect that support for Israel is really a Trojan horse. They fear that having failed to win Jewish converts through direct appeals, evangelical Christians have undertaken a two-stage initiative. First, they will win the trust of the Jews by supporting the cause of Israel to which they are so attached. Then, once the Jews have let their guard down, the Christians will move in for the conversion. To these critics, Christian Zionism is just the latest in a long history of efforts to turn Jews into Christians. It is the Inquisition with a smiley face.

The fact is that most evangelical Christians *do*, in their heart of hearts, want to see Jews accept Christ. They would also like to see Hindus, Muslims, Buddhists, and Zoroastrians accept Christ. For that matter, they would like to see the vast multitudes of secular Christians truly accept Christ through the experience of being born again. Spreading the gospel is, literally, an article of faith for evangelical Christians. Like it or not, these Christians believe in the universality of their message and feel obligated to share it with all humanity. Missionary activities in every corner of the globe over the course of centuries were not undertaken on a whim.

While Christians may want to see Jews accept Christ, however, there is simply no evidence to connect their zeal for evangelism to their support for Israel. The suggestion that the two are somehow related rests on a strange conspiracy theory. This argument presumes that Christians—millions of them—have agreed to a plan that they are now implementing church by church across America. Somehow, Christians from the Deep South all the way north to Minnesota, from Los Angeles all the way east to New York, know that they must support Israel—something they presumably would not otherwise do—in order to harvest Jewish souls at some point down the road. Why hasn't someone leaked the memo to the press? Or has this grassroots plan to convert the Jews been orchestrated by a sleeper cell?

If this allegation were true, if support for Israel were merely a means to soften and convert Jews, then one would expect the first targets to be those Jews who have worked longest and closest with Christians. Yet the Jewish veterans of interfaith Zionism—some of whom have collaborated with Christians for decades—relate to a person that no such conversion efforts have taken place. Not one of the Jewish leaders interviewed for this book can remember a time when one of their Christian allies attempted to convert them.* Instead, these Jews describe their relations with their Christian counterparts as being marked by mutual respect and tolerance.

While there is no evidence that the Christian-Jewish alliance in support of Israel facilitates the conversion of Jews, there is evidence that the alliance

---

* While interviewing these Jewish leaders, I was at first concerned that there might be some element of spin to these answers. Jews who work with Christians might have a motive to make light of conversion efforts. Yet after more than three years of attendance at evangelical churches and conferences as an open Jew, I have yet to be subjected to a serious effort to convert me to Christianity.

actually works to *impede* efforts to convert Jews. Christian Zionist leaders who work closely with Jews are exposed to Jewish sensitivities and concerns. Upon discovering that Jews find "Jesus talk" to be offensive, these Christians tend to be far more circumspect when discussing their faith around their Jewish friends. These Christian leaders then teach their grassroots to understand and respect these Jewish concerns.

While most Jews are aware of the centuries of pain caused by Christian efforts to convert them, few evangelicals are as well versed in their Jewish history. For evangelicals, sharing the gospel comes as naturally as sharing a hidden treasure: they have found something that has brought them great joy, and with the best of intentions they want to pass it on. What Jews call *proselytizing*, evangelicals earnestly call "sharing the good news." Most evangelicals cannot imagine that someone would take offense at such a gesture. Sensitivity here, as in so many instances, must be taught. And the teachers, the ones sharing the Jewish perspective with the evangelical grassroots, are typically those who have come to understand these concerns through their close collaboration with Jews.

Fear of the Right

Jewish fears of an ongoing Christian drive to convert them explain much, but not all, of the Jewish discomfort with Christian Zionism. There remains another line of criticism of the Christian Zionists that focuses not on their theology but on their politics. Christian Zionists are usually stalwarts of the Christian Right. As such, they espouse conservative political views on both domestic and international issues that differ with those of a Jewish community that is still largely liberal.

Such differences of opinion are a normal part of political discourse in a democratic society. Yet the Jewish response to these policy differences often exhibits a level of emotion that indicates something deeper at work. Like other aspects of Christian-Jewish relations, the Jewish critique of evangelical Christian politics is turbo-charged by memory and fear. With nerves still raw from the long history of Christian anti-Semitism, Jewish critics of the Christian Right are quick to see sister hatreds behind current policies. From this perspective, Christian support for prayer in the schools and school vouchers is seen as a demonstration of continuing Christian disdain for all religions not their own. Likewise, Christian support for West Bank settlements is viewed as part of a Christian effort to spark the bloody wars of Armageddon. Many Jewish critics thus conclude that Christian Zionists are extremists who must be excluded from the broad pro-Israel coalition.

Support for right-wing politics in America

Many American Jews are wary of Christian Zionists because of their positions on domestic issues. Christian Zionists are typically pro-life and against gay marriage. They usually support faith-based initiatives, school vouchers, and prayer in the schools. Such views on these controversial domestic issues are sharply at odds with those of a Jewish community that is still largely liberal.

These social issues resonate deeply in the Jewish community. Most Jews believe that the separation of church and state has enabled Jewish success in a majority Christian America. Moreover, such Jews typically equate the "separation of church and state" with the broad interpretation thereof embraced by the Supreme Court in a series of opinions in the 1960s and 1970s. Jews tend to see efforts to move the wall of separation from where it was at that time placed as an attack on the very foundations of their status in America. Even conservative initiatives that have nothing to do with Establishment Clause jurisprudence, such as opposition to abortion, are perceived as efforts to erode this all-important church-state divide. In the words of Abraham Foxman, national director of the Anti-Defamation League, the domestic agenda of the Christian Right threatens to make American Jews "second-class citizens in our own country."[10]

Because of these differences on domestic policy, many leaders of the Jewish community have expressed reservations about working with Christian Zionists in support of Israel. David A. Harris, executive director of the American Jewish Committee, summed up the mixed feelings many Jews have toward joining a coalition with evangelical Christians in support of Israel:

> On the one hand, here are fervent supporters of Israel and that is a precious commodity. On the other hand, on so many domestic issues we profoundly disagree, and many American Jews are unsettled by the theological underpinning of the Christian fundamentalist support.[11]

The views of leaders such as Mr. Harris reflect a rather pristine view of coalition building. The halls of Congress are packed with coalitions taking stands on hundreds of issues. What unites these coalitions is not the fact that they agree on *every* issue, but the fact that they agree on *one* issue—the one on which they are collaborating. The members of such coalitions are not expected to change their positions or dampen their zeal when it comes to issues outside the narrow one that has brought them together. The oft-expressed suggestion that the Jewish community must choose between support for Israel and its heartfelt domestic agenda is simply false—they can simultaneously serve both.

Why, then, are so many American Jews so uncomfortable with a broad coalition in the case of support for Israel? One explanation is that they fear that such collaboration will confer legitimacy upon the Christian Right and, thereby, strengthen its hand when it comes to domestic battles. Yet, the fact is that the Christian Right already enjoys legitimacy. Conservative Christians comprise the largest single voting bloc in the Republican Party, and they have learned to wield their political power with considerable aplomb. A decision by the American Jewish Committee or other Jewish groups to agree to collaborate with conservative Christians in support of Israel will hardly tip the scales in the debate over domestic issues.

There is often a deeper reason for the hesitation. To many in the Jewish community, the rejection of Christian Zionists as coalition partners is driven not by legislative strategy but by moral outrage. In their eyes, the views of Christian conservatives are so repugnant, so beyond the pale of civil society, that people who espouse them are simply not legitimate partners for *any* coalition.

No doubt there are certain issues on which we must not tolerate dissent. It is evil to fly a plane filled with innocent civilians into an office tower filled with innocent civilians. Anyone who argues otherwise is beyond the pale of civil discourse. Likewise, it is wrong to hate an entire group of people on the basis of their skin color or ethnicity. Racists must not be legitimized by inclusion in any coalition. The same rule applies, of course, to anti-Semites.

In contrast, the Christian political agenda focuses on issues about which reasonable people can and do disagree. The abortion debate, for example, implicates two values at the very core of Western society: respect for human life on the one hand, and reverence for individual liberty on the other. These two values happen to conflict when it comes to this issue, and it is not surprising that people differ over which value should be supreme. The only thing extreme about the abortion debate are those who are so absolute in their positions that they deny the humanity of those who disagree.

DESPITE THE DISCOMFORT, some Jewish leaders have taken the position that they are open to partnering with the Christian Zionists provided that the Christian Zionists do not ask the Jews to back away from their liberal views on social issues. According to Rabbi David Saperstein, the Reform Movement's representative in Washington:

> If the American Jewish community buys the support of the religious right [for Israel] by its acquiescence on domestic policies, that would damage our religious freedom and our tradition of pluralism and tolerance. It will be a disaster for America and for Jews.[12]

Rabbi Saperstein has it backwards. Evangelical Christians already support Israel—no one has to buy their support. Furthermore, Christians have not asked the Jewish community for anything in return for their support of Israel—not even a thank you. It is the Jewish community, more than the evangelical, that has been reluctant to join hands in support of Israel with people who do not share their views on social issues.

Those Jewish leaders who have worked most often with the Christian Right confirm that these Christians have never placed conditions on their support for Israel. Mort Klein, president of the Zionist Organization of America, notes that:

> No Christian leader—and I talk to almost all of them—has ever asked me, "If I speak out in favor of Israel, will you support me on this?" Never.[13]

According to Abraham Foxman, national director for the Anti-Defamation League:

> Importantly, at no point have we heard them [Christian Zionists] place any conditions on their support. There is no quid pro quo. At no point have we had to choose between our fundamental principles concerning the role of religion in America and our appreciation for their standing with Israel.[14]

Support for the Israeli Right

Yossi Alpher, a former Mossad agent, served for years as director of the American Jewish Committee's office in Israel.* Alpher is not bashful about expressing his feelings toward the Christian Zionists:

> God save us from these people. When you see what these people are encouraging Israel and the U.S. administration to do—that is, ignore the Palestinians, if not worse, if not kick them out; expand the settlements to the greatest extent possible—they are leading us into a scenario of out-and-out disaster.[15]

Strong words these. Especially when uttered by an Israeli patriot about people who are ostensibly devoted to Israel. Alpher is an eloquent proponent of a critique of the Christian Zionists that focuses on the positions they take on issues of war and peace in the Middle East. These critics argue that Christian Zionists tend to support right-wing politicians and policies that will block Israel from making the territorial concessions necessary for peace. Naturally, this particular complaint is voiced only by those who still favor territorial compromise.

This argument was echoed by Peter Beinart, editor of *The New Republic,* in commentary appearing in his magazine. Beinart argued that:

> American Jews should shun the Christian Right because Zionism is not only a national tradition; it's also a moral one. And Christian conservatives... don't merely misunderstand the moral tradition, they disfigure it beyond recognition.[16]

As these examples indicate, those who make this argument tend to overstate the case. It is an effort to project onto an entire group the views of its lunatic fringe or, in this case, its extreme right wing. Yes, there certainly are some Christian supporters of Israel who ignore the legitimate rights of the Palestinians and the moral traditions of Zionism. There also happen to be many Jewish supporters of Israel who are guilty of the same ignorance. Much as the

---

* Alpher, an Israeli, reflects a mentality far more common among Jewish Americans than their Israeli cousins.

extremist Jews don't disqualify all Jewish Zionists, the existence of extremist Christians is hardly an indictment of the Christian Zionist movement.

While they cannot be dismissed as extremists, most Christian Zionists can fairly be categorized as right wing in their approach to the peace process with the Palestinians. The question is, however, whether these Christians hold views that are substantially different from those of the Israeli Right. If not, why should the Christians alone be ostracized? While many Israelis and American Jews seriously disagree with the right-wing policies of Benjamin Netanyahu and Natan Sharansky, few have proposed that these leaders be shunned or excluded from the pro-Israel coalition. There is no reason why a Christian supporter of Israel should be judged by any different standard.

When discussing the Middle East peace process, most Christian Zionists do in fact hew closely to the arguments and rhetoric of the Israeli Right. For starters, Christian Zionists did not trust the late Yasser Arafat as a peace partner. Jerry Falwell, for example, believed that Yasser Arafat was an unrepentant terrorist and that concessions did nothing to divert him from seeking Israel's destruction. Gary Bauer echoed the point. Since Arafat did not really seek peace, Bauer argued, territorial concession would only serve to strengthen an enemy of Israel.

Pat Robertson shared the skeptical assessment of Arafat. According to Pat Robertson:

> I'm for Israel. And I want that nation to be strong. I want them to be free and I want them to exist as a nation in the midst of the other nations of the earth. And I think if they make compromises with a thug like Arafat, they're going to wind up so weakened that they will not be able to resist an attack.[17]

This skeptical view of Arafat, once terribly gauche during the early days of the Oslo process, gained greater currency following the Camp David Summit of 2000. When Arafat turned down Prime Minister Barak's offer of a Palestinian state in almost all of the West Bank and Gaza, many observers were forced to revisit their initial assumptions. Ehud Barak himself, along with the Bush administration, joined the leaders of the Israeli Right in concluding that it was futile to continue negotiating with Arafat.

The Christian Zionist critique of the peace process goes beyond the specific personality of Yasser Arafat. Both Pat Robertson and Jerry Falwell note that without the West Bank, Israel would be so narrow near its population center in Tel Aviv that it would have no territorial margin for error.[18] Falwell further argues that Israel's Arab neighbors are governed by dictators, not democracies, and that a new dictator will in no way feel bound by a peace agreement signed by the previous dictator whom he has overthrown. Given these factors, Falwell is wary of trusting "the ephemeral good will of Arab leaders."[19]

Gary Bauer has linked his opposition to a Palestinian state more to issues of timing. Like so many others in Washington and Jerusalem, Bauer has asserted that it would be a terrible mistake to create a Palestinian state in response to Palestinian terror. Speaking in 2003 Bauer stated:

> To set in motion a state now, when the Palestinians have not met any of the markers set out by the President, will in fact make Israel less secure because it sends a signal that if the Palestinians keep blowing people up they will eventually be rewarded.[20]

But what if President Abbas proves himself to be a more responsible leader than Arafat? What if the Palestinians reconciled themselves to the existence of Israel and renounced terrorism? Could conditions arise under which a Christian Zionist would support the creation of a Palestinian state in the West Bank? Bauer admits that this is a difficult question, and one with which he wrestles. He is "ambivalent" and "goes back and forth"[21] on how to reconcile Israel's security needs with the rights of the Palestinians. His opposition to a Palestinian state is nuanced and rooted more in the realm of policy analysis than in that of biblical certainty. In this regard, Bauer resembles the majority of American Jews and Israelis.

Pat Robertson too leaves the door open to concessions when and if there is a more moderate Palestinian leadership. Says Robertson:

> If that's the case, then something might work out. But right now the Palestinian Authority...is an oppressive regime. It doesn't know how to manage its own finances or its own people. But you know, the last thing I want to do is sit here in America and dictate domestic politics to the people of Israel.[22]

As Robertson's comment indicates, Christian Zionists typically know their place when it comes to issues of war and peace in the Middle East.

Like most American Jews, Christian Zionists view themselves as friends of Israel who provide support for Israel when called upon to do so. But they also understand that, ultimately, decisions about trading land for peace must be left to the people who will bear the brunt of the outcome—the Israelis. According to Jerry Falwell:

> If Israel desires to give part of her land to her neighbors, that is her business.... The government of Israel as represented by its people will have to decide what is best. It is a democratic society and the final decision will be as a result of the democratic process within Israel.[23]

Such moderate talk is well and good. But are Christian Zionists really so moderate in practice? Are they truly able to hold their tongues when it comes to the disposition of the land that God promised to Abraham and his progeny in the Bible? One of the major concerns about Christian Zionists is that they will use their significant political weight to work against the peace process and the territorial concessions that it would necessitate. In the words of Rabbi David Saperstein, director of the Religious Action Center for Reform Judaism:

> It is not the theology that bothers us. It is the way that some of these people have, and will, implement that theology into concrete American support, or opposition to an American role on the peace process and on issues of compromise and on issues of military conflict in the Middle East. If it [Christian Zionism] manifests itself by saying they should not give back one inch of land, of historic, biblically promised Israel, as part of a peace agreement to create a two state solution to resolve the conflict in the Middle East, it could have very dangerous implications.[24]

The question of how American supporters of Israel should approach the Middle East peace process has been the subject of great debate within the Jewish community. The American Israel Public Affairs Committee (AIPAC), the preeminent pro-Israel lobby organization in America, has chosen a course that captures the consensus view. AIPAC does not adopt an independent position on the issue of how best to achieve peace in the Middle East. Instead, AIPAC supports the policies of Israel's democratically elected governments. AIPAC reasons wisely that since the Israelis are the ones who will bear the consequences of decisions about war and peace, then it must be the Israelis who make these decisions. Thus when a right-leaning Israeli government seeks to stop or slow the pace of territorial concessions, AIPAC will apply its considerable weight to block American pressure to the contrary. When a left-leaning Israeli government seeks to trade land for peace, AIPAC supports the peace process.

The Christian Zionists have largely followed AIPAC's lead. When Israel has been governed from the right, the Christian Zionists have enthusiastically embraced their role as defenders of the Jewish State. When Prime Minister Netanyahu wanted to slow the pace of troop redeployments under Oslo, Christian Zionists gave him a hero's welcome in Washington. When Prime Minister Sharon wanted to crack down on Palestinian militants, the Christian Zionists mobilized to persuade the administration to give him a free hand.

Such Christian support for Netanyahu and Sharon is, of course, no surprise. The more interesting question is how Christian Zionists would react to a left-leaning Israeli government dedicated to making territorial concessions. While this question is often posed as a hypothetical, it need not be. Twice in the decade of the 1990s, Israeli leaders have actively pursued efforts to trade the biblical lands of the West Bank for peace with the Palestinians. Prime Minister Rabin embraced this policy when he launched the Oslo Peace Process in 1993. Upon his election in 1999, Prime Minister Barak picked up the standard of territorial concessions and at Camp David offered to relinquish almost all of the West Bank and even parts of Jerusalem.

Throughout the terms of both Rabin and Barak, the Christian Zionists respected the traditional boundaries of American pro-Israel activism. So long as the Israelis were behind it, the Christian Zionists did not seek to obstruct the peace process. Instead, they deferred to the Israelis and largely faded into the background. This does not mean that the Christian Zionists morphed into peace enthusiasts. They remained largely skeptical and sometimes expressed their doubts and concerns. Yet they at all times remained more circumspect in their criticism than the leading Jewish opponents of Oslo.

Typical of the Christian response was Ralph Reed. When commenting on the Middle East shortly after Ehud Barak's victory on a dovish platform, Ralph Reed said:

> I recognize that Barak won and pretty strongly, and if—without compromising Israeli security—he can accelerate the peace process and bring about an end to the killing, I'm certainly supportive of that.[25]

Reed, a Christian conservative skilled at sounding moderate, merely implied what many others expressed openly—a doubt that Barak could actually bring about an end to the killing. Unfortunately, the events that followed Camp David proved the wisdom of such skepticism.

This same pattern repeated itself in 2005 when Ariel Sharon, a stalwart of the Israeli Right, shocked many of his supporters in Israel and abroad by ordering the unilateral withdrawal of all Israeli soldiers and settlers from the Gaza Strip. The Gaza withdrawal led to weeks of massive protests in Israel and, eventually, to a major realignment of Israeli politics. Yet Israel's Christian friends remained largely silent. While some questioned the wisdom of Israel's actions in the absence of a responsible Palestinian leadership to govern Gaza, no Christian Zionist leader took steps to oppose a choice made by a sovereign Israeli government. Once again, the loudest opposition to Israeli territorial concessions came from Jewish, not Christian, Zionists.

AFTER THE OSLO Accords were signed in 1993, Congress took up legislation called the Middle East Peace Facilitation Act to help fund the often expensive steps called for in that agreement. Yet while a contagious optimism reigned in the initial post-Oslo period, not everyone was infected. As Congress debated the funding legislation, a small band of conservative lobbyists descended upon Capitol Hill. Waiting in office lobbies and outside hearing rooms, these skeptics successfully pressed for an amendment that conditioned U.S. aid to the Palestinians on their full compliance with their obligations under Oslo. Both AIPAC and the Israeli government had supported a more flexible framework for the flow of aid, and they were furious at these freelancers who had so trumped them.

The people involved in this effort to condition Palestinian aid were all Jews. Morton Klein, president of the Zionist Organization of America, led the effort together with a handful of his supporters. To this day, Morton Klein sits on the board of AIPAC and is a full member of the Conference of

Presidents of Major American Jewish Organizations. He crossed a line that Christian Zionists have not crossed. Yet even he has not been shunned.

As this story indicates, American Jews have not always followed AIPAC's example. Some American Jews think that they know what is best for Israel and seek to enlist the support of the White House and Congress to help them impose their will upon a recalcitrant Jewish State. Such individuals are not confined to the right. Groups such as the Israel Policy Forum and American Friends of Peace Now believe that it is in Israel's best interest to trade land for peace. They further believe that if Israel lacks the wisdom to make these concessions on its own, then America should pressure Israel to do so. Toward this end, these groups lobby Congress and the administration to play a more active role in the Middle East peace process.

Such supporters of the peace process are naturally among the most vocal critics of Christian Zionists. By seeking to block American pressure on Israel to make concessions for peace, the Christian Zionists work directly against the efforts of the peace camp to elicit such pressure. As Rabbi Eric Yoffie, a long-time leader of Reform Judaism in America, said of the Christian Zionists, "They see any concession as a threat to Israel, and in this they strengthen the hardliners in Israel and the United States. That may make it difficult for the peace process to go forward."[26]

In expressing this concern, the peace camp is not exaggerating. In fact, this left-wing complaint that Christian Zionists block American pressure on right-wing Israeli governments is the one Jewish complaint about Christian Zionism that is entirely accurate. Yet, while their facts may be correct, their premise is questionable. The mainstream Jewish community has comfortably embraced the AIPAC view that they should defer to Israelis on the big issues of war and peace. When supporters of territorial concessions place themselves above the Israelis on the front lines and seek to impose their views of what is best for Israel by means of American pressure, they break with this communal consensus and go out on a limb. For the peace camp to sit out on that limb and criticize Christian Zionists for standing with most of the Jewish community in support of the Israeli government is to exhibit what a true Jew might call *chutzpah* (nerve).

So long as the Christian Zionists continue to join the Jewish community in deferring to Israel on the direction of the peace process, they will remain well within a safe and time-honored consensus. If they decide to follow certain Jewish leaders out into dissent from the Israeli position, however, they would be crossing a very bright red line. If the Christian Zionists ever changed their policy and openly worked against an Israeli government that chose to trade land for peace, they would find themselves at odds with the majority of Jews in America and Israel. Such a blatant disregard for the will of the Israeli majority by such a powerful bloc would raise troubling questions about Christian Zionism.

To date, there is little indication that the Christian Zionists will abandon the AIPAC approach that has served them and the Jewish community so well. The Christian Zionists have already demonstrated the depth of their commitment to these limitations during the aggressive peace initiatives of Prime Ministers Rabin and Barak. When Prime Minister Ariel Sharon began to call for the creation of a Palestinian state and the removal of Jewish settlers from Gaza in 2004 and proceeded to implement the Gaza withdrawal in 2005, the Christian Zionists continued to maintain their traditional deference.

There is no guarantee, however, that past practices will be continued into the future. The Christian Zionist community is not a monolith. The debate that has been underway for years in the Jewish community over how supporters of Israel should react when they disagree with Israeli policy can now be heard in the Christian Zionist community as well. Yet the voices calling most loudly for Christian Zionists to break with the AIPAC approach and oppose those Israeli policies that they believe to be too "dovish" are often Jewish, not Christian. Right-leaning American Jews such as Mort Klein and Herbert Zweibon of Americans for a Safe Israel are encouraging the Christian Zionists to join them in more actively opposing the creation of a Palestinian state and the withdrawal of Jewish settlements from the Gaza Strip. Since Klein and Zweibon are among the few Jewish leaders to warmly embrace the Christian Zionists, they have developed close working relationships with them and exercise far more influence over them than other American Jews. Ironically, by shunning the Christian Zionists for being too hawkish when it comes to Israel, many moderate American Jews are simply abandoning the field to those who would push these Christians even further to the right.

In the same century in which the Holocaust occurred, to be accused of anti-Semitism is the most serious and grave charge that can be leveled against a citizen in a free society.[1]

—Ralph Reed, 1995

Chapter Nine

EVANGELICAL ANTI-SEMITISM?

IN A VERY old book, the author sounds some very familiar themes. The Jews, he writes, are an "unfaithful" and "blasphemous" people. They are guilty of "abominations" and "evil," and they "defile themselves" through "harlotry," "dishonesty," "lust," and "lewdness." He concludes that, in a word, the Jews are *scum*.

The author then threatens the Jews with great punishments for their bad behavior. He promises to "pour out fury" on the Jews and "deal furiously" with them by "devouring" them "with fire." He tells them that he will deliver them "naked" into the hands of "those who hate you."

The author is the prophet Ezekiel conveying the words of God. Ezekiel was hardly alone in his harsh criticism. All of the Hebrew prophets had some very tough things to say about their fellow Jews. In fact, Moses himself referred to the Jews as "stiff-necked" people. Yet the Hebrew prophets were by no means anti-Semites. They were Jews who spoke harshly to their own people in an effort to save them from the wrath of God. Tough love is not a modern concept.

Were Ezekiel's exact words to issue from someone else's mouth, however, the statement could mark the height of anti-Semitism. Hitler used similar language when discussing the Jews, but toward an altogether different end. Thus in judging whether a statement is anti-Semitic, context is crucial. The actions and intent of the speaker are typically far more important to the analysis than the words themselves.

Echoing this theme, Protestant scholar Franklin Littell cautioned his fellow Christians:

> John the Baptist or Paul of Tarsus, who would have perished in a Death Camp, had the right to speak harshly to their fellow Jews.... An American Gentile Christian, whose government was silently complicit in the Holocaust and whose cobelievers...shared in the operation of the camps, has no ground on which to stand validly to criticize "the Jews."[2]

ANTI-SEMITISM PROVED ITSELF to be the most deadly hatred of the twentieth century. The record from prior centuries only confirms the danger. The charge of anti-Semitism, therefore, remains a charge of enormous severity. It is a point of view for which no excuse can be made.

The charge of anti-Semitism has been leveled against some of America's leading Christian Zionists. This claim is of an entirely different nature than the standard critique of Christian Zionism discussed in the prior chapter. Any Christian Zionist found guilty of this crime must be shunned by civil society. Such individuals are not fit to be allies in any cause or partners in any coalition.

These allegations must be thoroughly examined. Jews have learned through bitter experience never to ignore possible signs of anti-Semitism. Those who dismissed Hitler's anti-Semitism as meaningless talk likely perished in his gas chambers. Those who took his words seriously were often able to escape the consequences of his actions. They lived to share their lesson that anti-Semitic speech must never be taken lightly. As Abraham Foxman has noted, "The gas chambers and crematoria in Auschwitz did not begin with bricks, they began with words."[3]

Yet while maintaining this heightened vigilance, the Jewish community must also maintain its common sense and decency. If the charge of anti-Semitism is to retain its enormous power, then it must not be leveled frivolously. Distinctions must be made between this hatred so grave and lesser crimes of insensitivity or ignorance. All suspect comments must be taken seriously. But conclusions must be reached, not jumped to.

Above all, the inquiry into anti-Semitism must focus on context. In the absence of confessed anti-Semitism, comments must be examined in light of all relevant evidence to determine what they reveal about the speaker's heart. A critical comment spoken by someone who has a history of such remarks and has never lifted a finger to help the Jewish people is likely anti-Semitic. The same comment by a committed Jew or a lifelong friend of the Jews is probably more benign. The fact that the same comment is often perceived so differently by members of the same community largely reflects the different assumptions they are making about context. Those who presume that the speaker harbors ill intent are far more likely to find fault with that speaker's words.

EARLY DISPENSATIONALIST ANTI-SEMITISM

IN 1933, A leading dispensationalist named Arno Gaebelein wrote a book titled *The Conflict of the Ages*. Here, Gaebelein warned of a number of conspiracies threatening Christian America. Among those he cited were conspiracies orchestrated by a secret society called the Illuminati, the Roman Catholic Church, international socialists, and the Jews. In support of his assertion of an international Jewish conspiracy, Gaebelein cited the *Protocols of the Elders of Zion*, a notorious czarist forgery alleging a Jewish plot to control the world.[4] When Henry Ford published excerpts of the *Protocols* in his *Dearborn Independent* newspaper, Gaebelein applauded the disclosure, remarking that "all true Jews will be grateful for an exposé like the one published by the *Independent*."[5] A few other dispensationalist leaders, including Charles C. Cook and William Riley, also embraced the *Protocols* and used them to argue that the Jews played a central part in the international threat to American civilization.[6]

In expressing these anti-Semitic views, these Christian leaders were not introducing any new ideas to the American public. Such opinions were common at the time, especially in conservative, anti-Roosevelt circles. The only surprise was that some dispensationalists were joining the chorus. The dispensationalists, after all, had broken with replacement theology and embraced the Jews as God's chosen people. Now some of the movement's leaders were turning their backs on this core message to single the Jews out as a source of evil.

Dispensationalism, it appears, does not completely inoculate its adherents from anti-Semitism. They are still fallible human beings, subject to infection by the anti-Semitism prevalent in the surrounding culture. In fact, there may be something inherent in dispensationalism itself that works counter to its other teachings and opens the door to a belief in such conspiracy theories. Dispensationalists typically view the world as a battlefield between the forces of Satan and the forces of God. This belief that Satan is actively plotting in the world may predispose the believer to see plots and conspiracies where others do not. As religion scholar George Marsden has asserted about the dispensationalists:

> The conspiracy theories did...appeal to their general disposition of thought. Like their premillennialism, the political threats could be placed in the framework of the conflict between the forces of God and Satan. The two types of conspiracy theory, the political and the religious, might well have appealed to a single mind-set in such a way as to override the difficulty of reconciling specific details.[7]

Thus Gaebelein cannot be simply dismissed as a dispensationalist aberration. Gaebelein stands instead as a sign that anti-Semitism can infiltrate even an inherently philo-Semitic movement. Decades after Arno Gaebelein was dead and buried, another leading dispensationalist would write another book warning of a very similar international conspiracy.

PAT ROBERTSON AND *THE NEW WORLD ORDER*

IN 1991, PAT Robertson wrote a book called *The New World Order,* which rose to number four on the *New York Times'* best-seller list. The book was timely. America had just won the Gulf War at the head of a large, international coalition. The Bush administration had announced that this successful effort marked the beginning of a "new world order" in which the international community would work in concert to enforce the rule of international law. While Pat Robertson agreed that a new world order was in fact emerging, he dissented sharply from the prevailing optimism. Robertson warned that the new world order would be one in which a small cabal of international bankers seized control of the world and all of its wealth.

Robertson neither alleged nor believed that President Bush and his predecessors were willing participants in this dark conspiracy. He knew some of these men, after all, and had in some cases been their political ally. Instead, Robertson suggested that these leaders were unwitting dupes of the plotters. In Robertson's words:

> It may well be that men of goodwill like Woodrow Wilson, Jimmy Carter, and George Bush, who sincerely want a larger community of nations living at peace in our world, are in reality unknowingly and

> unwittingly carrying out the mission and mouthing the phrases of a tightly knit cabal whose goal is nothing less than a new order for the human race under the domination of Lucifer and his followers.[8]

Robertson explains in *The New World Order* that this conspiracy is centuries old. We are told that the Illuminati, a Bavarian secret society, launched the conspiracy in the late eighteenth century to gain control of the world's wealth. The first phase of their plot required establishing strong central governments, with centralized financial institutions, that could extract the wealth of the nations under their control and deliver it to the conspirators. Toward this end, Robertson writes, the Illuminati and their partners in crime—the Freemasons and certain financial elites—established the Bank of England and engineered the French Revolution and the Russian Revolution.

According to Robertson, the United States, with the power of its government limited by the Constitution, posed a special challenge to the conspirators. In order to extract America's vast wealth efficiently, the conspirators needed to create a central bank that could borrow money from international finance. They also needed to impose a federal income tax to generate the revenue to pay off these debts. Accordingly, Robertson explains, the conspirators engineered the election of Woodrow Wilson as president in 1912. Wilson supported both the creation of the Federal Reserve and a Constitutional amendment legalizing a federal income tax.

Once the requisite institutions were in place in the world's financial centers, the next step was to create a pretext for these central banks to engage in large-scale borrowing. Robertson claims that the conspirators therefore provoked two world wars and a cold war and in each case engineered the entry of the United States into the conflict. As planned, these wars were financed by large public debts owed to international financiers. Since the conspirators controlled the leading houses of international finance, they were the ones to reap the enormous profits that poured in through the payment of compound interest on these large debts.

Robertson warns that the final step in this conspiracy is to combine these strong central governments into one world government with one centralized economy. Then the citizens of the world will be nothing more than tax serfs earning money and sending it through their taxes to the new masters of the universe. To Robertson, the great international cooperation under UN auspices during the Gulf War was startling evidence that this final phase of the conspiracy was under way.

Among the individuals Robertson places at the center of the global conspiracy are a group he refers to as the "European bankers." Robertson mentions many of these bankers by name. He writes that the Rothschild banking family likely provided the Illuminati with their first entrée into the world of high finance, and that a "German radical" named Moses Hess first connected the Illuminati with the budding Communist movement. Robertson notes that the Rothschilds worked hard to accomplish another key component of the conspiracy: saddling the United States with a central bank. According to Robertson, the Rothschilds were instrumental in creating the Bank of the United States in 1816, but were foiled when Andrew Jackson later shut it down. Not a family to give up easily, the Rothschilds allegedly sent their "associate" Paul Warburg, of Kuhn, Loeb and Company, to the United States in 1902 to resuscitate the national bank in the form of the Federal Reserve. Robertson further notes that Jacob Schiff, the head of Kuhn, Loeb and Company, gave $20 million to the struggling Russian Communists in 1917 and "no doubt saved their revolution."

Not all of the "European bankers" that Robertson names in *The New World Order* have Jewish last names. But as the examples given above indicate, many of these individuals were in fact Jewish. The most serious critiques of *The New World Order* focus on the fact that so many of the key participants in Robertson's conspiracy theory are Jews.

In *The New World Order,* Pat Robertson writes that, "Authors who expose subversive secret organizations are usually ridiculed. . . ."[9] This is one of the only predictions Robertson made in the book that turned out to be accurate. His book has been widely criticized for indulging in conspiracy theory and for failing to document many of its central allegations. More seriously, some critics of Robertson's book have argued that it is anti-Semitic.

A few years after *The New World Order* had climbed to number four on the *New York Times'* best-seller list, two critiques of the book appeared in the *New York Review of Books.* On February 2, 1995, Michael Lind published an article titled "Rev. Robertson's Grand International Conspiracy Theory." On

April 20, 1995, Jacob Heilbrunn followed up with a piece titled "His Anti-Semitic Sources." These belated reviews sparked a major controversy over Robertson's work.

Lind and Heilbrunn both argue that the Robertson's theory about an international plot for world domination is substantially similar to the theories of a handful of openly anti-Semitic writers. Lind focuses on the parallels between Robertson's thesis and the views of a Canadian writer, William Guy Carr, whom Lind describes as a defender of Hitler and fascism. Heilbrunn documents the even closer parallels between Robertson's work and the books of an anti-Semitic author named Nesta Webster.

Through a close textual comparison, Heilbrunn demonstrates that Robertson clearly paraphrases Webster's work in certain passages of *The New World Order*. Robertson by no means denies this reliance upon Webster: he lists her as a source in his bibliography and quotes directly from her books in his text. In introducing one of these quotes, Robertson notes that "British author Nesta Webster researched and wrote extensively on subversive movements."[10]

Having established this connection, Heilbrunn then reveals some troubling details about Nesta Webster. Heilbrunn points out that Webster's book *Secret Societies and Subversive Movements*—the book that Robertson cites in his bibliography—contains a chapter entitled "The Real Jewish Peril." Here Webster suggests that the notorious anti-Semitic czarist forgery *The Protocols of the Elders of Zion* may in fact be genuine, and she includes a copy of this work in her appendix. Another chapter in Webster's book—the chapter from which Robertson takes a direct quote—includes a series of anti-Semitic passages. Among these is the observation, in reference to the rise of Communism, that:

> There is another power at work, a power far older, that seeks to destroy all national spirit, all ordered government in every country, Germany included. What is this power? A large body of opinion replies: the Jewish power.[11]

There is one major difference between Robertson's book and the anti-Semitic books it borrows from. As both Lind and Heilbrunn note, Robertson eliminates all of the overt references to Jews. Where Webster and others explicitly reference Jews and Jewish plots, Robertson mentions only individual actors by their names—many of whom are recognizably Jewish.

PAT ROBERTSON PUBLICLY responded to the controversy provoked by the Lind and Heilbrunn articles in two communications to the *New York Times*. While he renounced neither his sources nor the central thesis of *The New World Order*, he directly challenged the charge of anti-Semitism. In a letter to the editor of the *New York Times* printed on March 5, 1995, Robertson defended his book by focusing on the work's pro-Israel theme. Robertson notes that:

> My primary objection was that a United Nations–driven foreign policy could ultimately be directed against the security interest of Israel. That there was enormous international pressure on Israel not to respond to Iraqi Scud missile attacks against its civilian population during the Persian Gulf war demonstrates that my concern is legitimate.[12]

Robertson notes that he has been a long-standing friend and defender of Israel and concludes, "If that is anti-Semitism, then it is the most bizarre and self-defeating anti-Semitism ever uttered."[13]

In a "statement" to the *New York Times* published on March 4, 1995, Robertson denied that his references to "European bankers" were coded anti-Semitism:

> I deeply regret that anyone in the Jewish community believes that my description of international bankers and use of the phrase "European bankers" in my book refers to Jews. As chairman of one of the nation's largest and most widely respected cable television companies whose stock is traded daily on the New York Stock Exchange, it has been my experience that the international financial community is very diverse and can hardly be characterized as Jewish. Further, I have never intentionally used what some would describe as code words to portray Jewish business interests. I condemn and repudiate in the strongest terms those who would use such code words as a cover for anti-Semitism.
>
> If my statements were misunderstood, I offer my sincere regrets. I never intended to offend my Jewish colleagues who I consider to be dear friends and allies.[14]

To PROPERLY JUDGE the charge of anti-Semitism against Pat Robertson, all of the relevant facts must be placed in their proper context. The first and most immediate context is that of the book itself. As Robertson accurately notes in his letter to the *New York Times*, there is nothing overtly anti-Semitic in *The New World Order*. Quite to the contrary, the Jews—and Israel in particular—are among the heroes of the piece.

Robertson writes that humanity can be divided into two camps. On the one side are those of the "Abrahamic, monotheistic" tradition, the people whose beliefs "flowed from Abraham to the Jewish race and then to the Christians of the world."[15] These people put God in the center of the world and seek to serve Him. To Robertson, these Christians and Jews are the good guys.

In the opposing camp are people who put man at the center of the world and seek to rebel against God. To Robertson, these are the people who staged the "first attempt to build a new world order" when they started building the Tower of Babel. And, according to Robertson, these are the people responsible for the current attempt to build a new world order through the United Nations. Robertson notes that the Gulf War was significant in that the United Nations action to authorize the use of military force against Iraq was "the first time since Babel that all of the nations of the earth acted in concert with one another."[16]

Robertson warns that, once in power, the enemies of God will target the people of God. In his words, "This means very simply that the world government of the new world order will one day become an instrument of oppression against the Christians and Jews around the world."[17]

In particular, Robertson fears that the growing power of the United Nations is a threat to Israel. He argues, convincingly, that Israel is likely to be the next victim of such concerted international military action:

> It is also clear that Satan's strategy will include a frontal assault on Israel. Rest assured that the next objective of the presently constituted new world order, under the present United Nations, will be to make Israel its target....
>
> A recalcitrant nation whose action does not accord with United Nations policy may be disciplined by military force. That is the newest

> law of world order. The United Nations General Assembly has already voted to brand Zionism as racism. Surely we can expect, sooner or later, an unreasonable demand for Israel to vacate control of the West Bank and the half of her capital city in East Jerusalem.... And if Israel refuses to vacate the Holy City, there will be war—under the world order as it is even now constituted.[18]

Beyond *The New World Order*, the charge of anti-Semitism must also be examined in a second, broader context: that of Robertson's long career. *The New World Order* was hardly the first time that Robertson spoke or acted in reference to the Jews.

During a 2003 visit to Israel, Pat Robertson was invited to address the prestigious Herzliya Conference on Security. Here, Robertson started off with some observations about Jewish history:

> One day in the late 19th Century, Queen Victoria of England reportedly asked her Prime Minister, Benjamin Disraeli, this question: "Mr. Prime Minister, what evidence can you give me of the existence of God?"
>
> Disraeli thought for a moment and replied, "The Jew, your majesty."
>
> Think of it. According to Disraeli the primary evidence that God exists is the existence of the Jewish people. A people who in 586 BC were deported to Babylon, yet returned after seventy years to rebuild a nation. Who were again brutally massacred and dispersed by the Romans in 70 AD, yet after countless centuries of Diaspora, expulsions, pogroms, ghettos, and attempts at genocidal extermination, have clung to their faith, their customs. And now after some 2,500 years of wandering have returned to the land promised by God to their ancestors. A new nation began in that land in 1948 named after their ancestor Jacob, whose divinely appointed name means "Prince with God"...
>
> Yes, the survival of the Jewish people is a miracle of God. The return of the Jewish people to the land promised to Abraham, Isaac and Jacob is a miracle of God. The remarkable victories of Jewish armies against overwhelming odds in successive battles in 1948, 1967 and 1973 are clearly miracles of God.[19]

In Herzliya, as he has done in many other places on many other occasions, Pat Robertson demonstrated a passion for Jewish history that few other speakers can muster. Such enthusiasm for Jewish survival is the antithesis of anti-Semitism. Anti-Semites simply don't see Jewish victories as "miracles of God."

Robertson closed his Herzliya speech with a story he has told many pro-Israel audiences.

> On Christmas Day in 1974, I had the privilege of interviewing Prime Minister Yitzhak Rabin for my television program, *The 700 Club*. Rabin lamented the fact that after Israeli military victories, the nation had been stopped from achieving a peace treaty....
>
> That evening...I began to recall the feeling of sadness which had come from the Prime Minister—the sense of isolation of his nation. That evening, I made a solemn vow to God that, despite whatever might happen in the future, I and the organizations I headed would stand in support of Israel and the Jewish people. Ladies and gentlemen, I am proud to say that I have kept that vow each year since 1974.[20]

The audience in Herzliya that day was filled with Israel's sophisticated, mostly secular elite. Upon hearing these words from an evangelical preacher, the crowd rose to their feet in a standing ovation.[21]

Robertson's closing flourish happened to be a statement of fact. He has been a steadfast and consistent supporter of Israel ever since that 1974 meeting. Robertson has repeatedly lobbied presidents and members of Congress to support Israel and has intensified this effort in recent years. He constantly speaks out in defense of Israel to his massive Christian Broadcasting Network audience. At his Regent University, he educates new generations of Christian leaders to support the Jewish State. Robertson has visited Israel so many times that he has lost count—he thinks it is around sixteen times.[22] And he has given hundreds of thousands of dollars to Jewish charities.[23]

THUS WHEN PLACED in its proper context, *The New World Order* emerges as an overtly pro-Israel book written by an outspoken friend of Israel and the Jews. In order to find anti-Semitism in Robertson's work, one must connect a series of dots with the help of some significant research. Unfortunately, true anti-Semites tend to be far less subtle. As Robertson himself has noted, it is a bizarre anti-Semitism indeed that seeks to attack the Jews by making a passionate argument in their defense.

Still there remains some troubling aspects of *The New World Order*, namely Robertson's propagation of a conspiracy theory with anti-Semitic undertones and his reliance upon, and failure to denounce, some of the anti-Semitic sources upon which he relied. How does one reconcile these concerns with Robertson's lifetime of philo-Semitic and pro-Israel words and deeds? Robertson's critics suggest an explanation. They assert that Robertson loves Israel—a theological concept—not the Jews themselves. As we have seen, such critics suggest that Robertson and the other Christian Zionists support Israel only to speed the Second Coming of Christ, at which time the Jews will be killed or converted. The Robertson they conjure up is a profoundly psychopathic man, one capable of hiding his nefarious agenda beneath a smiling mask of love for the Jews.

This argument is unsatisfying. As we've seen in chapter three, dispensationalists like Robertson do not believe that they can actually speed the Second Coming through their actions. Nor do they seek to use support for Israel as a wedge to convert Jews in the here and now. Christian Zionists support Israel for a series of more positive reasons, of which Robertson himself has been an outspoken advocate. Robertson often invokes the Christian debt to the Jews for the fundamentals of their faith. And he repeatedly reminds audiences that if they wish God's blessing, they had better bless the Jews.

There is another way of reconciling Robertson's pro-Israel career with his questionable book that conforms better to the record. Robertson is not an anti-Semite who happens to support Israel. Rather, Robertson is a friend of the Jews and Israel who happens to believe that individual Jews are capable of poor behavior. Just because an individual is born Jewish or Christian does not mean that they will walk blameless through life. Thus while to Robertson most Christians and Jews are indeed "God's people," he believes that others have strayed into the camp of Lucifer and the international plotters.

Finding fault with the actions of individual Jews does not make someone anti-Semitic. Such criticism crosses the line into the forbidden only when the criticism of individuals who happen to be Jewish spills over, explicitly or implicitly, into a criticism of the collective, the Jews. To disagree with a few Jews here and there is normal. To criticize only or mostly Jews for all of the ills of the world is anti-Semitic. The real question is, does Robertson in any way project criticism outward from the individuals to the people?

Robertson has avoided crossing this line. In *The New World Order* Robertson does not make any overt reference to a Jewish role in his great international conspiracy. He limits his critique to the actions of certain individuals, some of whom happen to be Jews. In fact, the only statements in *The New World Order* that refer to the Jews as a group are statements that *praise* the Jews. For Robertson, the collective, the Jews, are blessed.

Pat Robertson is not an anti-Semite. He is a friend of the Jewish community who sometimes criticizes the behavior of individual Jews. Yet even friends can embrace ideas that are dangerous for the Jews. For that matter, Jews themselves can embrace ideas that are dangerous for the Jews. Many Jews, for example, helped build the totalitarian Soviet state that later devoured much of its Jewish population. Before the enormity of his crimes against humanity came to light, Stalin's portrait occupied a place of honor in kibbutz dining halls and Jewish living rooms. These were not anti-Semites; they are just people with some dangerous ideas.

The problem with *The New World Order* is not that it is anti-Semitic, but that it contains some dangerous ideas. Spreading conspiracy theories involving Jews, even if Jews are not singled out, helps convince people that such conspiracies are real. If people believe in the general scenario, it will be that much easier for an anti-Semite to come along and fill in the blanks with Jewish details. *The New World Order* resuscitates, propagates, and lends credibility to some typically anti-Jewish conspiracy theories. Pat Robertson has never renounced the ideas expressed in his book or even the anti-Semitic sources he cites. He should have. Given his deep knowledge of Jewish history, Pat Robertson of all people should understand the danger of providing fodder to anti-Semites.

Norman Podhoretz, one of the deans of the neo-conservative movement, employed a helpful analogy from Jewish law to exonerate Pat Robertson from the charge of anti-Semitism in a 1995 *Commentary* article. According to the Talmud, food that is otherwise permitted by Jewish dietary law ceases to be kosher if a forbidden ingredient gets mixed into it. If a piece of bacon falls into your bowl of chicken soup, you're out of luck. But what if the bacon falls, not into a bowl of soup, but into a large vat of soup? Isn't there some point at which a contaminant is so small by comparison that it will no longer taint the larger, kosher portion?

This concept—that an impurity can represent so minute a percentage of the whole as to be nullified—is captured in the rabbinic rule of *batel b'shishim* (literally "canceled by the rule of one-sixtieth"). Under this principle, if the nonkosher contaminant has slipped into the food unintentionally, and if it represents no more than one-sixtieth of the whole, then the food remains kosher. An Orthodox rabbi can eat it with gusto.

Employing this concept, Podhoretz reached the following conclusion about the problematic passages in *The New World Order*:

> Taking it all for all...I would still maintain that the contamination represented by those passages, when set within the context of Robertson's record as a whole, can be considered *batel b'shishim*, and that Robertson can and should be absolved on that basis of the charge of anti-Semitism.[24]

PAT ROBERTSON AND *THE NEW MILLENNIUM*

The New World Order is not the only controversial book Pat Robertson has written. In his article for the *New York Review of Books*, Michael Lind is highly critical of a passage from Robertson's 1990 book, *The New Millennium*. In his otherwise supportive *Commentary* article, Norman Podhoretz takes exception to the same words. Both men quote the objectionable lines from *The New Millennium* as follows:

> The part that Jewish intellectuals and media activists have played in the assault on Christianity may very possibly prove to be a grave mistake....For centuries, Christians have supported the dream of Zion, and they have supported Jews in their dream of a national homeland. But American Jews invested great energy in attacking these very allies. That investment may pay a terrible dividend....[25]

As quoted, Robertson appears to be making a chilling, thinly veiled threat against his Jewish critics. The reader is left with the distinct impression that

Robertson is warning that continued Jewish criticism of conservative Christians will be a "grave mistake" because it will drive the Christian masses to "pay a terrible dividend" to the Jews in some form of Christian backlash. Robertson seems to be trying to stifle Jewish political speech with the threat of a modern-day pogrom. As presented, this is a profoundly troubling comment.

Yet there is a serious problem with the way this quote is presented. The quote combines text from two different paragraphs in *The New Millennium*. In two places, noted by the ellipses, key sentences that more fully explain the thrust of Robertson's comments are left out. When one reads the full text of the quote, it becomes clear that Robertson is making no so such threat of Christian retribution against Jews.

As quoted above, Robertson writes: "The part that Jewish intellectuals and media activists have played in the assault on Christianity may very possibly prove to be a grave mistake." Why is this a mistake? The next line, left out of the quote used by Lind and Podhoretz, continues: "It is beginning to appear that support for Israel in America may already have been weakened in the political arena, and soon the Christians may be in no condition to help."[26]

In the following paragraph, Robertson writes, as quoted above, that the Jewish effort to attack Christians is an investment that "may pay a terrible dividend." Then the next sentence, also left out of the Lind and Podhoretz quote, reads "If a shift should come in America's public opinion toward Israel, the Christians who stood for them throughout the ages may not be able to reverse the trend."[27]

When the full text is provided, it is clear that Robertson is not threatening any Christian retaliation against the Jews. Instead, he merely notes that to the extent Jews help weaken conservative Christians as a political force in America, these same Christians will be less able to help Israel when that support is needed most. He is appealing to Jewish self-interest, asking the community not to attack its true friends. In Robertson's words, liberal attacks will weaken "the moral consensus that has supported Israel from the start."[28] This is a fair point.

Ironically, the quotes at the center of this controversy come from a chapter of *The New Millennium* entitled, "The Rise of Anti-Semitism." Here, Robertson warns about the spread of anti-Semitism across Europe. Robertson fears that this rising tide of anti-Semitism will eventually lead the world to turn against Israel and that even Israel's one true friend, the United States, may one day abandon her. This is a result that Robertson desperately wants to avoid. Robertson notes that:

> So long as this nation has any concern for God's favor, we cannot turn our backs on Israel. Throughout scripture, the prophets warned that God will judge the nations that stand against Israel. Intolerance in any quarter is wrong, but insomuch as we are able, we must ensure that the trend throughout the 1990s remains in favor of a Jewish homeland in Israel and not for the elimination of the Jews.[29]

Thus Pat Robertson's oft quoted anti-Semitic threat is actually part of a plea to America not to abandon Israel in the face of increasing global anti-Semitism and for Jews not to hobble their own cause by weakening their strongest defenders. Placed in its proper context, Robertson's quote turns out to be the exact opposite of what it is purported to be. Such an outcome lends support to one rabbi's observation that, "If Pat Robertson is an anti-Semite, then we need more anti-Semites like him in this country."[30]

JERRY FALWELL

THE OTHER DEAN of American Christian Zionism, Jerry Falwell, has also been accused of anti-Semitism. In Falwell's case, criticism has centered on two allegedly anti-Semitic comments he made over the course of his career. As with Robertson, context is the key to determining just how seriously these comments should be taken.

At a pastor's conference in early 1999, Jerry Falwell rose to address the gathered churchmen. The speech was largely unremarkable until Falwell told the crowd that, in his view, the Antichrist is probably alive today, and, "Of course, he'll be Jewish."[31]

The Antichrist—for those who believe in such a thing—is someone who will pretend to be the Messiah and deceive the world in general and the Jewish community in particular. Since the Old Testament dictates that the Messiah must be Jewish, it would certainly be helpful for a pretender to this role also to be Jewish. There is a certain logic to Falwell's thesis.

The problem with this statement is not in Falwell's logic but in how his words may be interpreted by a broader audience. If the Antichrist is a Jew, and the Antichrist is evil, then there are some who may conclude from Falwell's words that the Jews as a whole are evil. Anti-Semites, after all, are not known for the clarity of their logic.

When confronted with this charge, Falwell did not retract his statement. His beliefs had not changed. But Falwell did apologize for the way in which his words were perceived. As he later noted:

> If I had known that the statement would be publicized widely and misconstrued as anti-Semitic, I would never have made it. I have since publicly apologized to any persons who were offended thereby, since expressing my opinion on such a sensitive matter is unimportant and serves no useful purpose. I continue to live and learn, and hopefully to develop greater sensitivity to the feelings of my dear Jewish and Christian friends worldwide.[32]

Falwell's apology satisfied his most vocal critics in the Jewish community. For example, Abraham Foxman, national director of the Anti-Defamation League, stated that Falwell's original comment regarding the Antichrist "borders on anti-Semitism at best, and is anti-Semitic at worst."[33] Foxman later welcomed Falwell's apology and expressed "appreciation" for Falwell's recognition that his comment had consequences for Christian-Jewish relations. According to Foxman, "The matter is now behind us."[34]

This first comment—on the religious affiliation of the Antichrist—is at least something that Falwell did in fact say. As for the second of Falwell's allegedly anti-Semitic comments, Falwell never actually said it. The words were wrongly attributed to him.

In August 1980, the Reverend Bailey Smith, then president of the Southern Baptist Conference, told an audience of 15,000, "With all due respect to those dear people, my friends, God Almighty does not hear the prayer of a Jew."[35] In discussing the quote, some news accounts mistakenly attributed this statement to Jerry Falwell.[36] Even after the mistake was clarified, and

Falwell stated point-blank that "I believe God hears the prayers of Jews,"[37] he continued to be criticized for "his" comment.*

In the heat of the 1980 presidential campaign, this misinformation about Jerry Falwell was spread far and wide. The Carter-Mondale campaign produced a commercial stating:

> Dr. Jerry Falwell has said that God does not hear the prayers of Jews. If Reagan goes on to the White House, Falwell will come with him, and they'll purify the land as someone else did years ago.[38]

This thirty-second spot, complete with Hitler analogy, was run repeatedly on 252 radio stations in areas with heavily Jewish populations. The Moral Majority immediately filed an $11 million lawsuit against the Carter-Mondale campaign. When the Carter team confirmed that Falwell did not actually say the words attributed to him, they withdrew the commercial, and Falwell withdrew the lawsuit.[39]

WHILE THESE TWO comments have received the most media attention, it doesn't take much digging to find additional comments Falwell has made over the years that would strike some as anti-Semitic. The only difference is that these comments were never reported in the mainstream press. For example, in an August 2001 sermon before his Thomas Road Baptist Church, Falwell discussed the fact that the Jews have returned to their land—have been physically reborn—but have yet to undergo spiritual rebirth through the acceptance of Christ. He then asked, "But why should the Jews turn to Jesus as their Messiah now after all these twenty centuries of spiritual blindness?"[40]

---

* According to the Anti-Defamation League, Falwell himself made a statement similar to the one made by Rev. Smith. Falwell is quoted as saying that God "does not hear the prayers of unredeemed Gentiles or Jews." This quote raises the issue of what it means to be "redeemed" and, by its inclusion of unredeemed Gentiles, is less likely to be mistaken as anti-Semitic. Falwell later retracted this statement. (*The Religious Right: The Assault on Tolerance and Pluralism in America* [New York: The Anti-Defamation League, 1994], 71.)

Spiritual blindness? Falwell could certainly have chosen more respectful words to express the theological disagreement between Christians and Jews over the nature of Jesus Christ. He should have. But are such dogmatic comments really anti-Semitic? Or is there a lesser offense involved? Falwell, after all, believes that Christ was the Messiah foretold in the Old Testament. Falwell further believes that the Jews failed to recognize their own Messiah when He was standing right in front of them. There is a name for such a system of beliefs—it is called Christianity.* No matter how he chooses to phrase things, Falwell is a believing Christian. He believes that the Jews failed to recognize the Messiah every bit as much as an Orthodox rabbi believes that the world's two billion Christians are praying to a false messiah. No matter how careful each side is—and *should* be—to show tolerance for those who adhere to a different view, these deeply held beliefs will find expression from time to time.

Falwell is well aware of this tension. As he has noted:

> Obviously an Orthodox Rabbi feels that the Christian's Messiah has not come and therefore the Christian has no basic and vital faith. Obviously, the traditional Christian minister believes that the Messiah has come and the Orthodox Rabbi did not recognize him, but is yet looking for the Messiah to come. Neither view is anti-Semitic or anti-Christian. Both are matters of interpretation based upon the views that each has derived from the Book of Books, the Bible.[41]

For an expression of Christian religious beliefs to cross the line into anti-Semitism, there must be an added element. The historical record is helpful in isolating what characterizes such excess. In the words of Jules Isaac, the church has spread anti-Semitism over the centuries by engaging in a systematic "teaching of contempt" for the Jews. This teaching of contempt has centered on two major themes. The first has been the accusation of deicide, that the Jews killed Christ. The second theme has been that of replacement—that when the Jews rejected Christ, they were in turn rejected by God and

* In fact, Falwell was likely paraphrasing the apostle Paul, who wrote in Romans 11:25 that "blindness in part has happened to Israel until the fullness of the Gentiles has come in."

replaced by the church as God's chosen people. This traditional teaching of contempt provides a helpful context within which to evaluate accusations of theological anti-Semitism.

Falwell has been outspoken in his rejection of these core aspects of the teaching of contempt. On the issue of replacement, Falwell is a dispensationalist—he flatly rejects the concept that the church has come to replace the Jews and asserts instead that the Jews are "very definitely" still God's chosen people.[42] As for the Crucifixion, Falwell embraces the standard evangelical view that Christ "willingly laid down his life for the sins of all humanity" and that therefore "every human being in every age contributed to his crucifixion."[43] As for those who assert that the Jews are Christ killers, Falwell notes simply: "It has been my observation that those persons who refer to Jews as 'Christ-killers' have a personal axe to grind—namely anti-Semitism."[44]

AS WITH PAT Robertson, Jerry Falwell's controversial statements must be judged in the broader context of the man's life. Falwell readily acknowledges being raised in an anti-Semitic climate. According to Falwell, "As a boy, I never heard of Jews. If he was a Jew, he was always a 'damn' Jew."[45]

There were few Jews in Lynchburg, Virginia, during Jerry Falwell's youth. Nor did Baptist Bible College in Missouri afford Falwell an opportunity to make Jewish friends. Yet Bible college introduced Jerry Falwell to the promises and prophecies relating to the Jews contained in the Bible. It is the Bible that drives Falwell's commitment to the Jewish people and Israel.

Falwell relates that it took some work to overcome the negative stereotypes of Jews he learned as a child.* But he relates that he did overcome such views and, with the zeal of a convert, dedicated himself to defending the Jews both at home and abroad. In 1984 Falwell told interviewer Merrill Simon that:

* Falwell also admits to having been racist in his younger years. It was only after he had been in the ministry for a number of years, he relates, that the gospel supplanted these earlier views. Falwell notes that, "There are those people who say they were never prejudiced, but I doubt it."

> When all of that [prejudice] was flushed out of my system, my commitment to the Jewish people became more than theological. I began to internalize what the Jews had experienced for thousands of years. I began to realize that the great need for Christian people, who claimed to believe in the Bible, to take what is often an unpopular stand and work to reverse the attitudes of a predominantly non-Jewish society against a very small segment of the world's population. There was a particular time in my life, perhaps fifteen years ago, when this became an obsession with me. As a Zionist and as one who, in the Christian community, is probably the most outspoken supporter of Israel and the Jewish people the world over, I would say that I have become a radical on the issue. I think that radicalism is needed at this point in history to compensate for the injury that has been inflicted upon the Jewish family, often in the name of God, by religious zealots.[46]

Falwell has put these words into practice. When he founded the Moral Majority in 1979, he made support for Israel one of the group's four organizing principles. He has been an active and a forceful political ally of Israel ever since. Falwell preaches a pro-Israel message to his millions of television viewers and teaches a pro-Israel curriculum to thousands of future evangelical leaders attending his Liberty University. Falwell has traveled to Israel over thirty times.[47] On almost all of these visits, Falwell has brought large student groups with him to strengthen their bond to the Jewish State.[48]

In 1994, the Anti-Defamation League published a book that sharply criticized the Religious Right and escalated tensions between the Jewish and evangelical communities. In an effort to heal the rift, a meeting was arranged between leaders from each community. As the session got underway, the ADL's Abraham Foxman criticized evangelical leaders for referring to America as a "Christian nation." He explained to those assembled, "Every time you say this is a Christian nation, it raises our antennas because of the history of what Christian nations have done to the Jews."[49]

According to Foxman, Falwell was at first resistant to Foxman's critique. "Come on, Abe," Foxman quotes him as saying, "get over it. That's not what I mean." But then, Foxman relates:

> At the end of the day, Falwell was speaking a different tone. "You know," he said, "I think I understand your feelings a little better now. It's true that I'm not responsible for past anti-Semitism. But I am responsible if the things I say stir up hurts or hatred today. From now on I intend to refer to America as a Judeo-Christian nation, which describes our heritage accurately."[50]

JERRY FALWELL HAS made a few comments over the years that, standing alone, may raise concerns of anti-Semitism. But these comments do not stand alone. They were made during the course of over twenty-five years of diligent *action* on behalf of Israel and the Jewish people. This broader context makes it difficult to maintain that these comments reflect something darker within. The worst one can say about Jerry Falwell is that his comments have at times reflected a lack of sensitivity to the effect they will have on his listeners, both Jewish and non-Jewish. To equate such an occasional lack of circumspection with anti-Semitism cheapens what should be a most serious accusation.

For the first fifty years after the Holocaust survivors bore witness to evil, brutality and bestiality. Now is the time for us, for our generation, to bear witness to goodness.[1]

—Abraham Foxman

Chapter Ten

TOWARD A NEW APPROACH

IN THE HILLS outside of Jerusalem, the Israelis have built a memorial to the greatest tragedy in Jewish history, the Holocaust. This memorial, called Yad Vashem, houses a large and graphic exhibition detailing the murder of six million Jews. This display achieves its intended effect: it is impossible to walk through it and not be burdened by the enormity of the crime that the Nazis and their henchmen committed against the Jewish people. Visitors exit the hall carrying a heavy weight.

Outside the museum, nestled in a wooded campus, Yad Vashem hosts a more uplifting memorial: the Garden of the Righteous Among Nations. Here, scattered among the trees, are plaques in honor of the thousands of non-Jews who risked their lives to save Jews during the Holocaust. This part of Yad Vashem also impacts the visitor's state of mind. A detailed display of the depths of human cruelty ends, in this garden, on a note of hope.

The Garden of the Righteous was not an afterthought. It is integral to Yad Vashem's moral mission. The 1953 Israeli law that established Yad Vashem *required* that the museum also honor "the Righteous Among the Nations who risked their lives to save Jews."[2] Israel's legislators understood that moral accounting must use a two-sided ledger. The moral clarity that required condemnation of the great evil of the Holocaust also demanded a tribute to the great good that somehow survived in its midst.

These Israelis were no doubt cognizant of the larger lesson that such a display would impart to visitors. After the Holocaust, the Jewish people could have succumbed to anguish and rage. They could have turned their backs on a Europe that had perpetrated upon them an atrocity of such proportions. But instead, the Jewish people chose life. They chose to remain engaged in the world and open to all who extended their hands in friendship. Israel's founders chose to do the hard work of sorting friend from foe on the basis of individual—not group—attributes. By placing the Garden of the Righteous in between the museum of past atrocities and the exit, Yad Vashem subtly instructs its visitors toward this nobler path.

In building the Garden of the Righteous, the founders of Yad Vashem also embraced and communicated a second important principle. They decided that actions—not motivations—are the only relevant measure by which to judge righteousness. The Garden of the Righteous does not discriminate on the basis of motivation. It honors *all* who saved Jews from the Holocaust no matter what led them to do so. The playboy Oskar Schindler is honored there. So are Christians who saved Jews out of a religious imperative. These Israelis understood that any motivation that could produce acts of love so brave is *a priori* a worthy motivation. They did not dare sit in judgment upon heroism so sublime.

SADLY, MANY IN the American Jewish community have not followed the lead of their Israeli cousins. While they may visit Yad Vashem, they often miss its more subtle point.

During the 1970s, an English comedy troupe named Monty Python achieved fame in America through its successful television show. One of the show's most popular sketches featured a trio of men clad in red cardinal robes bursting into a modern-day business meeting and shouting, "Nobody expects the Spanish Inquisition!" The Monty Python troupe had clearly never spent a lot of time with American Jews. Many in the American Jewish community still harbor a deep suspicion of robust Christianity and its practitioners. Scratch the surface of a born-again Christian, they suspect, and beneath it you will find Torquemada.

The time has come for the American Jewish community to reassess their views of evangelical Christians in general and Christian Zionists in particular. American Jews must embrace the model of Yad Vashem and do the hard work of sorting people by their actions instead of their group affiliations. In judging these actions, they must have the humility to recognize acts of love and grace despite a lingering discomfort with the motives that produce them.

The Jewish community should go ahead and scratch the surface of some Christian Zionists. They will not find a Spanish inquisitor lurking beneath. Instead, they may very well find a righteous Gentile.

Indeed, far from following the careful approach of Yad Vashem, leaders of the American Jewish community have at times quite tragically thrown the evil and the righteous together in the same exhibit. A theological revolution took place in the twentieth century in which the replacement theology that contributed so much to European anti-Semitism was supplanted as the dominant Christian view. In its place, a new theology, which preaches love for the Jews, gained ascendance. Christian Zionists are not the modern descendants of the Christian anti-Semites who dominated the European church for centuries. On the contrary, in embracing this new theology Christian Zionists are the ideological heirs of the righteous Gentiles who saved Jews during the Holocaust.

To compare today's Christian Zionists with the righteous Gentiles of the Holocaust smacks of hyperbole. It is thus important to clarify the limits of the comparison. To say that Christian Zionists are the *ideological* heirs of the righteous Gentiles does not mean that they have also inherited their bravery or their selflessness. The presence of such extraordinary human qualities is impossible to gauge in the absence of the life-or-death situations that demand them. Nor does the comparison mean to imply that all who claim the title "Christian Zionist" are in fact righteous or even decent individuals. In any ideological movement there are scoundrels as well as saints. The comparison is simply, but significantly, one of theology. Sincere Christian Zionists are driven by the same theology that motivated righteous Gentiles during World War II.

Christian Zionists seek to apply the theology of the righteous Gentiles in a changed world. During World War II, Europe was the central front in the battle for Jewish survival. The Jews needed a place to hide, and helping them meant hiding them. Today, that front has shifted to the Middle East. While anti-Semitism continues to pose a very real danger for Jews around the world, it no longer threatens their communities with destruction. Instead, the larger questions of Jewish continuity and survival are now bound up in Israel. The true existential threats facing the Jewish people today are those directed at their Jewish State. It is no surprise, then, to find those seeking to fulfill the legacy of the righteous Gentiles rallying around the Israeli flag.

There is a surprisingly straight ideological line from the righteous Gentiles of the Holocaust down to the Christian Zionists of today. An exploration of what motivated some Christian rescuers and how their legacy is being interpreted by Christians today provides moving testimony to this continuity. A trip into the past sheds a very new light on these present-day friends.

THE TEN BOOM FAMILY

WHEN THE NAZIS invaded the Netherlands in 1940, Corrie ten Boom was sharing a comfortable, quiet life with her family in the city of Haarlem. Corrie lived with her father and her sister Betsie in a narrow townhouse built above their father's watch shop. Corrie and Betsie, both unmarried, cared for their aging father and helped him in the store. Corrie's sister Nollie and brother, Willem, and their children lived nearby and rounded out the tight-knit clan.

This peaceful existence was shattered when the Nazis started arresting Haarlem's Jews. According to Corrie, she and her family never made a conscious decision to hide Jews in their home. Jews simply started showing up asking for help, and the ten Booms could not refuse them.[3] As the early trickle turned into a steady stream, the ten Booms found themselves at the helm of a large and complex underground operation. At the time of their arrest in 1944, the ten Booms had organized a network of more than eighty volunteers who had rescued more than seven hundred Jews.[4]

The entire ten Boom family was involved in the rescue operation. Corrie and Betsie ran the operational center out of their small home and secured the extra ration cards needed to feed the constant stream of Jews passing through. Corrie's brother, Willem, found safe houses in the country to which to transport the Jews who came to the family home in Haarlem. Corrie's nephews, Kik and Peter, helped ferry the Jews out to the country under cover of darkness.

On February 28, 1944, the Nazis raided the ten Boom home. The Gestapo arrested Corrie ten Boom, her father, her brother, and her two sisters. At the time of the raid, there were six outsiders in the ten Boom home—two Dutch resistance workers and four Jews. All six ran to a hiding place in Corrie's bedroom built for such an emergency and escaped with their lives. Corrie's elderly father, Casper, was offered the opportunity to return home if he promised to stop saving Jews. He responded, "If I go home today, tomorrow I will open my door again to any man in need who knocks."[5]

The ten Boom family paid dearly for their heroism. Casper ten Boom became sick in prison and died ten days after his arrest. Corrie's nephew, Kik, was sent to a concentration camp from which he never returned. Corrie's brother, Willem, survived the concentration camps but emerged terribly ill. He died shortly after the war. Corrie and Betsie were deported to Ravensbruck, a female concentration camp in Germany. Betsie died there from the brutal conditions. Corrie survived to tell their story.

The ten Booms' motives

On February 28, 1968, the State of Israel formally recognized the ten Boom family as righteous Gentiles. An official ceremony in their honor was held at the Yad Vashem Holocaust memorial in Jerusalem. Corrie ten Boom planted a tree and gave a short address. In that speech, she shared what motivated her and her family to risk their lives to save Jews:

> I remember Nollie [her sister] telling me: "We love the Jews because we can thank them for the two greatest treasures. First of all, a Book written by the Jews. It is the Bible and we must thank Israel for it. It is the book which is almost bursting with good news and glorious promises. All its writers were Jews, except Luke, but he was converted through a Jew." I want to thank you, the Jews, for this Book. For the Bible has shown me the way to the second blessing which Nollie mentioned. It got me acquainted with my greatest Friend. He was a Jew. On His divine side He was the Son of God, but on His human side He was a Jew. And this friend is my Savior![6]

Corrie represented her family well at Yad Vashem. The ten Booms saved Jews because they felt a deep Christian devotion to the Jewish people. The family's love affair with "God's people" was actually a family tradition started by Corrie's grandfather. In 1844, Willem ten Boom initiated a weekly prayer meeting "for Israel" in his house. The group prayed for the peace of Jerusalem, the return of the Jews to their ancient homeland, and the welfare of the Jewish people. Corrie later observed that her grandfather's fervent prayers came true a century later when his son and four of his grandchildren were arrested in that very house for helping to save Jewish lives.[7]

Willem's son, and Corrie's father, Casper ten Boom, carried on the family tradition. In his words: "Love for the Jews was spoon-fed to me from my very youngest years."[8] Casper ten Boom did not merely love Jews on some abstract theological plain, but he treasured them as friends in the here and now. Corrie relates in her book *The Hiding Place* how as a young girl she used to travel with her father to visit watch wholesalers in Amsterdam:

> Many of these were Jews, and these were the visits we both liked best. After the briefest possible discussion of business, Father would draw a small Bible from his traveling case; the wholesaler, whose beard would be even longer and fuller than Father's, would snatch a book or a scroll out of a drawer, clap a prayer cap onto his head; and the two of them would be off, arguing, comparing, interrupting, contradicting—reveling in each other's company.[9]

When the Nazis occupied Holland, they forced the Jews to wear a yellow Star of David for easy identification. Casper ten Boom requested his own yellow star to stand in solidarity with the Jews, and he continued to doff his hat to every Jew he met.[10] When asked if he feared going to prison for saving Jews, Casper replied, "I am too old for prison life, but if that should happen, then it would be, for me, an honor to give my life for God's ancient people, the Jews."[11] Tragically, this was an honor that Casper ten Boom would receive.

Corrie's brother, Willem, inherited the family love for the Jews. After becoming a pastor in the Dutch Reformed Church, Willem became horrified by the new, racial anti-Semitism that was gaining strength in Europe. He returned to school to study the phenomenon and wrote a doctoral thesis titled *The Birth of Modern Racial Anti-Semitism in France and Germany*. Willem wrote his thesis in Germany, in 1925, while Adolf Hitler was still sitting in a Munich prison. Yet Willem could feel the coming storm in his bones. He wrote to his wife from Germany:

> I expect that in a few years time, there will be worse pogroms than ever before. Countless Jews from the east will come across the border seeking refuge in our country. We must prepare for that situation.[12]

Upon returning home to Holland, Willem put these beliefs into practice. While Corrie may never have planned to get into the Jewish rescue business, brother Willem most certainly did. The network of safe homes he developed during the prewar years, including his own home fitted with a hiding place under the floor boards, provided safe refuge for the hundreds of Jews that came to Corrie's Haarlem house seeking help.

Corrie's Legacy

Christians today seeking to fulfill the legacy of Corrie ten Boom and her family are faced with a challenge. What do righteous Gentiles do to demonstrate their love of the Jewish people when Jews no longer need to be hidden in their homes? What existential dangers do Jews face today, and what can Christians do to help? For most evangelicals seeking to walk in Corrie's footsteps, the path has led to Israel.

Immediately after her release from the Ravensbruck concentration camp, Corrie ten Boom returned to Haarlem, to the old, now empty, family home. And she began to share her experience with all who would listen. One night, she was invited to speak at the home of a local lawyer. With the shades drawn shut to keep the proceedings secret from the German soldiers still patrolling the streets, Corrie ten Boom told her story.

Among those listening that evening was the host's five-year-old son. The boy, Jan Willem van der Hoeven, still remembers that evening and the impression it made on him. Even as a youngster, he recalls, he began to pray for "Aunt" Corrie. And when he was a little older, he began to read the articles that Corrie wrote for a Dutch Christian magazine. Young Jan Willem had found his hero.[13]

Fast forward to the summer of 1980. Israel has declared the city of Jerusalem to be its "eternal and indivisible capital." By including contested East Jerusalem within the area so designated, the Israelis unleashed a storm of international criticism. In protest, thirteen nations closed their embassies in Jerusalem and moved them to Tel Aviv, where they joined the embassies of almost every other country that recognized Israel. From a diplomatic standpoint, the world had abandoned Jerusalem.

Enter Jan Willem van der Hoeven. After completing divinity school in the 1960s, Jan Willem had moved to Israel. He raised his family in Jerusalem, and both of his sons served in the Israeli army. From Jerusalem, Jan Willem helped to organize a network of Christian Zionists around the globe to provide political and moral support to Israel.

As the Jerusalem embassies closed down in 1980, Jan Willem and his Christian colleagues decided to open one. In September 1980, in a ceremony attended by Jerusalem mayor Teddy Kollek and more than five hundred visiting Christians, the International Christian Embassy in Jerusalem (ICEJ) officially opened for business.[14] Standing before the assembled crowd, clutching a small Bible in his left hand, Jan Willem prayed words that could have come straight from the mouth of his childhood hero, Corrie ten Boom:

> Dear Lord, we stand here as believers from many different nations, for your people, the Jews, to see a new day come over this nation, troubled and alone, standing with them in their time of forsakenness and isolation, in Jesus' name.[15]

The opening of the Christian Embassy was more than a symbolic gesture. The Christian Embassy has served as a center of international Christian Zionism ever since. In the 1980s, when Jews were not allowed to leave the Soviet Union, Jan Willem organized protest demonstrations around the world. When the Soviet Jews were finally allowed to leave, Jan Willem and the Christian Embassy helped transport them to Israel and to absorb them upon their arrival there.

In the same year Jan Willem opened the International Christian Embassy in Jerusalem, he also organized the first annual Christian celebration of the Feast of Tabernacles in Jerusalem. The Feast of Tabernacles is a seven-day Jewish holiday known by its Hebrew name *Succot*. The prophet Zechariah foretold of a day when the Jews would know such peace that the Gentiles who once attacked them would come to Jerusalem to help them celebrate this feast. Jan Willem decided that it would be a poignant act of solidarity with Israel to start fulfilling Zechariah's words in the here and now. In 1980, nearly a thousand Christians came to celebrate the Jewish holiday with study, prayer, song, and dance.[16] They have been coming, in increasing numbers, every year since.

The keynote speaker at the first Christian Feast of Tabernacles was an evangelical Christian from Holland named Peter van Woerden. Van Woerden is Corrie ten Boom's nephew, and during World War II he helped ferry the Jews hiding in her home to safe houses in the countryside. Like so many Christian Zionists, van Woerden seeks through his activism to fulfill the legacy of his famous aunt.

Before her death in 1983, Corrie ten Boom traveled the world, sharing her story and her message of religious faith. But Corrie's death has not stopped her story from being told. Corrie ten Boom still visits churches across America. She shuffles slowly up to the podium and, in her heavily Dutch-accented English, tells her story with humor and humility. Under the gray wig and padded dress is a young evangelical Christian from New Mexico named Susan Sandager.

Although she never met Corrie, Susan Sandager was so inspired by Corrie ten Boom that she has dedicated her life to continuing Corrie's work. Sandager's understanding of Corrie ten Boom's legacy comes from her interpretation of something mysterious that Corrie experienced. Corrie used to tell her audiences that while she and her sister Betsie were imprisoned in Ravensbruck, God spoke to them and told them, "It is for My people you must suffer this."[17] In this knowledge that there was a purpose to their pain, Corrie and Betsie ten Boom found comfort in a Nazi concentration camp.

Susan Sandager struggled with this statement. Corrie ten Boom believed that she had to suffer for the sake of the Jewish people. Yet what did her *suffering* accomplish for the Jews? Corrie had certainly helped Jewish people prior to being arrested. But she could no longer help them from behind the barbed wire of Ravensbruck. What positive purpose could her suffering possibly serve?

In time, Sandager came to her own understanding of the riddle. She decided that Corrie's suffering was the key that would unlock Christian hearts and open them to her message of love for the Jewish people. It is the very poignancy of Corrie's suffering and loss that gives her story the power to transform. Sandager elaborates on this theme:

> Israel is in extreme crisis. She is threatened by terrorists, undermined by Arab propaganda, attacked by anti-Semitic voices in the U.N. and in Europe. It doesn't take much creative thinking to surmise that Israel needs help. The millions of Christians around the world are potentially the best friend Israel has, yet most of the Church is sound asleep or deceived with regard to Israel's growing crisis.

> Miss ten Boom's message speaks volumes to the Church about how a true Christian should relate to Israel and God's People. Her family modeled Christ's example of laying down one's life for another. The ten Boom family shows us how to love Israel unconditionally. Like Ruth said to Naomi, the ten Booms said to the Jews, "Where you go, I go." The Church may miss her highest calling if she does not prepare herself to say also to Israel when and if the time ever comes, "Where you die, I will die."[18]

Susan Sandager has made it her mission in life to ensure that Corrie ten Boom's suffering serves its intended purpose. For this high calling Sandager leaves her family behind in New Mexico and takes to the road much of the year. By impersonating Corrie ten Boom and sharing her story, she hopes to inspire her fellow Christians to follow Corrie's example of love for the Jewish people and action in their defense. The specific action she seeks, what is to her the modern-day equivalent of sheltering hunted Jews, is support for the State of Israel.

SUSAN SANDAGER IS right. Corrie ten Boom's suffering can serve the Jewish people today by overcoming Christian apathy and inspiring Christians to stand in solidarity with Israel. But this is only half of the story. Corrie's suffering can also serve the Jewish people more directly, by opening their hearts to receiving this Christian embrace.

For Jews who remain wary of their Christian allies, Corrie ten Boom's story presents a most difficult challenge. Even those most cynical about Christian friendship must recognize that the risks Corrie took and the price Corrie paid were sublime acts of love. Once it is acknowledged that Corrie was a true friend, however, it becomes harder to dismiss those who seek to walk in her footsteps. Because she suffered alongside the Jews, Corrie's story has the power to penetrate hearts cast iron hard in the flames of a Holocaust.

AN OBSESSION WITH THE HOLOCAUST

NOT EVERY CHRISTIAN Zionist is focused on the particular example of Corrie ten Boom. She is merely a compelling symbol of a deeper phenomenon. The fact is that most Christian Zionists are obsessed with the Holocaust. With the possible exception of the Jews themselves, no other community talks as frequently and as passionately about the Nazi genocide. Christian Zionists carry a heavy burden of guilt for this atrocity perpetrated by people claiming to share their faith. They are determined to make amends and in the process demonstrate how true Christians relate to Jews. This sentiment was captured well in a 2002 Bridges for Peace fund-raising letter:

> Throughout history, there have been many times when Christians turned a blind eye to the suffering of their brothers. Many of us have mourned over the suffering of the Jewish people during the Holocaust and wished we could somehow change what happened. Sadly, we can't change a single event of past history. But, we can make a difference in the future! Our acts of love and kindness in this difficult time can change the face of Jewish/Christian relations. We can be the generation of Christians who stood up for Israel in accordance with God's plan. Or we can be like many who went before us and turned a blind eye.[19]

Thus, while they may look forward to the future fulfillment of prophecy, it is the past that drives many of the most dedicated Christian Zionists. Their stories further demonstrate the ideological continuity between the righteous Gentiles of the past and the Christian Zionists of today.

In 1941, a group of 778 Romanian Jews seeking to flee Hitler's final solution boarded a cattle barge called the *Struma* on Romania's Black Sea coast and set sail for Palestine. The sputtering engine got the boat as far as Istanbul before giving out entirely. Turkey was determined not to become a refuge for Jews fleeing Europe, and it refused to let the passengers of the *Struma* disembark. Turkey also did not want to provoke the British, so it prevented the boat from being repaired and continuing on its way.* After a seventy-day standoff, the Turks seized control of the *Struma* and towed it out to international waters. There the boat drifted, with no engine and no food for its passengers, until

* In deference to Arab sensibilities, the British had barred practically all Jewish immigration to Palestine in 1939.

a Russian submarine torpedoed it the next morning without explanation. Every passenger except for one perished.

Fifty years later, a group of English Christian Zionists formed an organization called Operation Exodus to transport Jewish immigrants from the former Soviet Union to Israel. They leased a ship and opened up the only sea route to Israel via the Black Sea. As the ship passed by the port of Istanbul on its maiden voyage, the Christian organizers and crew gathered on deck. There they held a ceremony of "memorial and repentance." Fred Wright, a minister from England, spoke to the crowd:

> We from England are standing here to request forgiveness for the hardheartedness and lack of compassion that our country showed the passengers of the *Struma*. This was a sinful act, and we humbly ask forgiveness.[20]

The participants threw a tall wreath made from Jerusalem pine branches and flowers into the sea. The ship sounded a long, solemn blast of its horn. Commenting on the event in his book, the founder of Operation Exodus, Gustav Scheller, noted:

> I believe there will not be one reading this whose home country has not done harm to the Jewish people in some way. Many of us have repented; but in my understanding this is only the first step. The Lord has clearly shown us in His word that we should carry the Jews back home to Israel. What an opportunity we have to say to the nation of Israel how deeply we care and so turn past curses into blessings.[21]

To provide prospective immigrants with a place to live while awaiting departure, Scheller's Operation Exodus purchased a campground near the Ukrainian port of Odessa. Scheller recruited a number of Christian volunteers to run the camp, including a German couple, Hinrich and his wife, Elke. Hinrich's father was an officer in the German army who had taken part in the World War II occupation of Odessa in which most of the Jewish population was massacred. As he met with groups of Jews he was helping transport to Israel, Hinrich liked to remind them of the following quote from the prophet Isaiah: "Also the sons of those who afflicted you shall come bowing to you."[22]

WHEN THEN HOUSE Majority Leader Tom DeLay traveled to Israel to address the Israeli Knesset in July 2003, he arrived at a difficult time for Israel. Terrorism and suicide bombings continued unabated, and there was little hope that peace efforts would produce any tangible results. DeLay warned his audience of more bloodshed to come, but promised a brighter future. DeLay reached back to the Holocaust for the appropriate words:

> In the words of a fifteen-year-old girl hiding in Amsterdam less than a month before she was taken to Auschwitz, "I hear the approaching thunder that, one day, will destroy us... I feel the suffering of millions. And yet, when I look up at the sky, I somehow feel that everything will change for the better, that this cruelty too shall end, that peace and tranquility will return once more."
>
> One day, Israel—with the United States by her side—will live in freedom, security and peace. And terrorism will perish from the earth. But until that day dawns, free men the world over—whether of the cross, the crescent, or the Star of David—will stand with Israel in defiance of evil.[23]

THE OTHER RIGHTEOUS GENTILES

IN ESTABLISHING THIS link between the righteous Gentiles of the Holocaust and today's Christian Zionists, an imprecise shorthand has been employed. The Christian Zionists are not the spiritual heirs of all righteous Gentiles but of one category of righteous Gentiles: those who, like Corrie ten Boom, acted out of a theologically based love for the Jewish people. Of course, many righteous Gentiles did not share Corrie ten Boom's Bible-based philo-Semitism.

To categorize broadly, there were two other types of Gentiles who saved Jews during the Holocaust. One such group, while also devout Christians, embraced a theology that assigned no special role to the Jews. A third group of righteous Gentiles was a secular people who were not motivated by religious faith in any appreciable sense.

This book focuses on Corrie ten Boom's category of righteous Gentiles because this was the only one to produce ideological progeny still devoted to the Jewish people. Corrie and others like her were motivated by a Judeo-centric ideology. They saved Jews because of a worldview that assigned a special significance to them. Even after the emergency of the Holocaust passed, individuals who inherited this worldview remained devoted to the Jews.

The other two categories of righteous Gentiles were never dedicated specifically to the Jewish people. These individuals saved Jews not because they were Jews but because they were human beings in danger. Once the immediate danger passed, so too did the focus. These righteous Gentiles quickly shifted their attention to new victims and what they viewed as more pressing causes.

Pastor Andre Trocme and the village of Le Chambon-sur-Lignon

Most righteous Gentiles operated on their own or as part of small networks. The village of Le Chambon-sur-Lignon in south central France provided a miraculous exception to this rule. Over the course of four years, this small village of three thousand souls worked in concert to save the lives of approximately five thousand Jews by hiding them in their homes, schools, and farms.[24] The village of Le Chambon perpetrated an astonishingly successful conspiracy of righteousness.

The residents of Le Chambon were Protestant Huguenots. Their own history as a persecuted religious minority in Catholic France no doubt made them sympathetic to the suffering of another religious minority. The residents of Le Chambon were also greatly influenced by their charismatic pastor, a man named Andre Trocme. Pastor Trocme was an outspoken pacifist who preached to the village the supreme value of every human life. To Trocme, the Jews were simply persecuted human beings who needed help. When asked about the Jews being hidden in his village, Trocme once replied, "We do not know what a Jew is. We know only men."[25] If Trocme ever uttered the words "chosen people," it is nowhere recorded.

Pastor Trocme occupied the same moral stratosphere as Corrie ten Boom. Both risked their lives to save other human beings from certain death. Yet in a sense these two Christian saints preached opposing messages. Corrie ten Boom stressed a love for a specific tribe—the Jews—and as a result her ideological heirs can be found planted firmly in the pro-Israel camp today. Pastor Trocme was a universalist who eschewed narrow loyalties to any one tribe or ethnicity. Trocme's followers thus inherit no particular commitment to Israel or the Jewish people.

Far from being Zionists, many of Trocme's ideological heirs are today among Israel's most vocal critics. Trocme believed that the only moral response to Nazism was the rejection of nationalism and armed force. The good pastor thus preached that the only justifiable resistance to the Nazis was one conducted with "weapons of the spirit." The Zionists learned very different lessons from their experience with the Nazis. They decided that Jewish survival necessitated *embracing* nationalism—Jewish nationalism—and building their own country and army. From the very start there was a tension between Trocme's pacifism and Zionism.

Unfortunately, this ideological tension has devolved into something far uglier. Among those who claim the pastor's mantle today are many who have replaced his love with rage. Europe's pacifist Left has been a loud, often shrill, opponent of Israel. Yet these pacifists maintain a disturbing silence when it comes to the terrorism directed against Israeli civilians. While Trocme showed pity for Jewish victims, many of his ideological heirs express only contempt for Jews who possess an army, tanks, and guns.*

In setting up Le Chambon as a city of refuge, for example, Trocme turned early on to his fellow pacifists, the Quakers, for financial and logistical support. The Quakers provided crucial assistance to Trocme in his heroic mission. Yet today Quaker organs such as the American Friends Services Committee have become one-sided critics of Israel. Like its pacifist brethren in Europe, the committee typically blames Israel alone for the violence in the Middle East and musters little enthusiasm for the condemnation of Palestinian terror. What to many Christian Zionists is a just war on terror is, to the Quakers, just another war.

Oskar Schindler and the secular righteous

The third category of righteous Gentiles could best be described as secular rescuers. These people may have been Christian by birth or loose affiliation, but it was not religious faith that motivated them to save Jews. Instead, these righteous Gentiles were driven by a secular moral code that did not permit them to sit idly by while innocents were slaughtered.

---

* Under the guise of a universalist embrace of humanity, Europe's Left often espouses some of the very same anti-Semitic ideas that Trocme himself so bravely opposed.

The most famous righteous Gentile, Oskar Schindler, belonged to this category of the secular righteous. The subject of Steven Spielberg's blockbuster 1993 movie *Schindler's List*, Oskar Schindler was an accomplished industrialist and an equally accomplished playboy. But when confronted with the evil of the Holocaust, he evolved into a hero. Oskar Schindler risked his life and went into bankruptcy to save more than one thousand Jews from death in the Nazi concentration camps by employing them in his factory.

Schindler's heroism placed him on the same high moral plain as Corrie ten Boom and Andre Trocme. Yet, as with Trocme, Schindler's secular righteousness transcended loyalty to any particular tribe or clan. Thus there is no group of later-day Schindlers devoted to helping the Jewish people today. For that matter, Schindler's philosophy does not appear to have spawned any identifiable set of followers. Such personal heroism, unconnected to any particular religious or philosophic tradition, does not easily lend itself to replication. While Schindler serves as an example to all humanity, he has bred no movement or following of his own.

WHILE OSKAR SCHINDLER has no identifiable ideological heirs, he does have a literal, physical heir who is a devoted supporter of Israel. Unlike her uncle Oskar, however, Rosemary Schindler is a devout evangelical Christian. She is also the founder of Schindler's Ark, a California-based organization of Christians and Jews dedicated to supporting Israel. According to Rosemary Schindler, "I feel as a Christian, we bear the guilt that we helped bring about the death camps. The worst oppressors of the Jewish people have been Christian."[26] Schindler has described her organization's mission as follows:

> [T]o bring restitution in both money and in esteem and honor [to the Jewish people], and also to acknowledge that Israel is a blessing to all the world. Jewish people are a blessing to all the nations they've ever been in. Those countries have all been blessed.[27]

Schindler's Ark sponsors an annual Judeo-Christian Zionist Conference featuring a number of Christian Zionist and Israeli speakers. At the group's 2003 convention, one of the featured guests was Susan Sandager doing her impersonation of Corrie ten Boom. While she may be the biological heir of

Oskar Schindler, Rosemary Schindler is the ideological heir of Corrie ten Boom.

The Education of Abe Foxman

At the 1995 annual meeting of the Anti-Defamation League (ADL), Abraham Foxman was about to publicly embrace a profound reversal of policy. Foxman and the Anti-Defamation League he directed had for years been vocal critics of America's Religious Right. When this criticism reached its peak in 1994 and 1995, an emergency interfaith meeting was called to pull the parties back from the brink. As a gesture in support of this rapprochement, Foxman invited Ralph Reed, executive director of the Christian Coalition, to give the keynote address at the ADL's upcoming annual meeting. Instead of lambasting Reed, the ADL would now listen to him.

While Abe Foxman appeared to have had a change of heart regarding Christian conservatives, he had yet to persuade his community or even his wife. Before departing for the leadership meeting, Foxman's wife, Gloria, warned him, "Abe, I know you. You're a hugger. But if I see you hugging Ralph Reed on the TV news, don't bother coming home tonight."[28]

That night, the Jewish embrace of the Christian Right would be strictly symbolic.

The Anti-Defamation League was founded in 1913 "to stop the defamation of the Jewish people." Ever since, the ADL has been the American Jewish community's leading anti-Semitism watchdog. As the executive director of the ADL since 1987, Abraham Foxman has come to personify both the ADL and its mission. Foxman is a pillar of the Jewish establishment. As such he helped craft, and echoed, the community's policy toward the Christian Right.

Throughout the 1980s and well into the 1990s, Foxman consistently expressed his community's great apprehension at the steady rise of conservative Christians as a political force in America. Like so many Jews who embraced liberal views on issues of abortion and church-state separation, Foxman did not view his differences with the Religious Right as mere policy disagreements. To him, the Religious Right was trying to undermine the very pluralism that enabled Jews to thrive in America. For Foxman, the rise of the Religious Right was a direct threat to the American Jewish community.

In 1994, the ADL directly engaged this emerging threat. The ADL published and widely distributed a 200-page book entitled *The Religious Right: The Assault on Tolerance and Pluralism in America*. As the title indicates, this book was not simply a dissent from the Religious Right's position on abortion and prayer in the schools: it was a frontal attack on the Religious Right and its leaders. Foxman set the tone in the book's foreword, where he wrote that the report would demonstrate that:

> The religious right brings to cultural disagreements a rhetoric of fear, suspicion, even hatred. The result is not surprising: real debate over the problems afflicting American society is eclipsed by the blare of grievance and blame and chauvinism, and the fragile structures of consensus are bulldozed by sectarian, absolutist declarations. In this way, we proceed down the road to the "Christian nation" trumpeted by these prophets of rage.[29]

The ADL report did not go so far as to claim that the Religious Right as a movement was anti-Semitic. Yet here was a long and detailed report from the nation's leading anti-Semitism watchdog warning about an "assault on tolerance and pluralism" by the Religious Right. The symbolism was profound. Rarely in its history has the ADL issued so lengthy and detailed a report about an organization or movement perceived to be inimical to the American Jewish community. The only analogous publications in the ADL library are a report on the international Skinhead Movement and another on Muslim terrorists.

The ADL book sparked a firestorm. The leading organ of the Religious Right, the Christian Coalition, issued a forty-page rebuttal, and angry letters were exchanged between Abe Foxman and the Coalition's president, Pat Robertson.[30] A group of seventy-five mostly neoconservative Jews published a full-page advertisement in the *New York Times* denouncing the ADL report.[31] Relations between evangelical Christians and the organized Jewish community were badly frayed. Years later, both Robertson and Reed expressed their feelings about the ADL report in surprisingly personal terms. According to Reed, he was "deeply hurt"[32] by the book, and Robertson acknowledged that "it hurt me terribly."[33]

The parties were pulled back from the brink by a man respected in both camps: Rabbi Yechiel Eckstein. Eckstein organized a meeting between Jewish leaders, including Foxman, and evangelical leaders, including Robertson and Reed. The parties talked, and many misperceptions were clarified. Dialogue worked its healing power. By the end of the day, Foxman had invited Reed to address the ADL's upcoming leadership conference.

Since that time, Abraham Foxman has continued to move from confrontation with Christian conservatives toward reconciliation and alliance.* To be sure, Foxman still disagrees with many policy positions of the Religious Right and is not shy about voicing those differences. Yet the disagreements now take place without much of the underlying distrust and fear that had characterized prior relations. Of Reed, Foxman now says, "He's not an enemy of the Jewish people, he's someone to listen to.... I consider him a friend."[34]

In April 2002, Ralph Reed wrote an article for the *Los Angeles Times* entitled "We People of Faith Stand Firmly With Israel," in which he noted that:

> Christians... saw support for Israel through the prism of a proud tradition that included Corrie ten Boom and Dietrich Bonhoeffer, who sacrificed their own lives while resisting Nazi tyranny and protecting Jews from the Holocaust. The depth of such feeling in the Christian community is difficult to overestimate.[35]

Foxman was so impressed with Reed's article that he had the ADL pay to reprint it as an advertisement in both the *New York Times* and the *Washington Post*. In July 2002, Abraham Foxman issued an explicit call for the Jewish community to embrace evangelical support for Israel. In an article entitled "Why Evangelical Support for Israel Is a Good Thing," Foxman noted that:

---

* In November 2005, after this book had been completed but before it went to press, Abraham Foxman made a speech before the ADL leadership in which he reprised some of the negative themes from the ADL's controversial 1994 critique of the Christian Right. Among other things, Foxman warned of "an emerging Christian Right leadership that intends to 'Christianize' all aspects of American life...." At this writing, it remains unclear if Foxman's words were merely an unusually passionate expression of his long-standing policy differences with the Christian Right or if they signaled an abandonment of the reconciliation achieved in 1994.

> American Jews should not be apologetic or defensive about cultivating Evangelical support for Israel. The need for support by an Israel under siege is great. Fortunately, Evangelical support is overwhelming, consistent and unconditional.[36]

ABE FOXMAN HAS undergone an important evolution. While every liberal political bone in his body leads him to condemn the Christian Right, something deeper has enabled him to recognize them as true friends of the Jewish community. He has gone against his political instincts and the views of his supporters, family, and friends to extend an olive branch. In his own very personal way, Abraham Foxman learned the lesson of Corrie ten Boom, internalized it, and has acted on it. To anyone who knows Foxman's own story, his ability to see through stereotypes to the moral core of these Christian Zionists should come as no surprise. While he may have ignored it for a period, Foxman learned an important lesson about righteous Gentiles a long time ago, in another country.

Abe Foxman's rescue

Abraham Foxman was born in 1940 to Jewish parents living in Poland. In a futile effort to stay ahead of the advancing Nazi army, Foxman's parents fled with him east to Lithuania. The Germans soon occupied Lithuania and ordered all Jews to report to the ghetto in Vilna. Hoping to save their child's life, the Foxmans decided to leave baby Abraham in the custody of his Polish nanny, Bronislawa Kurpi.

Kurpi was a devout Catholic, and she decided to raise Abraham in her faith. She had him baptized, taught him Catholic prayers, and gave him a little cross to wear around his neck. She not only cut him off from his Judaism, but she taught him to hate Jews. Whenever a Jew passed on the street, Abraham Foxman, future executive director of the Anti-Defamation League, would spit and mutter, "Dirty Jew."[37]

Foxman's parents survived the Holocaust, and they came back to reclaim their son. But Bronislawa Kurpi wanted to keep Abraham, and she was ruthless in her quest to do so. Kurpi went to the local Soviet officials who occupied Lithuania after the war and accused Foxman's father of having collaborated with the Nazis—an accusation that could have gotten the elder Foxman killed. After being arrested and interrogated, Foxman was released for lack of evidence. Kurpi next accused Foxman of having stolen government property from his place of work. Again he was arrested, and again he was freed for lack of evidence. By the third time Kurpi accused Foxman of a crime, the police knew to ignore her.

Tiring of the continuing battles, the Foxmans decided to settle the issue by suing Kurpi for legal custody of their child. At trial, Kurpi resorted to more dirty tricks. She claimed that the Foxmans were not who they claimed to be, but merely imposters using the Foxman name. After the Foxmans proved their true identity, Kurpi claimed that Abraham was actually her biological son and not theirs. The Foxmans were able to prove that this too was a lie.

Having lost the legal battle, Kurpi resorted to kidnapping. She had some of her relatives take young Abraham and hide him in their home. The Foxmans tracked their son down and had some friends kidnap him back. At this juncture, the Foxmans decided to take Abraham and leave Lithuania and Bronislawa Kurpi behind for good.[38]

Bronislawa Kurpi was no saintly Corrie ten Boom. She was a bitter woman capable of great evil. Yet Abraham Foxman disregards her ugly behavior because of one basic fact—Kurpi risked her life to save his. Foxman refers to Kurpi as "my dear old nanny."[39] Rather than condemn her actions, Foxman demonstrates an incredible ability to put himself in her shoes and understand why she acted as she did. Foxman seems to excuse the fact that she taught him to hate Jews by noting that, "After all, she shared the anti-Semitic assumptions of her world."[40] Foxman even excuses her efforts to steal him from his parents, pointing out that "Frau Kurpi had a simple, sincere acceptance of the dogma that only a faithful Catholic could hope to be saved, and she wanted me to be part of that fold."[41]

Addressing a conference of children rescued by righteous Gentiles during the Holocaust, Abraham Foxman certainly had his nanny in mind as he made an important statement:

> For the first fifty years after the Holocaust survivors bore witness to evil, brutality and bestiality. Now is the time for us, for our generation, to bear witness to goodness. For each one of us is living proof that even

> in hell, even in that hell called the Holocaust, there was goodness, there was kindness, and there was love and compassion.[42]

For much of his professional life, Foxman's "witness to goodness" ended when it came to the domestic political arena and those with whom he differed on social policy. Abraham Foxman was unable to see an echo of his nanny or the other righteous Gentiles in America's Christian Zionists. It is quite likely that, on the contrary, he sensed in their conservative and devout Christianity an echo of past persecutors, not rescuers. Policy differences were thus perceived as yet another assault on the Jews from the Christian camp. While he could excuse his nanny for teaching him to be an anti-Semite, Foxman could not excuse the Religious Right for differing with his strongly held views on the separation of church and state.

But as the real threats to the Jews and the Jewish State increased, Abraham Foxman's perspective changed. His love and understanding for Kurpi stemmed from the basic fact that she risked her life to save his in a dangerous time. Foxman could understand and accept differences on lesser issues because this woman stood with a small Jewish boy against a hostile world. Today, Abe Foxman sees the Christian Zionists standing with a small Jewish State against a hostile world. In this light, the moral continuity from his nanny down to these present-day Christians stands out more clearly. Once this connection is made, the policy differences between the two communities appear far less menacing. Abraham Foxman's evolution provides an example that the American Jewish community should follow.

RECOGNIZING THIS CONNECTION between Christian Zionists and righteous Gentiles requires an abstract analysis that spans two very different eras and historical milieus. This connection would have been far clearer had time and circumstances not conspired to prevent more concrete examples. Like most evangelicals of their era, Corrie ten Boom and other rescuers never got involved in politics. But what if they had? Though her style may have been gentle and her rhetoric inclusive, a Senator Corrie ten Boom would most certainly have supported the domestic agenda of the Christian Right. Yet Corrie's past heroism would have pierced the balloon of assumptions that critics typically make about people who hold such conservative views. Even those who opposed it would likely have been able to see Senator ten Boom's domestic agenda as an expression of Christian love and not of ancient hate. Thus drained of its emotional charge and historical baggage, such a domestic agenda would not have obscured Senator ten Boom's status as a true friend of the Jewish people.

To be sure, the issues of abortion, gay rights, and prayer in the schools are important, and the debate over these issues will be among the most contentious in America for years and even decades to come. Yet the stories of Corrie ten Boom and Abe Foxman bring us to a different, more rarified moral plane. And from these moral heights such policy differences fade dramatically in significance. The fact is that these domestic issues are ones about which reasonable people can—and do—disagree. Yet when it comes to the fundamental issues over which reasonable people cannot disagree—such as the survival of a Jewish boy in Nazi-occupied Europe or the survival of a Jewish State in a turbulent Middle East—many evangelical Christians are steadfast allies. From the ground level of day-to-day politics, Christian leaders often loom large in the Jewish imagination as dangerous adversaries threatening to shut out the light. When we view the forest from on high, however, these same leaders can be recognized as mighty oaks providing shelter from an ominous wind.

Conclusion

STRANGE BEDFELLOWS OR BLOOD BROTHERS?

THERE ARE FEW surprises in political Washington. For the most part, Democrats and Republicans stick to their partisan scripts. The dance is a familiar one.

Thus the scene that took place on the evening of April 2, 2003, came as a surprise. A crowd of approximately three hundred was assembled for a dinner at the posh Mayflower Hotel in downtown Washington. An organization named Stand for Israel had organized the event to present its Friend of Israel Award to two members of Congress: Tom DeLay and Tom Lantos.

These two honorees could not have been more different from one another. Tom DeLay, a devout Baptist, is a conservative Republican from Texas. At the time, DeLay was the House Majority Leader and, before this, had served for years as the Republican Whip. In these roles DeLay was the driving force behind the most controversial Republican congressional initiatives of the day, from cutting taxes to impeaching President Clinton. Tom DeLay is not a conservative; he is *the* conservative, and there are few men more despised and vilified in liberal circles.

Tom Lantos is a liberal Democrat from California. He is a Jew who speaks with the accent of his native Hungary. Lantos is a Holocaust survivor who spent much of World War II as a partisan fighting the Nazis. Much of that partisan spirit remains in him today. Lantos is a loyal Democrat and passionate proponent of the liberal party line. He was an outspoken opponent of the impeachment of President Clinton and before that had been a consistent critic of the independent counsels investigating the president. To many conservatives, Lantos is just another liberal attack dog.

Upon rising to accept his Friend of Israel Award, Tom DeLay set the tone for this unusual evening. He told the crowd that he was proud to share the honor with Tom Lantos and that he greatly appreciated his friendship with his colleague from across the aisle. DeLay then spoke words that went well beyond professional courtesy. Referring to Lantos, DeLay told the crowd, "I do love him. He is a really wonderful, wonderful man."[1] DeLay proceeded to give a rousing speech in support of Israel.

Tom Lantos rose next to accept his award. Lantos reciprocated DeLay's kind words of collegiality and then launched into a profound tribute to DeLay:

> It's not so difficult to be a friend of Israel when you are a survivor of the Holocaust. And I think there is a fundamental disparity between my support for Israel, which comes so naturally, and Tom's support for Israel, which stems from his deep Christian values and his sophisticated and principled view of the world. I am a Jew, and he is a Christian, and I admire him and I admire all of you who are Christians who have chosen to stand by this small, beleaguered, democratic, value-rich State of Israel.[2]

Tom Lantos is uniquely positioned to recognize and appreciate Christian values. His life was saved by Raoul Wallenberg, the Swedish diplomat who rescued thousands of Hungarian Jews during the Holocaust. As Lantos described so poignantly that night:

> In 1944, I was a sixteen-year-old boy who was convinced, with good reason, that he would not survive the Second World War—none of my family did. And a Christian, far away from Budapest, acted on the same Christian values that permeate my friend Tom DeLay. My wife Annette and I are here, our two daughters are alive and our seventeen grandchildren live because of a Christian.[3]

Upon descending from the podium, Tom Lantos approached Tom DeLay. The two men embraced, and they held on to one another far longer than a symbolic gesture or a photo opportunity would have required.

Tom Lantos shared a crucial insight that night. He did not merely praise Tom DeLay as a pro-Israel congressman. Instead, he illuminated the far deeper phenomenon at work. Lantos recognized DeLay as a modern-day righteous Gentile, the moral progeny of Raoul Wallenberg. Lantos made it clear that it is not despite his Christianity but *because* of it that Tom DeLay stands with Israel.

At first blush, it seems ironic that European Jews who survived the Holocaust, such as Tom Lantos and Menachem Begin, would be at the forefront of embracing Israel's Christian allies. After what these men suffered at the hands of Christians, it would be eminently understandable if they long ago closed their minds to the idea that anything good for the Jews could emanate from Christendom.

But on further reflection, the embrace makes eminent sense. Men like Lantos and Begin, after all, experienced the pitch darkness of a world loosed from the Judeo-Christian moral code. Having searched for the light, their eyes perhaps became more sensitive to it. In the long night of the Holocaust, they grew hyperopic. Thus they gained the ability to see beacons of morality in the distance before most others can.

In story after story, the media have invoked the term "strange bedfellows" to describe the emerging alliance between Jews and evangelical Christians in support of Israel. This is a mischaracterization. "Strange bedfellows" implies more than just an unlikely alliance; it suggests an uncomfortable one. Strange bedfellows share a bed in a marriage of convenience, not one of true love. It is a utilitarian embrace.

As the relationship between Tom Lantos and Tom DeLay indicates, however, the alliance of Jews and Christians in support of Israel is no temporary coincidence of interests. A connection far more profound is in evidence. There is at the heart of this alliance a shared passion for a shared moral code that transcends differences of culture and ritual.

The Lantos-DeLay friendship is hardly unique. Since the birth of the Zionist movement in 1896, Christians and Jews have been discovering deep bonds of kinship through their efforts on behalf of the Jewish State. The following three vignettes capture the true depth of these Christian-Jewish relationships. All three take place in the declining days, or on the deathbeds, of one of the protagonists. These are not stories about strange bedfellows. These are stories about brothers.

We start in Vienna. The year was 1904. Theodor Herzl, the father of modern Zionism, lay dying. He had worked almost nonstop for eight years to build the Zionist movement. Although only forty-four, his weak heart was finally giving out.

As he lay on his deathbed, Herzl permitted only one visitor from outside of his immediate family. This visitor was William Hechler, Herzl's first Christian ally. It was Hechler who introduced Herzl to the German kaiser, and it was with Hechler that Herzl first traveled to Jerusalem. Historian Paul Merkley relates what happened next:

> On 2 July, Hechler spent considerable time recalling with his friend their visit to Palestine. Taking to heart the encouraging diagnosis of Herzl's doctor, Hechler sought to cheer Herzl with the promise that they would return together to the Holy Land, "But," Hechler recalled, "he seems to have known that there was no hope for him. He placed his right hand on his heart, and holding my right hand in his left he said: 'Greet all of them for me, and let them know that I gave all my life for my people.'"[4]

Theodor Herzl died the next day.

We now shift location to London, England. The year was 1930. Lord Arthur Balfour, the author of the Balfour Declaration, lay on his deathbed. Like Herzl, Balfour limited his visitors to his immediate family, but he made one exception. He called for Chaim Weizmann, the Zionist leader who helped persuade Balfour to embrace the Zionist cause. Weizmann rushed to his bedside. According to Balfour's niece, Blanche Dugdale:

> No words passed between them, or could pass, for Balfour was very weak, and Dr. Weizmann much overcome.
>
> But I, who saw the look with which Balfour moved his hand and touched the bowed head of the other, have no doubt at all that he [Balfour] realized the nature of the emotion which for the first, and only, time showed itself in his sick room.[5]

For our third scene, we move to Jerusalem. The year was 1983. Menachem Begin had resigned as prime minister of Israel and gone into seclusion. For the next nine years, until his death in 1992, Begin lived alone in his apartment, venturing outside only once a year to visit his wife's grave on the anniversary of her death. During this entire period, Begin allowed only his children, grandchildren, and old comrades from his underground days to visit him. With, of course, one exception: the Reverend Jerry Falwell.[6]

YOU DON'T INVITE a stranger to visit you at your deathbed. One's last moments of life are not the time for political gestures or networking. In all three cases discussed above, what may have begun as a pragmatic political alliance ended as something far deeper. In the face of much talk of strange bedfellows, these stories clarify the true nature of the relationship that has existed between Jewish and Christian Zionists.

As Jews and evangelical Christians contemplate an alliance in support of Israel today, they must keep in mind these instructive examples. What is taking place is not so much a union as a reunion. It is true that Christians and Jews differ in their religious doctrine and ritual. These religious differences have bred a host of derivative disagreements on issues of domestic and international policy. These policy differences are deep and heartfelt, and they will likely persist for decades to come.

Yet circumstances have changed in ways that should render such differences less significant. World events have flipped the telescope around. What was once so menacing now appears very small and distant. During World War II, people united in fighting the Nazis likely disregarded as irrelevant one another's position on abortion. Since September 11, the new threats facing Americans and Israelis should likewise work to bring into sharp relief the fundamental values that evangelical Christians and Jews share while making their disagreements appear small by comparison. None of the differences between Jewish and Christian Zionists impact upon the larger questions at the core of what it means to be a moral actor in the world today. Christians and Jews share bedrock beliefs in basic morality and the value of human life that make them natural allies in the face of attacks from enemies who share neither.

As the Jewish community faces the new dangers of a new century, it must break free from its fixation on past traumas. American Jews must look forward, assess the circumstances on the ground today, and make objective judgments. The anti-Semitic Christians of past generations have been eclipsed in America by Christians who enthusiastically embrace the Jewish people and the Jewish State. As the Jews confront the latest threats to their existence, they will find standing alongside them Christian soldiers who passionately share their concerns not despite their Christian faith, but because of it. While the Jewish embrace of these new allies may not be imminent, it is certainly overdue.

Notes

Introduction
The Righteous Then and Now

1. Claire Huchet Bishop, "Jules Isaac: A Biographical Introduction," in Jules Isaac, *The Teaching of Contempt* (New York: Holt, Rinehart and Winston, 1964), 9.
2. Jules Isaac, *Jesus and Israel* (New York: Holt, Rinehart and Winston, 1971), xxiii.
3. Ibid., 399.
4. Cited in Claire Huchet Bishop's foreword to Isaac, *Jesus and Israel*, xvii.
5. Isaac, *Jesus and Israel*, 400.
6. David Gushee, *The Righteous Gentiles of the Holocaust* (Minneapolis: Fortress Press, 1994), 120.
7. Cited in Gushee, *The Righteous Gentiles of the Holocaust*, 119–120.
8. Cited in William Claiborne, "Begin Threatens to Destroy Any Reactor Menacing Israel," *Washington Post*, June 10, 1981.
9. John Hagee, *Final Dawn Over Jerusalem* (Nashville: Thomas Nelson Publishers, 1998), 12.
10. Ibid., 15.
11. John Hagee, speech at the Israeli embassy, Washington DC, December 14, 2002.
12. Bishop, "Jules Isaac: A Biographical Introduction," in Isaac, *The Teaching of Contempt*, 10–15; and Rabbi Harold M. Schulweis, "A High Holiday Response to the Outreach of Pope John Paul II," October 17, 2000, downloaded from the Rabbi Harold Schulweis Archives (www.vbs.org) on December 19, 2003.
13. Cited in Gushee, *The Righteous Gentiles of the Holocaust*, 120.

Chapter One
The Rise of Replacement Theology

1. Franklin Littell, *The Crucifixion of the Jews* (Macon, GA: Mercer University Press, 1996), 30.
2. David Kertzer, *The Popes Against the Jews* (New York: Alfred A. Knopf, 2001), 25–31.
3. This language of "Gentile inclusion" and "Jewish exclusion" comes from Jeffrey Siker, *Disinheriting the Jews* (Louisville, KY: Westminster/John Knox Press, 1991), 185–198. Here Siker provides an insightful analysis of the shift in attitudes toward the Jews as expressed in the writings of the early church fathers.
4. Romans 11:17–20, *The Scofield Study Bible.*
5. Romans 9:6–8.
6. Romans 11:18.
7. Romans 11:1–2.
8. Romans 11:11, 28–29.
9. Romans 9:3.
10. In interpreting Paul's writings, I am in a sense seeking to emulate Paul (as I envision him) by embracing a nuanced, middle-of-the-road view of his message. There are people on both sides of the debate over Christian Zionism who see no such tension in Paul's writings. Christian Zionists often argue that, in Romans 11, Paul is clearly telling his fellow Christians that the Jews are still God's chosen people and

that they did not lose their status simply because the Gentiles have been grafted into their covenant. On the other hand, Christians who subscribe to covenant theology, a modern-day version of replacement theology, argue that Paul nowhere recognizes a special role for the Jews as a people. They believe, instead, that Paul makes it clear in Romans and elsewhere that "Israel" is comprised only of those who believe in Christ. Those Jews who accept Christ as their Savior will be grafted back into the covenant. In the absence of such faith in Christ, they assert, Jewish ethnicity alone has no covenantal significance.

11. James Carroll, *Constantine's Sword* (New York: Houghton Mifflin, 2001), 139–141. My own views on Paul's writings were definitely influenced by Carroll's heartfelt and persuasive analysis.

12. *Dialogue with Trypho*, cited in Siker, *Disinheriting the Jews*, 166–167. Siker provides an insightful overview and analysis of Justin Martyr's writings on the Jews and the distinctions between his views and those of Paul.

13. Ibid., 172.

14. Ibid., 13, 175.

15. Carroll, *Constantine's Sword*, 208.

16. Augustine, *Adversus Judaeos*, cited in Carroll, *Constantine's Sword*, 215.

17. Paula Fredriksen, "Augustine on Jews and Judaism" (lecture), and Carroll, *Constantine's Sword*, 212–213.

18. Fredriksen, "Augustine on the Jews and Judaism," and Carroll, *Constantine's Sword*, 216–218.

19. Augustine, *City of God* (London: Penguin, 1972), 828.

20. Ibid.

21. Carroll, *Constantine's Sword*, 219.

22. Scholars such as Rosemary Ruether have argued that Augustine and Chrysostom preached theological views of the Jews that were substantially the same except for their tone. (See *Faith and Fratricide*, cited below.) I have embraced the view of Fredriksen and Carroll that there is a significant substantive difference in the message of these two men.

23. Cited in Rosemary Ruether, *Faith and Fratricide* (Eugene, OR: Wipf and Stock Publishers, 1995), 146–147.

24. Ibid., 178–179.

25. Ibid., 180.

26. Cited in Littell, *The Crucifixion of the Jews*, 104.

27. Cited in John Cornwell, *Hitler's Pope* (New York: Penguin, 1999), 25.

28. List taken from Raul Hilberg, *The Destruction of the European Jews* (New York: Holmes & Meier, 1985), 10–11.

29. *Encyclopedia Judaica*, cited in John Hagee, *Should Christians Support Israel?* (San Antonio, TX: Dominion Publishers, 1987), 18–19.

30. Daniel J. Goldhagen, *A Moral Reckoning* (New York: Alfred A. Knopf, 2002), 70.

31. Ibid., 49.

32. Hilberg, *The Destruction of the European Jews*, 10–11.

33. Daniel J. Goldhagen, *Hitler's Willing Executioners* (New York: Alfred A. Knopf, 1996), 110–111; and Goldhagen, *A Moral Reckoning*, 59–60.

34. Kertzer, *The Popes Against the Jews*, 283.

35. Ibid., 287.

36. Ibid., 287–289; and Susan Zuccotti, *Under His Very Windows* (New Haven, CT: Yale University Press, 2000), 50–52.
37. Cornwell, *Hitler's Pope*, 308–309.
38. Ibid., 310.
39. Cited in Zuccotti, *Under His Very Windows*, 163–164.
40. Rabbi David Dalin, "A Righteous Gentile: Pope Pius XII and the Jews," *Weekly Standard*, February 26, 2001.
41. Goldhagen, *Hitler's Willing Executioners*, 111.
42. Victoria Barnett, *For the Soul of the People* (New York: Oxford University Press, 1992), 33–34; and James A. Zabel, *Nazism and the Pastors* (Missoula, MT: Scholars Press, 1976), 31.
43. Barnett, *For the Soul of the People*, 34.
44. Zabel, *Nazism and the Pastors*, 32.
45. Ibid., 41–42.
46. Goldhagen, *Hitler's Willing Executioners*, 112.
47. Ibid., 437.
48. Barnett, *For the Soul of the People*, 39–44.
49. Elliott Abrams, *Faith or Fear* (New York: The Free Press, 1997), 46.
50. Ibid., 51.

Chapter Two
The Return of the Jews

1. Clarence Wagner, "The Error of Replacement Theology," http://www.bridgesforpeace.com/modules.php?name=News&file=article&sid=1914 (accessed March 13, 2003).
2. This story is told in Philip Hallie, *Lest Innocent Blood Be Shed* (New York: HarperPerennial, 1994), 182–183.
3. My summary of Darby's life and theology is based largely upon the following works: Larry Crutchfield, *The Origins of Dispensationalism* (Lanham, MD: University Press of America, 1992); Larry Crutchfield, "John Nelson Darby: Defender of the Faith," downloaded from www.histable.com on November 25, 2003; E. Roy Coad, *A History of the Brethren Movement* (Vancouver, Canada: Regent College Publishing, 1968); Ernest Sandeen, *The Roots of Fundamentalism* (Chicago: The University of Chicago Press, 1970); Craig Blaising and Darrell Bock, eds., *Dispensationalism, Israel and the Church* (Grand Rapids, MI: Zondervan, 1992); Timothy Weber, *Living in the Shadow of the Second Coming* (New York: Oxford University Press, 1979); and Matt Costella, "The Historical Development of Dispensational Theology within Biblical Fundamentalism," *Foundation Magazine*, January/February 2002, downloaded from www.fundamentalbiblechurch.org on December 2, 2003.
4. Cited in Blaising and Bock, eds., *Dispensationalism, Israel and the Church*, 23.
5. Cited in Crutchfield, *The Origins of Dispensationalism*, 205.
6. My summary of the rise of American fundamentalism and the fundamentalist/modernist controversy is based largely on the following works: George M. Marsden, *Understanding Fundamentalism and Evangelicalism* (Grand Rapids, MI: Eerdmans Publishing, 1991); George M. Marsden, *Fundamentalism and American Culture* (New York: Oxford University Press, 1980); Ernest Sandeen, *The Roots of Fundamentalism*

(Chicago: The University of Chicago Press, 1970); Ernest Sandeen, *The Origins of Fundamentalism* (Minneapolis, MN: Fortress Press, 1968); and Ed Dobson, Ed Hindson, and Jerry Falwell, *The Fundamentalist Phenomenon* (Grand Rapids, MI: Baker Book House, 1986).

7. The term *evangelical* is widely used but rarely defined. The lack of definition likely stems from the difficulty of definition: evangelicals have never had a central body or platform to which they all adhere. Still, evangelicals do share a general approach to their Christianity that tends to differentiate them. Evangelical Christians embrace a core belief that the sole means of salvation is from a personal conversion experience in which one accepts Christ as Savior—that is, being "born again." Evangelicals also embrace the Bible as the inerrant Word of God, and they typically read the Bible literally. Accordingly, most evangelicals share a belief in the supernatural aspects of Christ's life, from His literal resurrection after the crucifixion to His literal return to earth in the Second Coming.

8. Cited in Weber, *Living in the Shadow of the Second Coming*, 14. Weber's book provides an extremely helpful review of the role of premillennialism in American Christianity.

9. Ibid.

10. "The Battle Hymn of the Republic" by Julia Ward Howe. Public domain.

11. Marsden, *Understanding Fundamentalism and Evangelicalism*, 32–36. In writing this chapter, I found Marsden's works to be extremely helpful. His books have the double blessing of being not only scholarly but also accessible to those, such as the author, who lack an academic background in Christian theology.

12. Ibid., 38.

13. Cited in Crutchfield, *The Origins of Dispensationalism*, 11.

14. Sandeen, *The Roots of Fundamentalism*, 71.

15. Crutchfield, *The Origins of Dispensationalism*, 12, 20, n. 65.

16. Weber, *Living in the Shadow of the Second Coming*, 32–33, 52.

17. Encyclopedia Britannica, Online Edition, s.v. "Sunday, Billy."

18. Dobson, Hindson, and Falwell, *The Fundamentalist Phenomenon*, 42–43; and Weber, *Living in the Shadow of the Second Coming*, 26.

19. Cited in Sandeen, *The Roots of Fundamentalism*, 276–277.

20. Dobson, Hindson, and Falwell, *The Fundamentalist Phenomenon*, 43.

21. Weber, *Living in the Shadow of the Second Coming*, 33–35.

22. Marsden, *Understanding Fundamentalism and Evangelicalism*, 40–41.

23. Sandeen, *The Roots of Fundamentalism*, 181–183; and Weber, *Living in the Shadow of the Second Coming*, 34–35.

24. James Barr, *Fundamentalism* (Philadelphia: The Westminster Press, 1978), 5, cited in Costella, "The Historical Development of Dispensational Theology within Biblical Fundamentalism."

25. Crutchfield, *The Origins of Dispensationalism*, 15.

26. Vern Poythress, *Understanding Dispensationalists* (Grand Rapids, MI: Zondervan, 1987), 19, cited in Costella, "The Historical Development of Dispensational Theology within Biblical Fundamentalism."

27. Ibid., 14.

28. Marsden, *Understanding Fundamentalism and Evangelicalism*, 9–10.

29. Marsden, *Fundamentalism and American Culture*, 68.

30. Hal Lindsey, *The Late Great Planet Earth* (Grand Rapids, MI: Zondervan, 1970), page opposite title page.
31. Ibid., 48–49.
32. Cited on back cover of Lindsey, *The Late Great Planet Earth*; Mark Silk, "Religious Books: Seven That Made a Difference," *New York Times*, March 30, 1986; and Stella Dong, "Faith in Trade Houses," *New York Times*, April 11, 1982.
33. Cited on front cover of Lindsey, *The Late Great Planet Earth*. Newspaper and magazine articles have asserted that Lindsey's book has actually sold closer to 35 million copies. See Daniel Pipes, "The End of Days," *Commentary*, April 1, 2001; Carl E. Olson, "No End in Sight," *First Things*, November 1, 2002; Christopher Howse, "What's All This About the Rapture?" *Daily Telegraph*, April 24, 2004; and Gwen Florio, "Christian Merchandise Wades Into Secular Waters," *Denver Post*, December 23, 2003.
34. Pipes, "The End of Days."
35. Biography of Dr. Tim LaHaye, http://www.leftbehind.com/channelbooks.asp?channelID=30&pageid=130#lahaye (accessed November 30, 2003).
36. Ibid.
37. Ibid.
38. Gershom Gorenberg, "Intolerance: The Bestseller," *The American Prospect*, September 23, 2002; and Tom Sine, "Who Is Tim LaHaye?" *Sojourners*, September/October 2001.
39. There remain millions of Protestants in America, many of whom are in fact evangelicals, who have not renounced replacement theology. On the contrary, these Protestants fervently embrace a form of replacement theology that they refer to by the more positive name of "covenant theology." Covenant theology stresses the familiar message that the true Israel is comprised of all people who have embraced Christ as their Savior. Jews who accept Christ are certainly welcomed back into the covenant. But in the absence of such Christian faith, the Jewish people and the modern State of Israel enjoy no special theological status. This view is not anti-Semitic, and those who adhere to it are not anti-Semites. Rather, it is my thesis that replacement theology creates the *potential* for anti-Semitism in the church. Human nature being what it is, this potential for anti-Semitism has in the past been fully realized. In America today, many who embrace covenant theology recognize this potential, and they are committed to opposing anti-Semitism in their churches.
40. Cited in Elliott Abrams, *Faith or Fear* (New York: The Free Press, 1997), 46–47.
41. Ibid., 52.
42. Ibid., 49–50.
43. Ibid., 53.
44. Ibid., 52–53.
45. Ibid., 53.
46. Ibid., 50.
47. Ibid., 59.
48. Alan Cooperman, "Israel Divestiture Spurs Clash," *Washington Post*, September 29, 2004.
49. Kevin Eckstrom, "World Council of Churches Endorses Divestment from Israel," *Religion News Service*, February 21, 2005; and Stephen Brown, "World Council of

Churches Gives Nod to Israeli Divestment Proposal," *Ecumenical News International*, February 21, 2005.

50. Alan Cooperman, "United Church of Christ Urges Economic Pressure on Mideast," *Washington Post*, July 6, 2005; and Mary Frances Schjonberg, "Positive Investment in Israel-Palestine Central to Council Action," *Episcopal News Service*, October 9, 2005.

CHAPTER THREE
MOTIVES

1. Netty C. Gross, "Theology Be Damned," *Jerusalem Report*, January 15, 2001.
2. Hagee, *Final Dawn Over Jerusalem*, 9.
3. Craig Horowitz, "Israel's Christian Soldiers," *New York Magazine*, September 29, 2003.
4. Cited in Kathy Kiely, "GOP's DeLay Garners Influence," *USA Today*, July 29, 2003.
5. Jeremiah 16:13, *The Scofield Study Bible*.
6. Ezekiel 34:12–13.
7. Jerry Falwell, *Listen, America!* (New York: Bantam Books, 1980), 93.
8. Hagee, *Should Christians Support Israel?*, 166.
9. Pat Robertson, "Why Evangelical Christians Support Israel," speech to the Herzliya Conference on Security, Herzliya, Israel, December 17, 2003.
10. Pat Robertson, interview by Bob Simon, *60 Minutes*, CBS, August 21, 2002.
11. Gary Bauer, interview with author, January 7, 2003.
12. Horowitz, "Israel's Christian Soldiers."
13. Cited in Merrill Simon, *Jerry Falwell and the Jews* (Middle Village, NY: Jonathan David Publishers, 1999), 64.
14. Cited in Martin Schram, "Jerry Falwell Vows Amity with Israel," *Washington Post*, September 12, 1981.
15. Hagee, *Final Dawn Over Jerusalem*, 34–42.
16. John Hagee, speech at the Israeli embassy, Washington DC, December 14, 2002.
17. Barbara Tuchman, *Bible and Sword* (New York: Ballantine Books, 1984), 316.
18. Gary Bauer, interview with author, January 7, 2003.
19. Pat Robertson, interview by Bob Simon, *60 Minutes*, CBS, August 21, 2002.
20. Cited in Michael Freund, "Cross His Heart," *Jerusalem Post*, September 5, 2003.
21. Hagee speech at the Israeli embassy, December 14, 2002.
22. Hagee, *Should Christians Support Israel?*, 2–4.
23. Hagee speech at the Israeli embassy, December 14, 2002.
24. Gustav Scheller, *Operation Exodus* (Kent, England: Sovereign World, 1998), 90.
25. Bridges for Peace, "Light in the Midst of Darkness," www.bridgesforpeace.com (accessed October 5, 2003).
26. Cited in Simon, *Jerry Falwell and the Jews*, 63.
27. Ibid., 65–66.
28. Samuel Huntington, "The Clash of Civilizations?" *Foreign Affairs*, Summer 1993.
29. Ibid.
30. Cited in Laurie Goodstein, "Seeing Islam as 'Evil' Faith, Evangelicals Seek Converts," *New York Times*, May 27, 2003.

31. Gary Bauer, interview with author, January 7, 2003.
32. Gary Bauer, speech to AIPAC Policy Conference, Washington DC, March 30, 2003.
33. Alan Keyes, "Standing Firm for Israel," *World Net Daily*, posted April 29, 2002.
34. Tom DeLay, speech to AIPAC Leadership Summit, Washington DC, July 23, 2003.
35. Ibid.
36. Tom DeLay, speech at "Night to Honor Israel," Cornerstone Church, San Antonio, Texas, November 24, 2002.
37. Gary Bauer, speech to AIPAC Policy Conference, Washington DC, March 30, 2003.
38. Robertson, speech to the Herzliya Conference on Security, December 17, 2003.
39. Bob Simon, "Zion's Christian Soldiers," *60 Minutes*, CBS, October 6, 2002.
40. Cited in Simon, "Zion's Christian Soldiers."
41. Ed Dobson and Ed Hindson, "Apocalypse Now?" *Heritage Foundation Policy Review*, Fall 1986.
42. Cited in Horowitz, "Israel's Christian Soldiers."
43. Pat Robertson, interview by Bob Simon, *60 Minutes*, CBS, August 21, 2002.
44. Cited in Simon, *Jerry Falwell and the Jews*, 45.
45. Matthew 24:36.
46. Dobson and Hindson, "Apocalypse Now?" and George Marsden, *Fundamentalism in American Culture* (New York: Oxford University Press, 1980), 141–149.
47. Dobson and Hindson, "Apocalypse Now?"
48. Ibid.
49. Ibid.

Chapter Four
The Deep Roots of Christian Zionism: Hechler and Blackstone

1. The Blackstone Memorial, 1891, viewed at American Messianic Fellowship International, http://www.amfi.org/blackmem.htm (accessed January 4, 2003).
2. Cited in Paul Merkley, *The Politics of Christian Zionism* (London: Frank Cass, 1998), 3.
3. Ibid. Merkley's book provides an excellent overview of Christian Zionism from 1891 up to the birth of the State of Israel. My discussion of Hechler, Blackstone, Wilson, and Truman in this chapter and the next has benefited enormously from Merkley's work.
4. Cited in Tuchman, *Bible and Sword*, 284.
5. Cited in Merkley, *The Politics of Christian Zionism*, 11.
6. Tuchman, *Bible and Sword*, 121–146.
7. Ibid., 175–207.
8. Merkley, *The Politics of Christian Zionism*, 16; and Michael Pragai, *Faith and Fulfillment* (London, England: Vallentine Mitchell, 1985), 58–59.
9. Lawrence Epstein, *Zion's Call* (Lanham, MD: University Press of America, 1984), 77–78; and Pragai, *Faith and Fulfillment*, 59.

10. Marvin Lowenthal, ed., *The Diaries of Theodor Herzl* (New York: The Dial Press, 1956), 105–107.
11. Ibid., 105.
12. Merkley, *The Politics of Christian Zionism*, 17–29; and Epstein, *Zion's Call*, 80–81.
13. Cited in Merkley, *The Politics of Christian Zionism*, 28, 30.
14. Lowenthal, *The Diaries of Theodor Herzl*, 291–294.
15. Cited in Epstein, *Zion's Call*, 82.
16. Merkley, *The Politics of Christian Zionism*, 34.
17. David Pileggi, "Vicarious Zionist," *Jerusalem Post*, November 8, 1988, cited in Merkley, *The Politics of Christian Zionism*, 34.
18. Peter Grosse, *Israel in the Mind of America* (New York: Alfred A. Knopf, 1983), 37.
19. Back cover of William Blackstone, *Jesus Is Coming* (Grand Rapids, MI: Kregel Publications, 1989). Similar numbers are also cited in Grosse, *Israel in the Mind of America*, 35, and Merkley, *The Politics of Christian Zionism*, 63.
20. Blackstone, *Jesus Is Coming*, 171.
21. Cited in Merkley, *The Politics of Christian Zionism*, 67.
22. Ibid.
23. The Blackstone Memorial, 1891.
24. Cited in Merkley, *The Politics of Christian Zionism*, 61.
25. The Blackstone Memorial, 1891.
26. Letter from William Blackstone to President Harrison and Secretary of State Blaine dated March 5, 1891, viewed at American Messianic Fellowship International, http://www.amfi.org/blackmem.htm (accessed December 8, 2005).
27. Merkley, *The Politics of Christian Zionism*, 69; and Grosse, *Israel in the Mind of America*, 37.
28. Cited in Merkley, *The Politics of Christian Zionism*, 20.
29. Blackstone, *Jesus Is Coming*, 135.
30. Cited in Merkley, *The Politics of Christian Zionism*, 15–16.
31. William E. Currie, "God's Little Errand Boy," originally published in *100 Years of Blessing*, 1987, viewed at American Messianic Fellowship International, http://www.amfi.org/errandboy.htm (accessed December 8, 2005).
32. Merkley, *The Politics of Christian Zionism*, 61.
33. Cited in Merkley, *The Politics of Christian Zionism*, 70.
34. Ibid.
35. Letter from William Blackstone to President Harrison and Secretary of State Blaine dated March 5, 1891.
36. Grosse, *Israel in the Mind of America*, 38.

CHAPTER FIVE
THREE CHRISTIAN ZIONISTS WHO HELPED TO CREATE ISRAEL: BALFOUR, WILSON, AND TRUMAN

1. Cited in Merkley, *The Politics of Christian Zionism*, 191.
2. Tuchman, *Bible and Sword*, 290–303.
3. Ibid., 302–309.
4. Ibid., 313–314.

5. Chaim Weizmann, *Trial and Error* (London: Hamish Hamilton, 1950), 144.
6. Arthur Balfour, Introduction to Nahum Sokolow, *History of Zionism* (New York: Longmans, Green & Co., 1919), xxix–xxx.
7. Weizmann, *Trial and Error*, 195.
8. Cited in Weizmann, *Trial and Error*, 225.
9. Tuchman, *Bible and Sword*, 321.
10. Cited in Tuchman, *Bible and Sword*, 337.
11. Merkley, *The Politics of Christian Zionism*, 48–49.
12. Tuchman, *Bible and Sword*, 337.
13. Weizmann, *Trial and Error*, 224–226.
14. Cited in Pragai, *Faith and Fulfillment*, 86–87.
15. Cited in Blanche Dugdale, *Arthur James Balfour* (New York: G. P. Putnam's Sons, 1937), Vol. 2, 158.
16. Ibid., Vol. 1, 324.
17. Ibid., 30.
18. Ibid., 28–29.
19. Cited in Pragai, *Faith and Fulfillment*, 86.
20. Cited in Tuchman, *Bible and Sword*, 323.
21. Ibid., 318.
22. Cited in Merkley, *The Politics of Christian Zionism*, 80.
23. Ibid., 79.
24. Grosse, *Israel in the Mind of America*, 67.
25. Merkley, *The Politics of Christian Zionism*, 88–89.
26. Ibid., 89.
27. Cited in Merkley, *The Politics of Christian Zionism*, 91.
28. Ibid., 88–92.
29. Cited in Grosse, *Israel in the Mind of America*, 67.
30. David McCullough, *Truman* (New York: Simon & Schuster, 1992), 347.
31. Cited in McCullough, *Truman*, 353.
32. Cited in Tuchman, *Bible and Sword*, 348.
33. Michael T. Benson, *Harry S. Truman and the Founding of Israel* (Westport, CT: Praeger, 1997), 120.
34. Michael J. Cohen, *Truman and Israel* (Los Angeles: University of California Press, 1990), 159–160; McCullough, *Truman*, 604; and Benson, *Harry S. Truman and the Founding of Israel*, 121.
35. McCullough, *Truman*, 598–604; Benson, *Harry S. Truman and the Founding of Israel*, 96–97; and Cohen, *Truman and Israel*, 183.
36. Cited in Merkley, *The Politics of Christian Zionism*, 185–186.
37. McCullough, *Truman*, 608; and Benson, *Harry S. Truman and the Founding of Israel*, 128.
38. Benson, *Harry S. Truman and the Founding of Israel*, 165–166.
39. Clark Clifford, *Counsel to the President* (New York: Anchor Books, 1992), 4.
40. Ibid., 13.
41. McCullough, *Truman*, 596.
42. Clifford, *Counsel to the President*, 24.
43. Ibid., 14, 189–194.

44. Grosse, *Israel in the Mind of America*, 300–301; and Benson, *Harry S. Truman and the Founding of Israel*, 176–180.
45. McCullough, *Truman*, 596.
46. Clifford, *Counsel to the President*, 7–8.
47. Cited in McCullough, *Truman*, 597.
48. Benson, *Harry S. Truman and the Founding of Israel*, 31.
49. Cited in Cohen, *Truman and Israel*, 5–6.
50. Cited in Merkley, *The Politics of Christian Zionism*, 159.
51. Cited in Cohen, *Truman and Israel*, 6.
52. Cited in Merkley, *The Politics of Christian Zionism*, 162–163.
53. Cited in Benson, *Harry S. Truman and the Founding of Israel*, 191.
54. Ibid., 190.
55. Ibid.
56. Ibid.
57. Ibid., 191.
58. Cited in Clifford, *Counsel to the President*, 25.
59. Cited in Merkley, *The Politics of Christian Zionism*, 191.
60. Ibid.
61. Ibid.

CHAPTER SIX
CHRISTIAN ZIONISM IN WASHINGTON

1. Jerry Falwell, comments on *60 Minutes*, "Zion's Christian Soldiers," October 6, 2002.
2. Jerry Falwell, *Strength for the Journey* (New York: Simon and Schuster, 1987), 337.
3. Pat Robertson, *Shout It From the Housetops* (South Plainfield, NJ: Bridge Publishing, 1972), 272.
4. Falwell, *Strength for the Journey*, 334.
5. Ibid., 334–337.
6. Ralph Reed, *Active Faith* (New York: The Free Press, 1996), 109.
7. Dinesh D'Souza, *Falwell: Before the Millennium* (Chicago: Regnery Gateway, 1984), 10.
8. Falwell, *Strength for the Journey*, 365.
9. Nina Easton, "The Power and the Glory," *The American Prospect*, May 20, 2002.
10. Martha Brant, "West Wing Story: A New GOP?" *Newsweek*, December 13, 2001; and Richard Berke, "Aide Says Bush Will Do More to Marshall Religious Base," *New York Times*, December 12, 2001.
11. D'Souza, *Falwell: Before the Millennium*, 8; and Falwell, *Strength for the Journey*, 363.
12. Falwell, *Listen, America!*, 98.
13. Pat Robertson, speech at the U.S.-Israel Solidarity Rally of the annual convention of the National Religious Broadcasters, Washington DC, January 30, 1994.
14. David Shipler, "1,000 Christian Zionists in Jerusalem," *New York Times*, September 25, 1980.
15. David Shipler, "Israel Is Cultivating Some Unlikely New Friends," *New York Times*, December 1, 1981; and William Claiborne, "Israelis Look on U.S. Evangelical Christians

as Potent Allies in Battle with Arab States," *Washington Post*, March 23, 1981.
16. Richard Cohen, "Allies," *Washington Post*, July 12, 1981.
17. Martin Schram, "Jerry Falwell Vows Amity with Israel," *Washington Post*, September 12, 1981.
18. Ibid.
19. Steven Erlanger, "Netanyahu, in U.S., Woos Conservatives," *New York Times*, January 20, 1998.
20. Laurie Goodstein, "Falwell to Mobilize Support for Israel," *New York Times*, January 21, 1998; and Gayle White, "Southern Baptists Rally to Support Netanyahu," *Atlanta Journal and Constitution*, January 22, 1998.
21. Caryle Murphy, "Jewish Leaders Assail Netanyahu; Meeting with Evangelicals Is Scored as a Mistake," *Washington Post*, January 22, 1998; and White, "Southern Baptists Rally to Support Netanyahu."
22. Jerry Falwell, "Pray for the Peace of Jerusalem," *World Net Daily*, posted March 30, 2002.
23. Cited in Martin Argles, "Israel for Beginners," *The Guardian* (London), January 5, 1999.
24. Cited in Simon, *Jerry Falwell and the Jews*, 29.
25. Gary Bauer, Jerry Falwell, John Hagee, et al., Letter to President George W. Bush, April 11, 2002, downloaded from the American Values Web site, www.ouramericanvalues.org, on November 21, 2002.
26. Howard Fineman and Tamara Lipper, "A Very Mixed Marriage," *Newsweek*, June 2, 2003.
27. Rabbi Yechiel Eckstein, "Christians, Jews on Same Page," *Chicago Sun-Times*, October 30, 2002; and "Stand for Israel," downloaded from the Web site of the International Fellowship of Christians and Jews (www.ifcj.org) on June 19, 2004.
28. Avram Goldstein, "Christian Coalition Rallies for Israel in Comeback Bid," *Washington Post*, October 12, 2002; and Janine Zacharia, "U.S. Christians Pledge 'We Love You Israel,'" *Jerusalem Post*, October 13, 2002.
29. Jerry Falwell, comments on *60 Minutes*, "Zion's Christian Soldiers," October 6, 2002.
30. Pat Robertson, interview by Bob Simon for *60 Minutes*, August 21, 2002.
31. Cited in Joshua Mitnick, "Christian Coalition Embraces Jewish State," *Washington Times*, November 27, 2002.
32. "Christian Coalition Leaders Return From Israel," Christian Coalition Media Advisory, November 27, 2002.
33. Ibid.
34. Tom DeLay, speech, Stand for Israel awards dinner, Washington DC, April 2, 2003.
35. Cited in Glenn Kessler, "Powell Able to Return Attention to Mideast Plan," *Washington Post*, April 24, 2003.
36. Gary Bauer, Jerry Falwell, John Hagee, et al., letter to President George W. Bush, May 19, 2003, downloaded from the American Values Web site, www.ouramericanvalues.org, on October 1, 2003.
37. Cited in Dana Milbank, "Bush's Shift on Israel Was Swift," *Washington Post*, June 21, 2003.
38. Ibid.

39. Herb Keinon, "The Christian Right Is Watching Bush on Israel," *Jerusalem Post*, July 7, 2003.
40. "H. Res. 294 Condemning the terrorism inflicted on Israel since the Aqaba Summit and expressing solidarity with the Israeli people in their fight against terrorism," 108th Congress, 1st session, introduced on June 25, 2003, http://www.imra.org.il/story.php3?id=17381 (accessed December 9, 2005). Also, Congressional Record 10 of 2000, page H5882, http://thomas.loc.gov/cgi-bin/query/D?r108:10:./temp/~r108IPxQwa:: (accessed December 9, 2005).
41. Cited in David Firestone, "DeLay Is to Carry Dissenting Message on a Mideast Tour," *New York Times*, July 25, 2003.
42. Tom DeLay, "Be Not Afraid," speech before the Israeli Knesset, Jerusalem, Israel, July 30, 2003.
43. Richard Hellman, president, Christians' Israel Public Action Campaign, interview by the author, January 14, 2004; and Julia Duin, "Israel Pits U.S. Politics Against Road Map Plan," *Washington Times*, August 18, 2003.
44. Helen Friedman, executive director, Americans for a Safe Israel, interview by the author, January 12, 2004; Duin, "Israel Pits U.S. Politics Against Road Map Plan"; and Committee for a One State Solution, downloaded from the Americans for a Safe Israel Web site (www.afsi.org) on January 12, 2004.
45. Ken Silverstein and Michael Scherer, "Born-Again Zionists," *MotherJones.com*, September/October 2002.
46. George W. Bush, *A Charge to Keep* (New York: Morrow, 1999), 136.
47. Stephen Mansfield, *The Faith of George W. Bush* (Lake Mary, FL: Charisma House, 2003), 119–121; Judy Keen, "White House Staffers Gather for Bible Study," *USA Today*, October 14, 2002; and Francine Kiefer, "The Private Faith of a Public Man," *The Village Voice*, September 6, 2002.
48. Mansfield, *The Faith of George W. Bush*, 109.
49. Howard Fineman, "Bush and God," *Newsweek*, March 10, 2003.
50. Kiefer, "The Private Faith of a Public Man."
51. Bush, *A Charge to Keep*, 138.
52. Mansfield, *The Faith of George W. Bush*, 124.
53. David Frum, *The Right Man* (New York: Random House, 2003), 249.
54. Lee Bockhorn, "Condi Crazy," *The Weekly Standard*, March 28, 2002.
55. John Adam, "Condi Rice: Presbyterian with Faith, Political Mettle," *The Presbyterian Layman*, November 22, 2000.
56. David Plotz, "Condoleezza Rice: George W. Bush's Celebrity Advisor," *Slate*, May 12, 2000.
57. Frum, *The Right Man*, 3.
58. "America's Stake in Israel's War on Terrorism," Senate Floor Statement by U.S. Senator James M. Inhofe (R-Okla), December 4, 2001, http://inhofe.senate.gov/pressreleases/terrorism.htm (accessed March 13, 2006).
59. "Peace in the Middle East," Senate Floor Statement by U.S. Senator James M. Inhofe (R-Okla), March 4, 2002, http://inhofe.senate.gov/pressapp/record.cfm?id=183110 (accessed March 13, 2006).
60. David Corn, "Wrath of the Right," *Working for Change*, April 22, 2002.

Chapter Seven
Christian Zionism's Good Works

1. Rebecca Brimmer, "Adoption Program Expands to Meet Increasing Needs," Bridges for Peace fund-raising letter, July 2002, downloaded from Bridges for Peace Web site (www.bridgesforpeace.com).

2. Jeffrey Sheler, "Odd Bedfellows," *U.S. News and World Report*, August 12, 2002; Ami Eden, "Pariah Rabbi Converts Foes of Evangelical Outreach," *The Forward*, July 12, 2002; Horowitz, "Israel's Christian Soldiers;" International Fellowship of Christians and Jews, financial statement, year ended December 31, 2002; and International Fellowship of Christians and Jews, financial statement, year ended December 31, 2003.

3. *Shoresh*, newsletter of the International Fellowship of Christians and Jews, Vol. 9, No. 8, August 2003, 4–5.

4. "A Concise Summary of Who We Are," Bridges for Peace, http://www.bridgesforpeace.com/h2n.php?fn=whoarewe.html (accessed December 9, 2005).

5. Rebecca Brimmer, "Come Home," Bridges for Peace fund-raising letter, April 2003, downloaded from the Bridges for Peace Web site.

6. Rebecca Brimmer, "I'm Bad, Just Because I'm Jewish," Bridges for Peace fund-raising letter, May 13, 2003, downloaded from the Bridges for Peace Web site.

7. Gustav Scheller, *Operation Exodus* (Kent, England: Sovereign World, 1998), 54.

8. Ibid., 73, 144–145.

9. Ibid., 115–143.

10. "The History of EEF," downloaded from the Web site of the Ebenezer Emergency Fund (formal name of Operation Exodus) (www.operation-exodus.org/UK) on October 4, 2003.

11. "What is Exobus," downloaded from the Exobus Web site (www.exobus.org) on October 4, 2003.

12. "Exodus II," downloaded from the John Hagee Ministries Web site (www.jhm.org) on June 20, 2004.

13. *The Religious Right: The Assault on Tolerance and Pluralism in America* (New York: Anti-Defamation League, 1994), 21.

14. Rebecca Brimmer, "Light in the Midst of Darkness," Bridges for Peace fund-raising letter, May 13, 2003, downloaded from the Bridges for Peace Web site.

15. Rebecca Brimmer, "We Need a Miracle," Bridges for Peace fund-raising letter, August 2003, downloaded from the Bridges for Peace Web site.

16. Ibid.

17. Rebecca Brimmer, "Restoring Zion," Bridges for Peace fund-raising letter, June 12, 2003, downloaded from the Bridges for Peace Web site; and Rebecca Brimmer, "When You Came, I Knew that God Was Real," Bridges for Peace fund-raising letter, June 2002, downloaded from the Bridges for Peace Web site.

18. *Shoresh*, newsletter of the International Fellowship of Christians and Jews, Vol. 1, No. 1, 7.

19. See Isaiah 58:7.

20. *Shoresh*, newsletter of the International Fellowship of Christians and Jews, Vol. 1, No. 1, 7.

21. "The Story of the International Fellowship of Christians and Jews" (promotional pamphlet).
22. Cited in Horowitz, "Israel's Christian Soldiers."
23. Silverstein and Scherer, "Born-Again Zionists."
24. E-mail message from Jodie Anderson, leader of the Battalion of Deborah, sent April 1, 2003.
25. E-mail message from Jodie Anderson, leader of the Battalion of Deborah, sent September 17, 2003.
26. Ibid.
27. Jodie Anderson, leader of the Battalion of Deborah, interview by the author, Washington DC, April 1, 2003.
28. Visitor Arrivals by Mode of Travel, tables prepared by the Israeli Ministry of Tourism and downloaded from the Ministry of Tourism Web site (www.tourism.gov.il) on December 26, 2003.
29. Jenny Hazan, "Birthright Summer Tours to Generate $25 Million Revenue," *Jerusalem Post*, July 11, 2003.
30. "Pat Robertson Visits Jerusalem," Press Room, Israel Ministry of Tourism, downloaded from the Ministry of Tourism's American Web site (www.goisrael.com) on December 25, 2003.
31. Richard Hellman, president, Christians' Israel Public Action Campaign, interview by the author, Washington DC, January 14, 2004.
32. "Join the BFP Solidarity Mission and Show you Care!" downloaded from the Bridges for Peace Web site on October 4, 2003.
33. Results from Inbound Tourism Survey 2001, table prepared by the Israeli Ministry of Tourism and downloaded from the Ministry of Tourism Web site on December 26, 2003; and Doron Geller, "Who's Coming," *Jerusalem Post*, December 29, 2000.
34. "What Is the Goal of the Jerusalem Prayer Team?" downloaded from the Jerusalem Prayer Team Web site (www.jerusalemprayerteam.org) on October 12, 2003.
35. "Stand for Israel," downloaded from the Web site of the International Fellowship of Christians and Jews (www.ifcj.org) on June 19, 2004.

CHAPTER EIGHT
THE RESPONSE FROM THE JEWISH MAINSTREAM

1. Cited in Carroll, *Constantine's Sword*, 366.
2. Cited in Roland Bainton, *Here I Stand* (New York: Meridian Books, 1995), 297.
3. *Luther's Works* (American Edition), Vol. 45, (published jointly by Fortress Press and Concordia Publishing House), 200, as cited in Mark Albrecht, "Martin Luther and the Jews," Middler Church History Paper, November 19, 1982.
4. *Luther's Works*, 229, as cited in Albrecht, "Martin Luther and the Jews."
5. Holmio, *Luther—Friend or Foe*, (Chicago: National Lutheran Council, 1949), 18, as cited in Albrecht, "Martin Luther and the Jews."
6. Cited in Hilberg, *The Destruction of the European Jews*, 14.
7. Gershom Gorenberg interviewed on *60 Minutes*, "Zion's Christian Soldiers," October 6, 2002.
8. Cited in Caryle Murphy, "Jewish Leaders in U.S. Assail Netanyahu; Meeting With Evangelical Is Scored as a Mistake," *Washington Post*, January 22, 1998.

9. Gershom Gorenberg, *The End of Days* (New York: Oxford University Press, 2002), 107–109.
10. Cited in Jonathan Broder, "Onward, Christian Soldiers!" *Jerusalem Report*, September 22, 1994.
11. Joan Lowy, "Some Conservative Christian Beliefs Are Disturbing to Many Jews," *Orange County Register*, April 29, 1998.
12. Cited in Horowitz, "Israel's Christian Soldiers."
13. Cited in Alana Newhouse, "Chicago ZOA Chapter Honors Televangelist Robertson," *The Forward*, July 12, 2002.
14. Abraham Foxman, "Why Evangelical Support for Israel Is a Good Thing," downloaded from the Anti-Defamation League Web site (www.adl.org) on November 6, 2002.
15. Yossi Alpher interviewed on *60 Minutes*, "Zion's Christian Soldiers," October 6, 2002.
16. Peter Beinart, "Bad Move," *The New Republic*, May 20, 2002.
17. Pat Robertson, interviewed by Bob Simon, *60 Minutes*, CBS, August 21, 2002.
18. Pat Robertson, *60 Minutes* interview; and Falwell in Simon, *Jerry Falwell and the Jews*, 82–83.
19. Cited in Simon, *Jerry Falwell and the Jews*, 84.
20. Gary Bauer, interview by the author, Arlington, Virginia, January 7, 2003.
21. Ibid.
22. Pat Robertson, *60 Minutes* interview.
23. Cited in Simon, *Jerry Falwell and the Jews*, 63, 82.
24. Rabbi David Saperstein interviewed on *Nightline*, "God and Country," ABC, November 26, 2002.
25. Cited in "The Rebirth of Ralph Reed," *Atlanta Jewish Times*, July 23, 1999.
26. Cited in Silverstein and Scherer, "Born-Again Zionists."

CHAPTER NINE
EVANGELICAL ANTI-SEMITISM?

1. Ralph Reed, "From Confrontation to Cooperation," speech before the Anti-Defamation League, New York, New York, April 3, 1995.
2. Littell, *The Crucifixion of the Jews*, 3.
3. Cited in "Anti-Israel, Anti-Semitic?" downloaded from the ABC News Web site (www.abcnews.com) on June 30, 2004.
4. Marsden, *Fundamentalism and American Culture*, 210.
5. Cited in Timothy Weber, *Living in the Shadow of the Second Coming*, 154–155.
6. Ibid., 155–156.
7. Marsden, *Fundamentalism in American Culture*, 211.
8. Pat Robertson, *The New World Order* (Dallas, TX: Word Publishing, 1991), 37.
9. Ibid., 72.
10. Ibid., 71.
11. Cited in Jacob Heilbrunn, "His Anti-Semitic Sources," *New York Review of Books*, April 20, 1995.
12. Pat Robertson, "Our Foreign Policy Should Put U.S. First," letter to the editor of

the *New York Times*, March 5, 1995.
13. Ibid.
14. "Two Letters and Excerpts from Book," *New York Times*, March 4, 1995.
15. Robertson, *The New World Order*, 257.
16. Ibid., 252.
17. Ibid., 258.
18. Ibid., 256–257.
19. Pat Robertson, "Why Evangelical Christians Support Israel," speech before The Herzliya Conference, Herzliya, Israel, December 17, 2003.
20. Ibid.
21. Craig Nelson, "Evangelicals a New Lifeline for Israelis," *Atlanta Journal-Constitution*, December 25, 2003.
22. Pat Robertson, interviewed by Bob Simon, *60 Minutes*, August 21, 2002.
23. *The Religious Right: The Assault on Tolerance and Pluralism in America*, 21.
24. Norman Podhoretz, "In the Matter of Pat Robertson," *Commentary*, August 1995.
25. Michael Lind, "Rev. Robertson's Grand International Conspiracy Theory," *New York Review of Books*, February 2, 1995; and Podhoretz, "In the Matter of Pat Robertson."
26. Pat Robertson, *The New Millennium* (Dallas, TX: Word Publishing, 1990), 292–293.
27. Ibid., 293.
28. Ibid., 290.
29. Ibid., 286.
30. Cited in "Jewish Leaders Denounce Attacks on Pat Robertson and Religious Conservative Voters," press release issued by the Christian Coalition on March 10, 1995.
31. Cited in Abraham Foxman, *Never Again?* (New York: Harper San Francisco, 2003), 146.
32. Jerry Falwell, preface to Simon, *Jerry Falwell and the Jews*, x.
33. Cited in "ADL: Rev. Falwell's Statement that the Antichrist Is a Jew Borders on Anti-Semitism and Is Rooted in Christian Theological Extremism," press release issued by the Anti-Defamation League on January 19, 1999.
34. Cited in "ADL Welcomes Falwell Apology on Antichrist," press release issued by the Anti-Defamation League on February 2, 1999.
35. Bailey Smith, quoted in *The Religious Right: The Assault on Tolerance and Pluralism in America*, 70.
36. D'Souza, *Falwell: Before the Millennium*, 123.
37. Ibid.
38. D'Souza, *Falwell: Before the Millennium*, 124.
39. Ibid.
40. Jerry Falwell, "Sharon, Arafat and the Coming War in the Middle East," sermon before the Thomas Road Baptist Church, Lynchburg, Virginia, August 26, 2001.
41. Cited in Simon, *Jerry Falwell and the Jews*, 9.
42. Ibid.
43. Ibid., 22–23.
44. Ibid., 23.
45. Ibid., 6.
46. Ibid., 5.

47. Falwell, preface to Simon, *Jerry Falwell and the Jews.*
48. Argles, "Israel for Beginners."
49. Foxman, *Never Again?*, 145.
50. Ibid., 145–146.

Chapter Ten
Toward a New Approach

1. Cited in Martin Gilbert, *The Righteous* (New York: Henry Holt, 2003), xvii.
2. "Yad Vashem—A Brief History," downloaded from the Yad Vashem Web site (www.yad-vashem.org.il) on December 21, 2003.
3. Carole Carlson, *Corrie ten Boom: Her Life and Faith* (New York: Guideposts, 1983), 78.
4. Alan Snyder, "Corrie ten Boom: A Protestant Evangelical Response to the Nazi Persecution of Jews," *Neo Politique*, downloaded from the Neo Politique Web site (www.neopolitique.org) on October 30, 2003.
5. Corrie ten Boom, *The Hiding Place* (New York: Bantam Books, 1971), 138.
6. Corrie ten Boom, *Father Ten Boom: God's Man* (Old Tappan, NJ: Fleming Revell, 1978), 154.
7. Ibid., 28–29.
8. Ibid., 33.
9. Ten Boom, *The Hiding Place*, 25.
10. Carlson, *Corrie ten Boom: Her Life and Faith*, 76.
11. Corrie ten Boom, *In My Father's House* (Grand Rapids, MI: Fleming Revell, 1976), 14.
12. Ten Boom, *Father Ten Boom: God's Man*, 107.
13. Carlson, *Corrie ten Boom: Her Life and Faith*, 124–125.
14. "Christians Open 'Embassy' in Jerusalem," Associated Press, September 30, 1980.
15. David Shipler, "1,000 Christian Zionists in Jerusalem," *New York Times*, September 25, 1980.
16. Ibid.
17. Cited in Susan Sandager, "Grant Proposal," provided to the author on October 28, 2003.
18. Sandager, "Grant Proposal."
19. Clarence Wagner and Rebecca Brimmer, "We Are Tired of Crying," solicitation letter dated May 13, 2003, downloaded from the Bridges for Peace Web site (www .bridgesforpeace.com) on October 4, 2003.
20. Cited in Scheller, *Operation Exodus*, 87–88.
21. Ibid., 90.
22. Ibid., 109 (citing Isaiah 60:14).
23. DeLay, "Be Not Afraid," speech before the Israeli Knesset, Jerusalem, Israel, July 30, 2003.
24. Philip Hallie, *Lest Innocent Blood Be Shed* (New York: Harper Perennial, 1979), xiii.
25. Ibid., 103.
26. Joe Eskenazi, "Christian Zionists and Jews Meet to Discuss Issues of Joint Concern," *Jewish Bulletin of Northern California*, April 26, 2002.
27. Ibid.

28. Cited in Foxman, *Never Again?*, 148.
29. Abraham Foxman, foreword to *The Religious Right: The Assault on Tolerance and Pluralism in America*, iv.
30. Foxman, *Never Again?*, 144.
31. Daniel Levitas, "A.D.L. and the Christian Right ," *The Nation*, June 19, 1995.
32. Cited in "The Rebirth of Ralph Reed," *Atlanta Jewish Times*, July 23, 1999.
33. Pat Robertson, interview by Bob Simon, *60 Minutes,* August 21, 2002.
34. Cited in "The Rebirth of Ralph Reed."
35. Ralph Reed, "We People of Faith Stand With Israel," *Los Angeles Times*, April 21, 2002.
36. Abraham Foxman, "Why Evangelical Support for Israel Is a Good Thing," downloaded from the Anti-Defamation League Web site (www.adl.org) on November 6, 2002.
37. Foxman, *Never Again?* 80.
38. Ibid., 78–87.
39. Ibid., 85.
40. Ibid., 80.
41. Ibid., 85.
42. Gilbert, *The Righteous*, xvii.

CONCLUSION
STRANGE BEDFELLOWS OR BLOOD BROTHERS?

1. Tom DeLay, speech at the Friend of Israel Award Dinner, Washington DC, April 2, 2003.
2. Tom Lantos, speech at the Friend of Israel Award Dinner, Washington DC, April 2, 2003.
3. Ibid.
4. Merkley, *The Politics of Christian Zionism*, 33–34.
5. Dugdale, *Arthur James Balfour*, Volume 2, 303–304.
6. Alexander Zvielli, "Begin: The Man, the Vision and the Deeds," *Jerusalem Post*, March 10, 1992.

INDEX

60 Minutes 81, 145, 262–263, 266–267, 270–272, 274
700 Club, The 142, 213
95 Theses 28, 181

A

Abbas, Mahmoud 147, 195
Abraham/Abram *xi*, 4, 13, 18, 20–22, 38, 42–44, 57, 68–70, 73–74, 94, 101, 126, 157, 175, 196, 211–212
Abrahamic covenant 13–14, 18–19, 21–22
Acheson, Dean 124
Afghanistan 153
Africa 97, 107
Al-Aqsa Mosque 186–187
al-Rantisi, Abd Al-Aziz 149
Alexandria 23
alliance of Jews and Christians 253
Alpher, Yossi 193, 271
America 5–6, 8–9, 13–14, 37, 42, 46–50, 52–56, 58, 60, 65–67, 70, 75–80, 82, 84–85, 91, 99–100, 113, 129, 137–140, 152, 168, 172, 174–175, 179–180, 188, 190, 192, 195–196, 199–200, 204–207, 217–218, 223–224, 228, 235, 243–244, 248–249, 256, 261
American Christian(s) 82, 168, 171
American Christian Trust 173
American Coalition for Traditional Values 60
American Friends of Peace Now 199
American Friends Services Committee 241
American Israel Public Affairs Committee (AIPAC) 91, 196–200, 263
American Jewish Committee 190–191, 193
American Jewish community 6, 133, 179, 192, 228–229, 243–244, 248
American Jews 6–8, 180, 187, 190–191, 193–196, 199–200, 216, 228, 246, 256
American Left, the 87
American Lutheran Church 37
Americans for a Safe Israel 200, 268
Anglican Church 42
anti-Christian 2, 221
Anti-Defamation League (ADL) 183, 190, 192, 219–220, 223, 243–246, 269, 271–272, 274
anti-Jewish 2, 17, 24–25, 27, 30–31, 33–35, 215
anti-Semitic 14, 24, 26–30, 35, 38, 72, 182, 203–205, 208–209, 211, 214–215, 218–222, 235, 241, 244, 247, 256, 261
anti-Semite(s) *xiii*, 35–36, 185, 191, 203, 213–215, 218–219, 229, 248, 261
anti-Semitism *xi*, 1–2, 5, 8, 14, 16, 29–33, 60, 72–74, 82, 92–94, 102, 143, 180–181, 189, 202–206, 210–219, 221–222, 224, 229, 232, 243–244, 261
anti-Zionist Jews 120
Antichrist 60, 85–86, 218–219, 272
Antioch 24–25
apocalypse 83, 185, 263
Aqaba summit 149, 268
Arab(s) 5, 13, 57, 75, 119, 121–124, 126, 147, 195, 235, 237, 266
Arab-Israeli conflict 63
Arabia 80
Arab Revolt, the 119
Arafat, Yasser 144, 194–195, 272
Argentina 97, 163, 169
Argentinean Jews 169
Armageddon 80–81, 185–186, 190
Armenia 165
Aryan 29–30, 36
assimilation 92, 99
Augustine 22–24, 26, 28, 258
Auschwitz 2, 6, 14, 32, 120, 204, 239
axis of evil 153

B

Babylonia 104
Baden, Grand Duke of 96, 102
Baghdad 3, 140–141
Baker, James 133
Balfour, Lord Arthur 57, 71–72, 107–110, 112–116, 118, 126, 254, 264–265, 274

Balfour Declaration, the 72, 108, 110–113, 116, 118–120, 122, 126, 254
Barak, Ehud 194, 197–198, 200
batel b'shishim 216
Battalion of Deborah 170–171, 269–270
Bauer, Gary 67, 69, 72, 77–80, 144–145, 148, 153, 172, 194–195, 262–263, 267, 271
Begin, Menachem 3, 140–142, 253, 255, 257, 274
Beinart, Peter 193, 271
Ben-Gurion, David 123, 129
Bible 4, 13–14, 17, 23, 35–36, 38, 42–43, 49–50, 52–55, 57–59, 65–69, 72–74, 82, 84–85, 92, 95, 98–99, 102, 114–115, 117–118, 120, 126–128, 135, 140, 142, 152, 155–157, 164, 167, 185, 196, 221–223, 231–232, 234, 239, 260, 268
Bible and Sword 112, 262–265
birth of Israel 57, 64, 72, 82, 84–85, 162, 183
Birth of Modern Racial Anti-Semitism in France and Germany, The 232
bishops 24, 31, 33, 36
Black Sea 237–238
Blackstone, William 90–91, 97–105, 117, 134, 263–264
Blackstone Memorial 99–101, 104, 117–118, 263–264
Blaine, James 99, 101, 104–105, 264
Blair, Tony 147
Bocquet, Germaine 2–5, 9
Bonhoeffer, Dietrich 37, 245
Boone, Pat 163
Brandeis, Louis 100, 116–118
Bridges for Peace 40, 163–165, 168, 172, 174, 237, 262, 268–270, 273
Briggs, Charles 50
Britain 57, 72, 79, 107–112, 115, 120, 126–127, 147, 152
British Mandate 119, 122–123
British Zionist Federation 110
Brownback, Sam 156
Bulgaria 101
Bush, George H. W. 133–134, 206
Bush, George W. 127, 133–135, 137, 143–155, 194, 266–268

C

Camp David 197–198
Camp David Summit 194
Canada 52, 168
Capitol Hill *xiii*, 156, 198
Card Jr., Andrew 155
Carr, William Guy 209
Carroll, James 24, 258, 270
Carter, Jimmy 152, 206, 220
Carter-Mondale campaign 220
Castel Gandolfo 32
Catholic Church 7–8, 23, 28, 30–32, 34, 37, 60, 72, 74, 181, 205
Catholic catechism 7
Catholic teachings 7
Center for Security Policy 151
Chafer, Lewis 59
Chamberlain, Joseph 107–108
Charge to Keep, A 151, 154, 268
Charismatic movement 175
Chicago Committee for Hebrew Christian Work 103
Christ 3–4, 9, 13, 16, 18–25, 29, 33–34, 37–38, 43–45, 47–50, 52, 55–56, 59–61, 67, 71–73, 81, 83, 85–86, 103, 152, 154, 156, 166, 170, 174, 181, 183–184, 186, 188, 214, 220–222, 236, 258, 260–261
Christendom 5, 27, 29, 72, 114, 182, 253
Christian-Jewish relationships 254
Christian allies *xi*, 188, 236, 253
Christian Broadcasting Network 166, 171, 213
Christian church 1, 13, 28–29, 71, 73, 182
Christian Coalition, the 84, 134, 137, 145–146, 156, 172, 243–244, 267, 272
Christian Europe 1, 24, 26, 180
Christian Friends of Israel 170
Christianity 2, 4, 7, 9, 18, 21–23, 26, 28–29, 35–36, 38, 44–45, 47–51, 58, 61, 66–67, 72–73, 82, 84, 103–104,

151–155, 167, 170, 180–182, 184–185, 188, 216–217, 221, 228, 248, 253, 260
Christian Right, the *xiii,* 60, 83, 134, 137, 142–145, 179, 189–193, 243, 245–246, 248, 267, 274
Christians' Israel Public Action Campaign 172, 268, 270
Christian Solidarity With Israel Rally 145
Christian theology 3, 6, 13–14, 21, 26, 28, 56, 61, 66–67, 71, 101–102, 183, 260
Christian X 8
Christian Zionism *xi, xiii,* 14, 44, 46, 66, 69, 80–82, 86, 89, 91–92, 102–103, 112–113, 115, 120, 131, 133–134, 154, 159, 174–175, 179–180, 183–184, 187, 189, 196, 199–200, 204, 218, 234, 257, 263, 266, 268
Christian Zionist(s) *xi, xiii–xiv,* 5–6, 42, 63, 65–67, 69, 71–75, 77–83, 86–87, 91, 95, 101–105, 107, 111, 120, 134, 140, 142–151, 155–156, 159–164, 166–167, 169–175, 179–180, 182–183, 186–187, 189–200, 204, 214, 228–230, 234, 236–239, 241–242, 246, 248, 255, 257, 264, 266, 273
Chrysostom, John 24–27, 34, 258
church doctrine 8, 22
Churchill, Winston 109–110, 119
Church of the Holy Sepulcher 154
circumcised 18–19
  uncircumcised 21
Civil War 48–50, 53, 55–56, 117, 152
Cizik, Richard 77
Clifford, Clark 125–126, 265–266
Clinton, Bill 141–142, 251
cold war 58, 67, 75–77, 82, 87, 124, 138, 207
Combs, Roberta 145–147
Communism 162, 169, 209
  Communist Party 87
  Communist(s) 75–76, 87, 164, 169, 208
Concordat 30–31
Conference of Presidents of Major American Jewish Organizations 198–199
Confessing Church, the 36, 37
Conflict of the Ages, The 205
Congress 5, 80, 100, 137, 148–149, 173, 190, 198–199, 213, 251, 268
conservative Christians 50, 136, 191, 217, 243
conspiracy theory 188, 206, 208, 214, 272
Constantine 13, 22, 26–27
conversion(s) 22, 28, 33, 47, 81, 103, 151, 167, 180, 182–184, 187–188, 260
  forced conversion 33, 180, 182
convert (verb) *xiv,* 13, 19, 22, 26, 31, 81–82, 142, 156, 167, 182–184, 187–189
convert(s) (noun) 18–19, 21, 31, 47, 53, 98, 135, 174, 187
Cook, Charles C. 205
Council of Basel 26–27
Council of Nicaea 26
Council of Oxford 27
Counsel to the President 125, 265–266
Cours d'histoire 1
covenant(s) 3, 13, 18–21, 23–24, 38, 43–44, 61–62, 67, 150–151, 258, 261
Cromwell, Oliver 94
crucifixion 25, 37, 71, 73, 154, 222, 260
Crusades 28, 97, 180
Cyrus 104–106, 128–130

D

Damascus 19
Danish Jews 8
Darby, John Nelson 41–46, 49, 52–54, 57, 59, 63, 94, 259
Darrow, Clarence 51
Darwin, Charles 49–50
Day of Prayer and Solidarity for Israel 173
Dead Sea 172
Dearborn Independent 205
death camp(s) 1, 204, 242
Defense of Philosophic Doubt 115
deicide 4, 6, 8, 25–26, 34, 38, 71, 221
DeLay, Tom 67, 78–79, 145, 148–150,

155–156, 159, 174, 239, 251–253, 262–263, 267–268, 273–274
democracy 6, 56, 67, 75, 80, 138
Democrat(s) 117–118, 149, 251
demographic shift 18
Denmark 8–9
Der Judenstaat 57, 93, 96, 102, 111
Der Stuermer 34
destruction 5, 23, 148, 185, 194, 229
Deutsche Christen 35 *see also* German Christians
Dialogue with Trypho 21, 258
Diaspora 68, 212
Disciples of Christ 61
dispensationalism 44–46, 52–55, 57–59, 63, 66, 98, 142, 205
Disraeli, Benjamin 212
Dobson, Ed 83, 87, 260, 263
Dome of the Rock, the 186–187
Dreyfus, Alfred 92–93
Dugdale, Blanche 114–115, 254, 265, 274

E

Eban, Abba 129–130
Eckstein, Yechiel 64, 145, 162–164, 168–170, 173, 245, 267
economy 6, 93, 169–172, 207
    economic 63, 70, 111, 121, 125, 163, 168, 171, 183, 292
Edwards, Jonathan 47
Egypt 70, 123, 139, 161–162
Elijah 4, 73, 104
England 46, 55, 70, 74, 94–97, 107, 111, 113, 166, 207, 212, 238, 254
Enlightenment 24, 29–30, 38, 67, 70, 92–93, 185
Episcopal Church 63
eschatology 82, 166, 184
Ethiopia 163
Europe 3, 5, 9, 29–30, 38, 57, 71, 74, 82, 90, 92–94, 97, 99–101, 107, 119–120, 128, 217, 227, 229, 232, 235, 237, 241, 249
European bankers 208, 210
European Jews 253
European Union 147
euthanasia 31, 138
evangelical Christian(s) *xiv*, 5, 7–8, 13, 46–48, 67, 69, 72, 75–77, 80, 84–87, 94, 133–134, 137, 140–141, 151–152, 155, 159, 162, 167, 173, 179, 183–184, 187–190, 192, 228, 234–235, 242, 244, 249, 253, 255, 260, 262, 266, 272
Evangelical Lutheran Church 37, 60
Evans, Mike 173
evil empire 67, 75, 77, 153
Exobus Project 166
Exodus II 166, 269

F

faith *xiii*, 18–19, 21–22, 25, 47, 49–50, 62, 65–68, 71–72, 79, 82, 94, 98, 104, 113–115, 117–118, 127, 135, 151–155, 167, 181, 188–190, 212, 214, 221, 235, 237, 239, 241, 245–246, 256, 258, 261
Falwell, Jerry 60, 69–70, 75, 83, 85, 91, 132, 135–145, 148, 159, 174, 182, 194–196, 218–224, 255, 260, 262–263, 266–267, 271–272
Farinacci, Roberto 31
fascism 209
Fascist Grand Council 31
father of many nations 21–22
Feast of Tabernacles 234
Federal Reserve 207–208
final solution 1, 31, 71, 237
Ford, Henry 205
Foreign Affairs 76, 262
foreign policy 67, 76, 110, 124, 127, 148–149, 154–155, 179, 210, 271
Forrestal, James 124
Fourth Lateran Council 27
Foxman, Abraham 183, 190, 192, 204, 219, 223, 226, 243–249, 271–274
France 1, 29, 33, 41, 73, 92–93, 240
Freemasons 207
French 1, 41, 92–93

French Revolution 17, 31, 207
Friend of Israel Award 251–252, 274
friends of Israel 6, 63, 138, 196
Frum, David 154–155, 268
fundamentalism 46, 51–52, 55, 58, 259
fundamentalist movement 46, 52–55

G

Gaebelein, Arno 205–206
Gaffney, Frank 151
Gamaliel 19
Garden of the Righteous Among Nations 227–228
Gaza 63, 194, 198, 200
genocide 29, 31, 41, 119, 180, 237
Gentiles 18–20, 34, 61, 158, 161, 167, 220–221, 234, 239, 258
George, David Lloyd 111–113, 115, 127, 152
Georgia 117, 165
German Christians 35, 36
German soldiers 1, 233
Germany 31, 34–37, 60, 94, 96, 209, 231–232
 Germans 1, 29, 34–35, 107, 246
Gerson, Michael 155
Gestapo 1, 230
ghetto(s) 6, 17, 27, 38, 57–58, 212, 246
 Jewish ghetto(s) 31, 92
Gilded Age 56, 100
global politics 76
Golden Age 46, 56, 70–71, 185
Gorenberg, Gershom 81, 183, 186, 261, 270
gospel 18–20, 47, 59, 65, 83, 143, 174, 181, 188–189, 222
Graham, Billy 53, 151, 156
Great Awakening(s), the 47
great exodus 161–162
Guide for the Perplexed, The 178
Gulf War 86, 141, 206, 208, 211

H

Haarlem 230, 233
Hadassah 4
Hadassah Hospital 140, 147
Hagee, John *xi*, 3–5, 65–66, 69–74, 79, 83, 144, 148, 166, 174–175, 257–258, 262, 267, 269
Halacha *xiii*
Hamas 144, 146–147, 149
Ha Pisga 104
Harris, David A. 190
Harrison, Benjamin 99, 101, 104–105, 117, 264
"Hatikva" 145
Hebrew(s) 33, 49, 104, 113, 145, 160, 170, 175, 203, 234
Hechler, William 91–92, 94–99, 101–103, 114, 254, 263
Heilbrunn, Jacob 209–210, 271
Herzl, Theodor 57, 91–100, 102, 107–108, 111, 254
Herzliya 212–213, 262, 272
Herzliya Conference on Security 212, 262–263
Hess, Moses 208
Hiding Place, The 232, 273
Hilberg, Raul 30, 258, 270
Hindson, Ed 83, 87, 260, 263
Hitler, Adolf 8, 29–31, 34–38, 71, 119–120, 203–204, 209, 220, 232, 237
Holland 232, 234
Holocaust *xiv*, 1–4, 6–7, 9, 14, 23, 29–30, 32–34, 37–38, 41, 57, 60, 62, 65–66, 119, 126, 175, 180, 202, 204, 226–231, 236–237, 239–240, 242, 245–248, 251–253
Holy City 212
Holy Land, the 22, 95–96, 118, 254
House Foreign Relations Committee 100
House of Israel 22
House of Representatives 100, 149, 156
Howe, Julia Ward 48, 260
Huguenots 240
Hungarian Jews 252
Hungary 74, 251
Huntington, Samuel P. 76, 262
Hussein, Saddam 140

I

Illuminati, the 205, 207–208
India 94, 111
Inhofe, James 156–157, 268
Inquisition(s), the 17, 28, 70, 94, 97, 111, 180, 187, 228
International Christian Embassy in Jerusalem (ICEJ) 174, 234
International Fellowship of Christians and Jews (IFCJ) 163, 168, 267, 269–270
intifada 168, 171
Iran 153
Iraq 3, 123, 147, 153, 211
Ireland 46
Isaac *xi*, 4, 13, 21, 68–69, 73–74, 126, 212
Isaac, Jules 1–2, 4, 6–8, 26, 221, 257
Isaiah 68, 115, 160–161, 164–165, 169, 238, 269, 273
Islam 76–78, 186
Islamic Jihad 147
Israel's Declaration of Independence 65, 123
Israel Awareness Day 175
Israeli embassy 173, 257, 262
Israeli policy(ies) 7, 63, 143, 200
Israeli Right, the 179, 193–194, 198
Israel Policy Forum 199
Italian Jews 32
Italy 31–32, 73

J

Jabotinsky, Vladimir 140
Jabotinsky Medal 140
Jacob *xi*, 4, 21, 68–69, 73–74, 126, 150, 212
Jacobson, Eddie 122–123, 130
Jenkins, Jerry 60
Jeremiah 68, 160–162, 164, 262
Jerusalem 18–19, 23, 57–58, 81, 93, 96, 98–99, 104, 109–110, 128, 139–140, 146–147, 160, 164, 168, 173, 186, 195, 197, 212, 227, 231, 233–234, 238, 254–255, 268, 273
Jerusalem Prayer Team 173, 270
Jesus and Israel 1–2, 257
Jesus Is Coming 98, 102, 264
Jewish Agency 164–166
Jewish community *xi*, 6–8, 23, 95, 103, 111, 123–125, 133, 142, 160, 164, 166, 170, 172, 179–180, 182, 189–192, 196, 199–200, 204, 210, 215, 218–219, 229, 244–246, 256
Jewish emigration 163, 165
Jewish history *xiii*, 14, 42, 107, 128–129, 175, 180, 189, 212, 215, 227
Jewish homeland 72, 97, 99, 111, 113, 125–126, 218
Jewish immigration 100, 119–121, 162, 164, 166, 237
Jewish law *xiii*, 18–19, 215
Jewish Messenger, The 104
Jewish State 5, 13–14, 63, 65–66, 69, 81, 97, 111, 117, 120–125, 138, 140, 143, 146, 155, 183, 197, 199, 213, 223, 229, 248–249, 254, 256, 267
Jewish Theological Seminary 130
Jewish vote(s) 117, 125–126
Jews and Their Lies, The 28, 182
jihad 186
Johnson, Lyndon 136
Jordan 123, 147, 149
Judah 21, 128
Judaism 2, 13, 18, 21, 61, 67, 73, 114, 164, 167, 185–186, 246, 258
Judaizers 21
Judeo-centric ideology 239–240
Judeo-Christian 77, 185, 224, 242, 253
Judeo-Christian Zionist Conference 242

K

Kazakhstan 165
Keyes, Alan 78, 263
Kfar Truman 129
KGB 162
kibbutz 215
Kissinger, Henry 155
Klein, Morton 192, 198, 200
Knesset 80, 150, 239, 268, 273

Kollek, Teddy 234
Kristallnacht 35
Kurpi, Bronislawa 246–248

L

LaHaye, Tim 59–60, 261
Land, Richard 69
Lantos, Tom 149, 251–253, 274
Late Great Planet Earth, The 58–59, 261
League of Nations 85, 111, 113
Lebanon 123
Le Chambon-sur-Lignon 240
liberalism 49, 85
  liberal(s) *xiii*, 7, 58, 85–87, 125, 184, 189–190, 192, 217, 243, 246, 251
liberal Jews 7
Liberty University 143, 223
Lind, Michael 208–210, 216–217, 272
Lindsey, Hal 58–60, 261
Listen, America! 138, 262, 266
Lithuania 246–247
Littell, Franklin 16, 203, 257–258, 271
Los Angeles Times 245, 274
Lovett, Robert 124
Luther, Martin 28, 34–35, 72, 74, 180–182, 270

M

Maimonides, Moses 178
Mandate for Palestine 97, 113, 122
Mansfield, Stephen 175, 268
March of the Living 14
Marsden, George 206, 259–260, 263, 271
Marshall, George 124
Martyr, Justin 21–22, 24, 258
martyr(s) 29
massacre(s) 28, 33, 97, 180
  massacred 212, 238
McAteer, Ed 144
McCullough, David 125–126, 128, 265–266
Mediterranean 19, 21, 120
Mein Kampf 34
Mengele, Josef 32
Merkley, Paul 92, 254, 263–266, 274
Messiah *xiii*, 3, 13, 18, 38, 43, 45, 58, 67, 72, 74, 167, 184–186, 218, 220–221
Messianic Age 103, 187
  messianic era 185
Middle Ages 17, 72
Middle East, the 63, 71, 75–76, 78–80, 87, 144, 147, 149, 156, 159, 193–197, 199, 229, 241, 249, 272
Middle East Peace Facilitation Act 198
Mideast policy 151
migration of Jews 161
Millennium, the 45–48, 55–56, 83–84
modernism 49–50, 52, 135
Moody, D. L. 53–54
Moral Majority, the 60, 84, 136–138, 220, 223
Moses 68–69, 160–161, 203
Mossad 193
Muller, Ludwig 36
Muslim(s) 56, 77, 157, 188, 244
Mussolini 31

N

nachtasyl 108
Napoleon 17, 92
National Association of Evangelicals 75, 77
National Socialism 33, 36
nations 13, 21–23, 29, 70, 75–80, 85, 90, 94, 100–101, 138, 161–162, 175, 194, 206–207, 211, 218, 223, 233–234, 242
Nazi(s) 1–2, 8–9, 29–31, 33, 35–37, 71, 74, 119, 169, 180, 227, 230, 232, 235, 237, 241–242, 245–246, 249, 251, 255, 273
Nazism 29–30, 33, 241, 259
Nebuchadnezzar 104
Negev Desert 121
neo-pagan 1, 29
Netanyahu, Benjamin 141–142, 175, 194, 197, 267, 270
Netherlands 230
Neue Freie Press 92
new Israel 13, 16
New Millennium, The 216–217, 272

New Republic, The 193, 271
New Testament 19, 33
New World Order, The 85, 206–216, 271
New York Times 59, 86, 157, 206, 208, 210–211, 244–245, 261–262, 266–268, 271, 273
Niagara Bible Conference 53
Niemoller, Martin 37
Night to Honor Israel 3–4, 174, 263
Nordau, Max 108
North Korea 153
Nostra Aetate 34
nuclear war 87
Nuremberg 31, 34

O

oil wealth 124, 126
Old Testament 23, 34–36, 42– 44, 68, 72, 83, 98, 112, 114, 126, 185, 218, 221
olive tree 19–20, 34
On the Origin of Species 49
On Wings of Eagles 163
Operation Exodus 165, 238, 262, 269, 273
Operation Iraqi Freedom 148
Orthodox rabbi(s) 216, 221
Oslo Accords, the 141, 198
Oslo Peace Process 197
Ottoman Empire, the 57, 71, 93, 96, 101, 107

P

pacifism 241
  pacifist(s) 240–241
Pakistan 78
Palestine 57–58, 91, 93–101, 104, 107–113, 115–117, 119–126, 181, 237, 254, 262
Palestinian Arabs 119, 122
Palestinian Authority 144, 146–148, 195
Palestinian(s) 62, 78, 141, 144, 147–151, 168, 171, 193–195, 197–198, 241
Palestinian state 147, 150, 194–195, 200
Palestinian terrorism 78
Palestinian terrorists 5, 150
Papal State 17
partition 121–123
Passover 26, 144, 170–171
Paul, the apostle 18–21, 23–24, 34, 43, 61–62, 167, 204, 221, 257–258
peace 56, 63, 72, 79, 104, 114, 139, 141–142, 147–150, 168, 173, 179–180, 193–200, 206, 213, 231, 234, 239
Pearl, Daniel 78
Pelosi, Nancy 149
Pharaoh 70–71
philo-Semitism 69, 94, 114, 239
  philo-Semitic 44, 179, 206, 214
Pileggi, David 97, 264
Plymouth Brethren 41–42, 46, 52, 55
Podhoretz, Norman 215–217, 272
pogrom(s) 23, 25, 28, 35, 71, 95, 108, 180, 212, 217, 232
Poland 14, 246
Pope John XXIII 8, 283
Pope Pius VII 17
Pope Pius XII 8, 259
Powell, Colin 147, 267
Presbyterian Church 37, 50, 60, 63
Prince, Derek 175
pro-Israel 5, 13, 91, 142–143, 154, 156, 174, 179, 190, 194, 196–197, 210, 213–214, 223, 240, 253
Promised Land 13, 43, 68, 160, 175
prophecy(ies) 14, 18, 23, 57–58, 64–65, 68–70, 83–84, 94–95, 98, 102, 138, 160–162, 164–165, 167, 170, 174, 182, 222, 237
prophet(s)s 3–4, 42–43, 65, 68–69, 73, 92, 115, 160–161, 181, 203, 218, 244
Protestantism 36, 46, 52, 181
Protocols of the Elders of Zion 205, 209
Puritan(s) 94, 112

Q

Quakers 241

R

rabbi(s) 3–4, 28, 71, 73, 99, 128–129, 145, 163, 218

Rabin, Yitzhak 133, 139, 141, 197, 200, 213
racism 212
Rapture, the 44, 59–60, 261
Ravensbruck 231, 233, 235
Reagan, Ronald 75, 77, 87, 127, 136, 140–142, 153, 220
Red Sea 65, 70
Reed, Ralph 136, 145, 173, 197–198, 202, 243–245, 266, 271, 274
Reformation 28–29, 72, 74, 181
Reform Judaism in America 199
Reform rabbi(s) 99
refugee(s) 41, 95, 100, 120, 161
refuseniks 162
Regent University 143, 213
Reich Church 35
Religious Action Center for Reform Judaism 196
religious minority(ies) 23, 26, 62, 240
Religious Right, the 134, 137–138, 142, 192, 223, 243–245, 248
Repairers of the Breach 168
replacement theology *xi*, 3–5, 9, 14, 17–18, 21–22, 24–26, 28–30, 33–34, 37–38, 40–42, 44, 46, 57–58, 60–63, 66, 71, 91, 98, 174–175, 205, 229, 258, 261
Republican(s) *xiii*, 5, 136–137, 156, 160, 251
Rice, Condoleeza 155, 268
right-wing 143, 190, 193–194, 199
righteous Gentile(s) *xiii–xiv*, 4–5, 9, 32, 229–231, 233, 237, 239–242, 246–248, 253
Riley, William 205
Roadmap for Peace 147–151
Robertson, Pat 69, 72, 80, 83, 85–86, 91, 135–136, 138–140, 142–143, 145–146, 166, 171, 174, 182, 194–195, 206–218, 222, 244–245, 262–263, 266–267, 270–272, 274
Robison, James 153
Roe v. Wade 136
Rohan, Dennis 187
Roman Empire 13, 23, 26
Romanian Jews 237
Rome 17, 22, 28–29, 31–32
Roman(s) 17–18, 21–22, 28, 68, 71, 90, 101, 104, 156, 212
Rosh Hashanah 171
Rothschild family 110, 208
Rove, Karl 137
Rusk, Dean 124
Russia 75, 95, 100, 102, 111, 147, 162, 166, 169
Russian Jewry 99
Russian Jews 93, 95, 99–101, 112
Russian Revolution, the 207
Ryrie, Charles 46

S

Sabbatarian movement 47
safe homes 232
Samuel, Herbert 111
Samuels, Dr. Larry 140
Sandager, Susan 235–236, 242, 273
Saperstein, David 192, 196, 271
Sasse, Martin 35
Satan 205–206, 211
Scheller, Gustav 74, 164–165, 238, 262, 269, 273
Schiff, Jacob 208
Schindler, Oskar 228, 241–243
Schindler, Rosemary 242–243
Schindler's Ark 242
Scofield, C. I. 54–55, 59–60, 98, 257, 262
Scofield Bible (Reference/Study) 54–55, 59, 98
Scopes, John 50–51, 135
Sea of Galilee 154
second-class citizens 190
Second Coming 21, 45, 48, 55, 59–60, 81–87, 102–103, 166, 170, 183–184, 186, 214, 260
second exodus 161
Second Vatican Council 34
Second World War 33, 252 *see also* World War II
Secret Societies and Subversive Movements 209

Senate 135, 137, 156, 268
separation of church and state 190, 248
September 11 (9/11) 66–67, 77–78, 80, 134, 140, 142–143, 145, 153, 255
Serbia 101
Sermon on the Mount 84, 127, 154
settlements 86, 133, 189, 193, 200
Shakespeare, William 78
Sharansky, Natan 194
Sharon, Ariel 80, 143, 145, 147, 174, 197, 198, 200, 272
Shop Israel 172
Siberia 162, 165
Silver, Abba Hillel 122
Simon, Bob 81, 262–263, 267, 271, 272, 274
Sinai 107
Sinai Peninsula 107
Six Days' War 75, 139
Skinhead Movement 244
sleeper cell 188
Smith, Bailey 219–220, 272
Solidarity Mission 172, 270
South Africa 63
Southern Baptist Conference 219
Southern Baptist Convention 70
Soviet Jews 169, 234
Soviet Union 67, 70, 74–77, 87, 133, 153, 159, 162–167, 169, 234, 238
Spain 28–29, 70–71, 73, 181
Stand for Israel 145, 251, 267, 270
Star of David 8, 232, 239
State Department 129, 142, 148
State of Israel 7, 13–14, 57, 62–63, 70, 91, 95, 102, 118, 121, 123–124, 127, 129–130, 143, 154, 161, 171, 173, 175, 231, 236, 252, 261, 263
Stowe, Harriet Beecher 48
Strang, Stephen 175
Streicher, Julius 34
Struma 237–238
Succot 234 *See also* Feast of Tabernacles
Sudan 78
Suez Canal 111
suicide bombings 5, 133, 146, 149, 239
Sunday, Billy 53
supersessionism 13, 21, 24, 61
Supreme Court 100, 116, 136, 190
Sweden 9
synagogue(s) 23, 25, 27–28, 35, 92, 142, 182
Synod of Breslau 27
Synod of Clermont 27
Synod of Elvira 27
Synod of Gerona 27
Synod of Ofen 27
Synod of Orleans 27
Syria 123, 139

T

Tajikistan 165
Talmud 28, 215
Tel Aviv 121, 123, 144, 195, 233
Temple Mount 162, 186
ten Boom, Corrie 230–236, 239–240, 242–243, 245–249
ten Boom family 230–236
terrorist(s) 5, 67, 133, 144–146, 148, 150, 153, 194, 235, 244
That Jesus Christ Was Born a Jew 181
theological shift 13–14, 66, 81–82
Third Lateran Council 27
Third Reich 30
tourism 160, 171–172, 270
  tourists 5, 14
Trocme, Andre 240–242
Truman, Harry S. 106–107, 118–130, 134, 151–152, 263–266
Tuchman, Barbara 112–113, 262–265
Turkey 19, 104, 237
Turkmenistan 165

U

U.S.-Israel alliance 79, 82, 86
Uganda 107–109
Ukraine 160, 162, 166
  Ukrainian 238
Uncle Tom's Cabin 48
UN General Assembly 121
United Church of Christ 61–63, 262
United Jewish Communities 5, 166

United Methodist Church 60
United Nations 75, 85–86, 121, 147, 210–212
United States 3, 6, 46–48, 52, 55, 59, 75, 77–80, 86, 99, 111–112, 116, 118, 120, 122–124, 129, 133, 141, 144, 147–148, 152, 155, 157, 166, 172, 199, 207–208, 217, 239
UN Special Committee 121
Uzbekistan 170

V

van der Hoeven, Jan Willem 233
van Woerden, Peter 234–235
Vatican 8, 17, 30–34
Vienna 32, 92–93, 95, 254

W

Wagner, Clarence E. 40, 259, 273
Wallenberg, Raoul 252–253
Walvoord, John 52
Warburg, Paul 208
War Memoirs 111–112
war of independence 123, 125
war on terror 67, 78, 82, 143, 149–150, 153, 241
war on terrorism 67, 134, 153
Washington 5, 66–67, 76–77, 91, 120, 122, 129, 133–134, 137, 141–142, 145, 150, 172–173, 175, 192, 195, 197, 251, 257, 262–263, 266–267, 270, 274
Washington Post 157, 245, 257, 261–262, 266–267, 270
Webster, Nesta 209
Weizmann, Chaim 108–111, 113, 115–116, 120–123, 254, 264–265
We Remember: A Reflection on the Shoah 33
West Bank 63, 81, 86–87, 133–134, 142, 144–146, 156–157, 189, 194–195, 197, 212
Western civilization 67, 77–78
Western Wall 154
White House 5, 77, 123, 125, 128–129, 133, 141–143, 145, 149–150, 152, 154–155, 160, 173, 199, 220, 268
White Paper, the 119
Wilhelm II 96
Wilson, Woodrow 107, 116–118, 127, 151, 206–207, 263–264
World Council of Churches 63, 261
World War I 1, 46, 48, 50, 53, 55–56, 97, 100, 109, 111, 116
World War II 1, 6, 8–9, 41, 118, 120, 124, 229, 234, 238, 251, 255 *See also* Second World War
Wright, Fred 238

Y

Yad Vashem 227–229, 231, 273
yellow star 8– 9, 17, 232
Yoffie, Eric 199
Yom Kippur 139
Yom Kippur War 139

Z

Zechariah 4, 73, 234
Zion 74, 95, 167, 205, 209, 216, 269
Zionism *xi, xiii,* 14, 44, 46, 66, 69–70, 80–82, 86, 91–92, 94, 97–100, 102–103, 105, 109–113, 115–117, 120, 122, 125, 134–135, 154, 174–175, 179–180, 183–184, 187–189, 193, 196, 199–200, 204, 212, 218, 234, 241, 254, 257, 263
Zionist movement, the 42, 57, 66, 91–92, 97, 102–103, 108–109, 187, 194, 253–254
Zionist Organization of America 192, 198
Zionist(s) 57, 91–97, 101–103, 108–110, 112, 116, 118–123, 125–126, 140, 148, 150, 159, 161, 187, 194, 198, 241, 254–255
Zweibon, Herbert 200